W9-BNY-162

Religion in America

*M*EMOIR

OF THE

*R*EV. *J*ESSE *L*EE

WITH EXTRACTS FROM HIS JOURNALS

ARNO PRESS & THE NEW YORK TIMES
New York 1969

Reprint edition 1969 by Arno Press, Inc.

*

Library of Congress Catalog Card No. 72-83428

*

Reprinted from a copy in the
Board of Missions of The Methodist Church Library

*

Manufactured in the United States of America

Memoir

OF THE

REV. JESSE LEE.

WITH

EXTRACTS

FROM HIS

JOURNALS.

—•—

BY MINTON THRIFT.

—•—

" Fight the good fight of faith, lay hold on eternal life."
2 *Tim.* vi. 12.

NEW-YORK:

PUBLISHED BY N. BANGS AND T. MASON, FOR THE
METHODIST EPISCOPAL CHURCH.

Myers & Smith, Printers.

1823.

PREFACE.

VOLUMES of Biography of late have flowed upon the public, so that Lord Bacon's complaint, as to the deficiency in the biographical department of literature in his day, is by no means applicable to the present times. Indeed frequent complaints are now made of the great number of books continually emitted from the press, entitled Memoirs, Journals, Travels, Tours, Experiences, Sketches, &c. These complaints, however, more frequently proceed from a certain fastidiousness of disposition than from any real or solid objections against the matter or method of those publications. To please all would require super-human abilities.

The Compiler of the following sheets, without ever feeling a wish to have his name affixed to the title-page of a book, has, from very different motives to that of ambition, or an expectation of worldly emoluments, been induced to make an attempt at writing the Memoir of the Rev. Jesse Lee. The trust confided to him by his brethren he has endeavoured to fulfil, to the best of his abilities.

That there are many imperfections cleaving to the performance, he will not attempt to deny; but he trusts that the candid reader will throw a veil over those faults which may be presented, and endeavour to profit by the excellencies, if any, which it may possess.

Where the subject of this Memoir was personally known, the Compiler trusts that this work will be read with interest. For it cannot be supposed that Jesse Lee will soon be forgotten by the thousands who have been benefitted by his labours. A remembrance of his successful efforts among them, will doubtless cause them to pay some respect to this simple monument raised to his memory.

Mr. Lee was a faithful servant of the Church of Christ for many years. During his ministry he saw that branch of the Church to which he belonged rise from obscurity into notice, and spread from state to state through this continent, with a rapidity encouraging to its friends, and appaling to its enemies.

That the cause may still prosper among us as a people, and that it may be blessed with a holy, zealous, and living ministry, is the fervent prayer of the

COMPILER.

CONTENTS.

CHAPTER I.

CHAPTER II.

CHAPTER III.

CHAPTER IV.

CHAPTER V.

CHAPTER VI.

CHAPTER VII.

CHAPTER VIII.

CHAPTER IX.

CHAPTER X.

CHAPTER XI.

CHAPTER XII.

CHAPTER XIII.

CHAPTER XIV.

CHAPTER XV.

viii CONTENTS.

MEMOIR

OF THE

REV. JESSE LEE.

—o++o—

CHAPTER I.

—o+o—

Preliminary remarks—His birth—Education—First religious impressions—Conversion of his parents—His Conversion—A revival—Seeks a deeper work of grace—The Methodist Preachers visit his neighbourhood—He joins Society.

To preserve the remembrance of men of worth, seems to have been the care of many in different ages of the world.

Men of science, or those who have acquired celebrity in arts, or arms, have not been left in total forgetfulness. Those too, who have borne a distinguished part in reforming the world, either by enacting or enforcing wise laws, have had historians to record their merits, and hand their names down to posterity.

Those who have been famous for piety and mental accomplishments, and have zealously devoted their lives to the advancement of religion, and have been eminently successful in a cause of such vital importance to the happiness of the world, deserve to be ranked amongst the benefactors of mankind. Neither their names, nor deeds, should be suffered to sink in oblivion, but should be held up as models for future generations.

In perusing the pages of profane history, we are often made to turn away in disgust from the description of those scenes of injustice, of wars and murders, practised by that race of human beings known by the name of kings, courtiers, and heroes; who, from time immemorial, have claimed for themselves a kind of superiority over the rest of mankind; and have exerted their strength in desolating the earth by their barbarous deeds. It affords us some relief to turn away from the contemplation of such characters, whose crimes, associated with their names, will render them odious to the latest generations, and mark the progress of those whose Christian virtues have procured for them the veneration of the wise and good.

The man who pursues that course which his own conscience approves, and which meets with the assent of good men, holds a dignified station in society, particularly when society has been greatly benefitted by his labours. In proportion as he has exercised his talents in doing good, and made personal sacrifices for the benefit of others, he should be admired and esteemed. The circumstance of his being removed from this sublunary abode, will only tend to extinguish the remembrance of his foibles, and set his virtues in the most agreeable point of view.

The individual whom we are now about to introduce to the notice of the public, was one, who, with respect to his acquirements in literature, we do not pretend to rank with some of his predecessors in the ministry.—But so far from doing him any injustice, or underrating his character by giving precedence to others in this respect, we intend to show in the following sheets, that he has been greatly useful to the church, and to society generally, without attaining to that eminence in human science which has adorned the brow of some, or of suffering imprisonment or death for the testimony of Jesus. Judging from what he did do and suffer, and from his acknowledged attachment to the cause of Christ, we may safely presume, that, had he been called, in the order of God's providence, to make greater sacrifices for his Divine Master, he would have done it with all cheerfulness.

JESSE LEE was born in the year of our Lord 1758, in Prince George County, Va. He was the second son of Nathaniel and Elizabeth Lee, whose forefathers came over from England soon after the first settlement of Virginia. His parents were respectable and moral ; and being members of the English Episcopal Church, dedicated their children to God according to its ceremonies.

It will not, it is presumed, be essential to record every circumstance relative to the education and early impressions of the subject of these memoirs ; some incidents of his early life shall, however, be noticed, and in doing this, reference will be had to manuscript journals, which were left in his own hand writing ; extracts from which we shall have occasion frequently to make in the following pages.

When he arrived to the proper age, he was put to a school in the neighbourhood, and as soon as he was capable of reading tolerably well, his teacher directed him to procure a prayer book, with a strict injunction to carry it to church every Sabbath, and out of which he was taught the catechism ; and the teacher,

prompted with a laudable ambition of improving the
morals of his pupils, had the morning service regularly performed in his school every Wednesday and
Friday. This custom had a tendency to familiarize
his mind to devotion, and to make the duty pleasant ;
for when summoned to church on Sunday, he would
seat himself in his pew, with his prayer book in his
hand, and repeat the service in a manner which did
credit to one of his age.

We shall not doubt his testimony, when he assures
us that he derived considerable benefit from this
course of religious instruction. " In a thousand instances (says he,) when I felt an inclination to act or
speak amiss, I have been stopped by the recollection
of my catechism, some parts of which I did not understand ; yet it was good upon the whole that I learned
it."*

He was also sent to a singing school in the neighbourhood : here it was he contracted a love for
sacred melody, which gave him a disrelish for
those vain songs which he had learned in his ear-
lier days—by this means he was enabled to join with
the congregation in singing the praises of God.
These circumstances are noticed with a view of showing the necessity of occupying the mind of youth with
religious instruction, so as to restrain the evil disposi-
tions of the heart, and to furnish the mind with strength
to overcome evil habits, which will always prevail, unless the faculties are employed in something
good.

It would be easy for parents generally to restrain
their children from the evil practices which prevail

* This circumstance evinces the importance and the utility of cat-
echetical instructions.

among the youth of the present age, were they with
due diligence and perseverance, to instil into their
minds early notions of piety. The mind is active;
it must have employment. Be it so; and are there not
ample opportunities afforded every parent, of furnishing the intellect with proper food? By using that substantial nourishment which the bible so plentifully
affords, and offering it in a way which will make it
acceptable and pleasant, and easily digested, even by
the most common capacity, is the most effectual
method to guard youth against the contagion of vice.
Young Lee was what may be called a moral youth.
"I do not (says he) recollect that I ever swore
in my life, except one night being in company
with some wicked young people, I uttered some kind
of oaths, for which I felt ashamed, and sorry all the
next day; and when alone, I felt that God was displeased with me for my bad conduct. I believe I
never did any thing in my youth, that the people generally call wicked. I used, however, to indulge bad
tempers, and use some vain words."

Although he had little inclination to indulge in the
vices which often prove destructive to youth, yet in
him as in all others, was realized the truth, so
solemnly announced by the prophet—"The heart is
deceitful and desperately wicked, who can know it?"
He was fond of amusement, whether it was the dance,
or the jovial company, when each one endeavoured
to display his talent in wit, to the best advantage;
and it but ill accorded with his own feelings when by
parental authority he was restrained from those
favourite scenes. We will quote his own words.

"When I was a little turned fourteen years of age,
my father refused to go to any place of amusement;

and withal, told his children they had better go no more. I thought, at times, that it was hard to be kept under such restrictions, inasmuch as I saw that other young people could go without being restrained; but it was not long before my father let us know that it was from religious motives that he was led to act as he did. From that time, I felt willing to forego the vain amusements of life, and to conform to my father's will."

His ready compliance with his father's request, is sufficient to put to the blush many of the children even of Methodist parents, who, in despite of all remonstrance, and the force of example, manifest a strong predelection to conform to customs and maxims prevalent in a vitiated and corrupted age. This evil, which seems to spread with rapidity, is ominous of nothing favourable to the progress of piety in the world ; and if parents who profess the religion of Christ, neglect to bring their children to feel the influence of religious precepts, we shall not be astonished if the name of religion should perish in their families after their heads are laid in the dust. But we will now notice a new era in the family of the subject of these memoirs.

"In the latter part of the year 1772, my father became much more serious, and more engaged with God than formerly.

"One day, when his conviction was deep, and his distress very great, he went into the woods, and continued travelling about, and mourning for his sins, till at length he claimed the promises of God, and by faith beheld the Lamb of God that taketh away the sin of world, and was justified freely by the blood of Jesus Christ. The joy he felt in his soul he could not describe with words. He had an inward evidence, that his sins were forgiven, and that he was born again. This was the beginning of religion in the family; and my father's conversation about religion from that time astonished us all.

"When my father informed my mother what the Lord had done for his soul, in the forgiveness of his sins, she believed it all, and began to weep; and from that time she became a broken hearted penitent. She sought the Lord in earnest prayer for some months. Some time in the following winter, while she was reading in the New Testament, the Lord spoke peace to her troubled soul; and there was, from that time, a visible alteration in her life and conversation. After the conversion of my father and mother, I frequently heard them talk about conversion, and being born again, of the comforts of religion, and the happiness they enjoyed, but nothing that I heard took hold of my mind for some time.

"One of my mother's relations came to my father's and stayed all night; the topic of conversation was experimental religion. While engaged on this interesting subject, my father observed, 'that if a man's sins were forgiven, he would know it.' That sentence, 'if a man's sins were forgiven him, he would know it,' took hold of my mind, and I pondered it in my heart. The next day, when alone in the field, it kept running across my mind, 'if a man's sins are forgiven, he will know it.' I thought it over and over again, and concluded it must be so, for my father said so, and I believe it. At length I began to reason with myself thus: are my sins forgiven? I hope so— but do I know it? No! no! I have no assurance of it; immediately it was impressed upon my mind with uncommon force, go and pray! The impression was repeated, and I went off into a large branch, which was surrounded with thick bushes; then I stopped and looked to see if any person was near me, but could see no one; yet I thought some one might pass that way and see me, so I set off to another place where the bushes appeared to be yet thicker, but when I came there I was afraid of being seen; I then went to another place with the same reasonings, and the same fears, but at length I ventured to kneel down, and began to pray that the Lord would forgive my sins.

"My distress of soul, at that time, was very great, and never wore off till my sins were forgiven.

"I would frequently, after that time, get by myself, and with many tears pray to God to have mercy upon my poor soul, and forgive my sins. Sometimes in the open fields I have fell on my knees, and prayed, and wept, till my heart was ready to break. At other times my heart was so hard that I could not shed a tear. It would occur to mind, 'your day of grace is past, and God will never forgive your sins.' It appeared to me that of all sinners in the world I was the greatest; my sins appeared to me greater in magnitude and multitude than the sins of any other person.

"All this time (says he) I kept my distress to myself, and *carefully* concealed it from all my friends. When in company, I would endeavour to be as cheerful as possible, to prevent any one from knowing my wretched state. There were no young people in the neighbourhood who were religious; and I could not take courage to talk to aged people on the subject; and withal, I saw myself to be such a desperate sinner, that I did not want any body to know how bad I was.

"When I was in company where religious people were talking about religion, I would frequently get near enough to hear what was said, and pay the greatest attention to what I heard, and yet would try to prevent the people from knowing my anxiety to hear and gain instruction: sometimes I would be writing on the ground, and at other times looking a different way.

"Sometimes I felt a fear that there was no mercy for me; but for the greater part of the time, I believed firmly that the Lord would in mercy forgive me. I relied on that promise, 'Seek, and ye shall find;' I was determined to seek as long as I lived.

"Thus I went on for about four weeks, in which time I never, for an hour, lost sight of my wretched condition. The cry of my soul was, 'how shall I escape the misery of hell?' I cared little about the sufferings of this life, if I could but escape eternal misery.—I read, that some 'asked, and received not, because they asked amiss;' the remembrance of this, made me, for a season, afraid to use many words* in prayer, for fear I should pray improperly, and, therefore, 'ask amiss.'

"One morning, being in deep distress, and fearing every moment I should drop into hell, and viewing myself as hanging over the pit, I was constrained to cry in earnest for mercy, and the Lord came to my relief, and delivered my soul from the burden and guilt of sin!

* How short, and how comprehensive was the prayer of the publican; "God be merciful to me a sinner." This prayer is a proper model for all true penitents.

"My whole frame was in a tremor from head to
foot, and my soul enjoyed sweet peace. The pleasure I then felt was indescribable. This happiness
lasted about three days, during which time I never
spoke to any person about my feelings. I anxiously
wished for some one to talk to me on the subject, but
no one did. I then began to doubt my conversion,
and to fear that I was deceived—I finally concluded
that if I were not converted, I would never rest without the blessing, and began to pray to the Lord to
show me my lost condition, and let me feel my danger,
as I had previously done ; but as I could not feel the
burden of my sins, the enemy of my soul suggested
to my mind that the Lord had forsaken me, and that
I had sinned away my convictions, and deceived my
own soul. Thus I was a prey to those doubts and
perplexities for about six months, before I could
assuredly believe that I was in the favour of God.

"One evening, travelling in company with a religious neighbour, he asked me if I was ever converted? I told him I believed I had been. He then
asked me several questions relative to the circumstances of the change, which I endeavoured to
answer. He then said, 'you are surely converted.'
I was much strengthened by that conversation, and so
much encouraged, as to tell other people, when they
asked me, what the Lord had done for my soul."

Soon after this he enjoyed such a manifestation of
the presence and power of God, as completely to
remove all his doubts, and enable him to say, " now I
know in whom I believe." This blessed assurance
he obtained by fervently besieging the throne of
grace—he proved successful, and was abundantly
blessed.

Nothing appears more evident than this, that those who have received the grace of justification, ought by no means to conceal it.—" Do men light a candle, and put it under a bushel?" was asked by Christ, when enforcing the necessity of the following precept : "Let your light so shine before men, that they may behold your good works, and glorify your Father which is in heaven."

The spirit of religious inquiry which was, at this time, wakened up in the minds of a few, was a favourable presage of what was about to follow ; the field was beginning to whiten for the harvest, and we are almost surprised, how the process of awakening, conviction and conversion, should be so regularly carried on at a time when those doctrines were so little understood, and but seldom enforced from the pulpit. But those who are acquainted with the history of religion in Virginia, will recollect that even in those days of moral darkness, there was a JARRET who did not fail to point sinners to the Lamb of God, who taketh away the sins of the world.

About this time, the Lord was raising up ministers, and thrusting them into his vineyard. The flame that had been kindled in England, under the ministry of Wesley, had already extended to America. It began in the city of New-York, and was gradually progressing towards the southern states.

Mr. Robert Williams was the first of the Wesleyan preachers who visited that part of Virginia where Jesse Lee resided. The doctrines of this minister of Christ, were just such as suited his state of mind ; he was comforted, and built up in faith and love. His soul was more than ever given up to God.

In the spring of the year 1774, Mr. Williams began
to form societies in the neighbourhood. It was then
that Mr. Lee, being about sixteen years of age, united
himself to the society of the Methodists, and was, perhaps, stimulated to it by the example of his father
and mother, and an elder brother. At that time the
number of Methodists, on the continent of America,
amounted to little more than one thousand.

In the following summer, the first circuit in Virginia
was formed, called Brunswick. His father freely
offered his house as a regular preaching place, which
was accepted ; and from that period to this,* continued
a home for the preachers, and a house of worship.
Like the house of Obed-Edom, the Lord blessed his,
because the ark of the Lord rested there. This son
often took sweet counsel with the preachers who
visited his father's. They not only imparted instruction by the public ministration of the word, but
in social conversation, they gave such advice as
was suited to the particular case of each individual.

It pleased God about this time, to show him the
necessity of a deeper work of grace than he had
hitherto experienced ; for, although he enjoyed the
blessed assurance of sin forgiven, he was at times
agitated with fears, darkness, and heaviness of soul.
Hearing the preacher speak of the evidences of the
Holy Spirit, and sanctification of soul, body and spirit ;

* Since writing the above, the author has to record the death of
this aged and long respected follower of Christ.
He died the 5th day of March, 1820, in the 90th year of his age.
He was married three times, had twelve children, and at the time of
his discease, there were 73 grand children and 66 great-grand children living. He had been a professor of religion 48 years, and acted
the greater part of that time as a class leader.—He came down to his
grave old and full of years.

he was incited to search the Holy Scriptures, that he might see the object after which all Christians should aspire. This he found to be holiness of heart and life, and a will entirely quiescent to the will of God. After having searched the divine records, and having seen the extensive privilege of the Christian, he resolved to seek for the enjoyment of the promised blessings. He often retired in secret, and poured out his soul to God in strong cries, and tears—he was blessed with an outpouring of the Spirit of God—he arose happy—freed from doubts and fears, and went on his way rejoicing.

We will close this chapter with one extract from his journal.

" In the latter part of the year, we had a great revival of religion in our neighbourhood, and many of my friends and acquaintances were brought to experience the favour of God. I felt greatly quickened, and comforted with the Divine Presence. I had little inclination to be in any other company but the religious. I was always glad to go to meeting, by night or by day, and sometimes went on foot many miles, and thought myself highly favoured in that respect."

CHAPTER II.

—◦+◦—

IN the year 1775, Messrs. Shadford, Drumgoole and Glendenning, succeeded Mr. R. Williams on Brunswick circuit, which, by this time, had become considerably enlarged.

The labours of these three men were greatly blessed. Mr. Shadford preached in a bold, energetic style, searching the heart, and stripping the sinner and false professor, of every subterfuge ; sometimes proclaiming the law from Sinai, to shake the conscience of the sinner, and then pointing him to the blood of Jesus Christ, to wash away his sins.

Mr. Drumgoole's talents were nearly of the same class with the former, calculated to awaken the conscience, and awe the mind into reverence. Under the ministry of these men, Mr. Lee sat with great delight.

" In the latter part of that year (says he,) we had the greatest revival of religion, I had ever seen. I have been at meetings where the whole congregation would be bathed in tears : and sometimes their cries would be so loud that the preacher's voice could not be heard. Some would be seized with a trembling, and in a few moments drop on the floor

as if they were dead; while others were embracing
each other, with streaming eyes, and all were lost
in wonder, love, and praise.

"During that season, my soul was greatly blessed.
and for the greater part of my time, I was 'strong in
faith, giving glory to God.' I had such confidence
in, and love to God, and his service, that I was willing to be any thing, or nothing, so that God might be
all in all."

He continued in a happy, and peaceful frame of
mind until the spring of 1776, when he attended a
quarterly meeting, held at Bisseau's Chapel, Dinwiddie County, where the Spirit of God was poured
out in a remarkable manner; many souls were
brought to the favour of God, and several persons professed sanctification. He now discovered that the
blood of Christ could, indeed, *cleanse from all sin*. To
use his own words, "I went home with a fixed determination to seek for a deeper work of grace, and to
hope, and pray, and wait for that perfect love, which
casteth out all fear. I did firmly believe that the
Lord was both able, and willing, to save to the
utmost all that would come to him. I felt a *sweet distress* in my soul for holiness of heart and life. I sensibly felt that while I was seeking for purity of heart,
that I grew in grace, and in the knowledge of God.
This concern of soul lasted for some time, till at
length I could say, I have nothing but the love of
Christ in my heart. I was assured that my soul was
continually happy in God. The world, with all its
charms, *is crucified to me, and I am crucified to the
world.*"

It may be truly said that these different manifesta-
tions of the Spirit of God, were an evidence of a growth

in grace, by which the soul ascends step after step,
towards the Christian's eternal inheritance—a continual progress in the knowledge and love of God.
His heart becoming thus the seat of holy affections,
of love to God and men, we are not surprised that he
should feel an anxious desire to do something for the
good of souls.

The Apostle of the Gentiles has represented the
church of Christ as a body, having many members,
and every member having not the same office. This
metaphor may serve to illustrate the necessity of a
faithful discharge of our duties, in the stations which a
wise Providence has assigned us. Each one should
use the gift which God has given him, knowing that
all must be accountable for the improvement of the
talents distributed in wisdom.

Our brother Lee, as a member of the spiritual
building of Christ, discovered the necessity of using
the gifts which were conferred upon him, in endeavouring to promote the Redeemer's kingdom. And
an ample field, at this time, opened to his view. He
did not, indeed, at that time feel it his duty to preach,
but he thought in the time of a revival, he might be
the means of helping some poor broken hearted sinner, to claim an interest in the blood of Christ. "It
was his desire, (he said,) to do all the good he could."

A glorious revival was still carried on in his neighbourhood, and among his most intimate acquaintances
and friends. He had frequent opportunities of pressing upon their minds the importance of religion, and
the necessity of fleeing the wrath to come. And
while some, whose hearts God had touched, were
prostrate on the earth, crying for mercy, he would

3 *

be engaged in pointing them to the Lamb of God, who taketh away the sin of the world.

His zeal, however, would prompt him sometimes, to exhort in public, but his diffidence kept him from it, for a considerable time. It is supposed that from an impression of mind that it would one day be his duty to preach the gospel, he commenced the study of religious authors, not forgetting, at the same time, the study of the best of all books, the bible. By this course, his stock of useful knowledge was increased, and he was enabled to converse with more ease and perspicuity, on the subject of religion.

In the year 1777, he makes mention of another glorious revival, which took place in his neighbourhood.—Surely they were a highly favoured people, who, while suffering the privations which generally attend a state of warfare, (for this was in the midst of our revolutionary struggle,) should still be visited, several years in succession, with such great outpourings of the Spirit of God.

In the latter part of this year, he, from motives of kindness to a near relation who was left in a widowed state, parted with his affectionate parents, and removed to North Carolina. In leaving, for the first time, his parental home, he felt all that sorrow which an affectionate son was capable of feeling, under such circumstances ; for he always cherished a most affectionate regard for his aged father and mother, and in all his subsequent peregrinations from the first day he took leave of them to go to North Carolina until his death, he did not forget to visit them whenever an opportunity offered.

We shall close this chapter with extracts from his journal, subjoining a few notes as occasion may offer.

"January, 1778. I began to write down some account of every meeting which I attended, where a sermon was preached.* I had no thought, at that time, of keeping a journal, or of writing any account of the exercise of my own soul; but being desirous of obtaining and retaining all the information I could, I was induced to adopt this plan: it has oftentimes been a source of satisfaction to me since.

"But I added to the first plan that of noting the place and time when the sermon was delivered, and manner in which the text was divided and enlarged upon by the minister.

"This plan of noting down the sermons I heard, was of great service to me.—It fixed useful things in my memory, and gave me a view of the method, and manner of preaching, and brought me to a much better judgment of the nature and substance of the doctrines to be raised from certain texts. All these things being put together, my mind was led thereby to the Lord Jesus Christ, as the meritorious cause of all the blessings that I enjoyed. The benefit which I have derived to my own soul from the above plan, causes me still to be thankful that he ever directed and guided

* The practice of noting down all the texts of Scripture which he had heard preached on, was attended to during his life. This was not the only proof of the minuteness of his observations, for it will be found in his M. S. journals that he duly registered the name of every author he read, with the number of pages the book contained. He also kept an exact account of every quarterly meeting which he attended, together with the number of love feasts at which he was present. General and annual conferences were regularly noticed, with the time, place, and every remarkable circumstance attending them. He likewise kept a regular account of the number of sermons and exhortations which he delivered; so that I have more than once heard him tell, from the pulpit, how many sermons he had ever preached. This I shall more particularly notice in the succeeding pages.

me in that way.—For, in these things, I took no man
for my pattern, and no man's plan for my guide.

" As soon as I united with the class at B. Dobs', the
preacher of the circuit* appointed me class leader. I
felt it to be a heavy cross, yet I dare not refuse. I
began with fear and trembling and often wished to be
excused : I loved the cause of God, and was willing
to do all I could ; but being young, not quite 20 years
of age, I was sensible of my danger and my own
weakness. When I met the class I frequently wept
much while I was talking to the people about the welfare of their souls. I was well received by the class,
and greatly united to them.

" On the 8th of March, I gave a public exhortation, which was my first attempt. I then lacked a
few days of being twenty years old. The Saturday
night following, I went to a watch night, at brother
Lock's, where F. Garrettson led the meeting; he
asked me to speak, and I exhorted, which was my
second attempt. The next evening I attended a
watch night, at C. Bustin's, where I exhorted again ;
but I felt truly sensible of my own weakness ; and
what made the cross heavier, was owing, probably, to
the circumstance of having many of my old friends
and acquaintances to hear me,

" From that time I frequently exhorted at prayer
meetings, and class meetings ; and sometimes I
appointed meetings in the neighbourhood, or among
the neighbouring societies, with a view of speaking to
the people, and of begging them to be reconciled to
God.

"I have often admired the providence of God in
opening the way for me to remove to North Carolina ;

for, had I continued among my relations in Virginia, I might not have began my public labours so soon ; for at that time of my life I was very timid. But when I removed among strangers, I lost, in some degree, my former fearfulness. I seldom gave an exhortation without weeping ; for my heart yearned over the souls of poor sinners.

"At that time I could truly say, ' *The zeal of thy house hath eaten me up.*'

" During these exercises I had very little thought of becoming a preacher : I only wished to exhort, and pray, and live to do good to the souls of the people. My soul was remarkably happy in general, both in private and in public. My chief wish and greatest concern was to know the will of God, and to do it in all things, both great and small.

" In the close of the year I went to visit my friends in Virginia, and was at meeting with them in different places, and exhorted them publicly, and with much earnestness, to flee the wrath to come, and prepare for a better world. I was much pleased to find many of my old friends steadily pursuing their journey to heaven.

" On Christmas day we had a precious love feast at my father's, where the Christians were highly favoured of the Lord, and greatly comforted together in hearing each other tell of the goodness of God to their souls.

" After spending a little time with my friends and relations in Va. I returned to N. Carolina and spent a few days with my relations and religious friends, and then went into business again.

" In the beginning of the year 1779, I engaged in business with G. L. with whom I expected to find much comfort in the course of the year; as he war, in my esteem, one of the best private Christians that I was acquainted with. It turned out according to my expectations; and my soul was greatly blessed, quickened and comforted during that year; and the man with whom I lived, acted towards me as a father, and a brother, and gave me much information, and encouragement in religious matters. I spent all the time I could spare from my common vocation, in reading or in going to meeting.

"On the 17th of November, 1779, I preached for the first time in my life, at a place called the Old Barn. My text was 1 John iii. 1, 2. 'Behold what manner of love the Father hath bestowed upon us, that we should be called the sons of God! therefore the world knoweth us not, because it knew him not,' &c.

"I felt more liberty in speaking from that text than what I expected when I began. I felt such a desire to please God and instruct the people how to serve him, that I was at that time. willing to spend my days in the service of God.

"I preached again for the second time, at Mr. Guthrey's, on the Saturday following, and several times after that in the course of two weeks; and found much of the Divine Presence with me in public, yet I was so sensible of my own weakness and insufficiency, that after I had preached, I would retire to the woods and prostrate myself on the ground, and weep before the Lord, and pray that he would pardon the imperfections of my preaching, and give me strength to declare his whole counsel in purity; although, at that period, I had no expectation of ever travelling, and preaching extensively in the work.

"About this time, John Dickins, who was the preacher of that circuit, having some writings on hand, and wishing for a few weeks leisure, in order to complete what he had taken in hand, requested me to take his place on the circuit, which I consented to do ; but it was to me a heavy cross to begin, and equally heavy to continue for the short space of time for which I was engaged. From that time I continued to hold public meetings in different places ; and in most places the Christians appeared to be blessed. It appeared to me, that if I was of any use at all in my public character, it was among the religious part of mankind.

"At the close of the year, I again visited my friends in Virginia, and spent some time with them, and attended all the public places of worship in the neighbourhood. I felt more pleasure in religious meetings than in visiting my own relations. This was supposed to be the coldest winter that had ever been known in Virginia. It has properly been called the cold winter of 1770—80.

"I returned home in January, 1780, and lived at the same place.

"In June, Mr. Asbury came through that part of North Carolina, and preached in many places. It was a little more than twelve months from the time that the Methodist preachers in the South had separated from their brethren in the North. This separation took place at the *Broken Back Church*, in Virginia, where the conference was held in 1779. The cause of the separation was this :—the preachers in Virginia, seeing and feeling the necessity of having the ordinances of baptism, and the Lord's Supper, and seeing no way of having them administered without ordination, determined to ordain ministers for that purpose, and the conference accordingly, made choice of a committee who first ordained themselves, and then proceeded to ordain and set apart other preachers for the same office.

" On the 8th May, 1780, the conference was held at the Manakin Town, on James' River, where Mr. Asbury attended, and by his advice, it was agreed to suspend the administration of the ordinances for twelve months, and in the mean time to write to Mr. Wesley in England for his advice. This plan being adopted, the separation was stopped, and a happy union restored ; and the preachers in the North and South were again united."

After this division was healed, Mr. Asbury travelled considerably through the different circuits in Virginia and North Carolina, where the preachers had been in favour of the new plan ; but the division was soon healed, and the hearts of the preachers were closely united together.

CHAPTER III.

—◦◆◦—

He serves a tour of duty in the army—Is put under guard—
Released by the Colonel—Preaches to the army—Is appointed wagoner—Appointed Sergeant of the Pioneers—A tory
hung—Apprehends an attack from the Enemy—Gets a discharge from the army, and returns home—Reflections.

M R. LEE, who heretofore had been quietly engaged
in the pleasing task of cultivating the soil, and of
improving his spare moments in striving to aid in the
reformation of his fellow men, now is suddenly interrupted in his career by an imperious summons given
by his country, to exchange the implements of agri-
culture for the weapons of war; or it must be
recollected that at this juncture, America was engaged
in a struggle for her national rights and liberties. The
clarion of war had for several years been sounding on
the continent; and the storm which had begun to
gather in the northern, now began to lowr dreadfully over the southern and middle states. An invad-
ing foe was marching through the country, tracking his
way with blood and devastation. On all hands was
heard the sound of the martial trumpet, calling the
friends of liberty to the banners of their country; but
few who had arrived at the proper age were exempt
from taking an active part in the conflict. The militia
were drafted, and it fell to Mr. Lee's lot to go. How
illy it accorded with his religious views and feelings,
may be seen in the following extracts.

4

" I weighed the matter over and over again, but
my mind was settled ; as a Christian and as a preacher
of the gospel I could not fight.   I could not reconcile
it to myself to bear arms, or to kill one of my fellow
creatures ; however I determined to go, and to trust in
the Lord ; and accordingly prepared for my journey.

" Monday July 17th, 1780, I left home and set out
for the army, and travelled about 25 miles to Mr.
Green Hill's, where I was kindly used—I tarried
there all night.

" Wednesday 19th, I set off early in the morning
and travelled about 16 miles to Mr. Hines'.   In the
afternoon we had much conversation on spiritual matters, and in the evening, felt my heart more engaged
with God in prayer than usual.   I felt my dependence
upon God, and though I believed that great difficulties
lay before me, yet I resigned myself into the hands of
God, and felt assured that he would protect and take
care of me.

" I did not join the army till the 29th.   On the
evening of that day I came in sight of the camp, and
was soon called on parade, and orders were given for
all the soldiers to be furnished with guns.   I then
lifted up my heart to God and besought him to take
my cause in his hands, and support me in the hour of
trial.

" The sergeant soon came round with the guns, and
offered one to me, but I would not take it.   Then the
lieutenant brought me one, but I refused to take it.
He said I should go under guard.   He then went to
the colonel, and coming back, brought a gun and set it
down against me.   I told him he had as well take it
away or it would fall.   He then took me with him and
delivered me to the guard.

" After a while the colonel came, and taking me out
a little way from the guard, he began to converse with
me, and to assign many reasons why I should bear
arms ; but his reasons were not sufficiently cogent to
make any alteration in my mind. He then told the
guard to take care of me, and so left me.

" Many of the people came and talked with me and
pitied me, and would leave me with tears in their eyes.
We lay encamped at a tavern a few miles from the
site of what was afterwards the seat of government
for North Carolina. After dark, I told the guard we
must pray before we slept ; and, having a Baptist
under guard, I asked him to pray, which he did. I
then told the people if they would come out early in
the morning, I would pray with them. I felt remarkably happy in God under all my trouble, and did not
doubt but that I should be delivered in due time.
Some of the soldiers brought me some straw to lay
upon, and offered me their blankets and great coats
for covering. I slept pretty well that night, which was
the first, and the last night I was ever under guard.

" Sunday 30th.—As soon as it was light, I was up
and began to sing, and some hundreds of people soon
assembled and joined with me, and we made the plantation ring with the songs of Zion. We then kneeled down
and prayed ; and while I was praying, my soul was
happy in God, and I wept much and prayed loud, and
many of the poor soldiers also wept. I do not think
that I ever felt more willing to suffer for the sake of
religion than what I did at that time.

" A little after we were done prayer, Mr. Thomas,
the tavern keeper, came out and talked with me, and
told me he was in bed when he heard me praying, that
he could not refrain from tears, and he had called to

see me, and know if I would be willing to preach to
them that day, it being sabbath ? I told him I would
preach provided he would procure a block, or something for me to stand upon ; which he readily promised to do. I told him, withal, I wished him to go
to the colonel, for we had no higher officer amongst
us, and obtain leave for me to preach ; which he did,
and liberty was granted. It is but just to state, that
Colonel Bru * * * was a man of great humanity,
although a profane swearer. When he heard that I
was about to preach, it affected him very much, so
he came and took me out to talk with me on the subject of bearing arms. I told him I could not kill a
man with a good conscience, but I was a friend to my
country, and was willing to do any thing that I could,
while I continued in the army, except that of fighting.
He then asked me if I would be willing to drive their
baggage wagon ? I told him I would, though I had
never drove a wagon before ; he said their main
cook was a Methodist, and could drive the wagon
when we were on a march, and I might lodge and eat
with him ; to which I agreed. He then released me
from guard, and said when I was ready to begin meeting I might stand on a bench by his tent. When
the hour arrived, I began under the trees, and took
my text in Luke xiii. 5. *Except ye repent, ye shall all
likewise perish.* After I had been speaking awhile it
began to rain, and we were under the necessity of
going into the house, where I resumed my discourse.
I was enabled to speak plainly, and without fear ; and
I wept while endeavouring to declare my message.
Many of the people, officers as well as men, were
bathed in tears before I was done. That meeting
afforded me an ample reward for all my trouble. At

the close of the meeting, some of the gentlemen went about with their hats to make a collection of money for me, at which I was very uneasy, and ran in among the people and begged them to desist. I could not at that time feel willing to receive any compensation for preaching. I thought if the people could afford to sit and hear me, I could well afford to stand and preach to them. I felt my heart humbled before God, and was truly thankful to him for the grace communicated to my soul at that time. I had no doubt but that all things would work for my good.

"On Monday I took charge of the wagon, and felt much resigned to the will of God."

It is obvious to every reflecting mind, that a good deal of religious boldness and enjoyment is necessary to support a mind disposed to seriousness amidst the noise and confusion of a camp. The army has always been a nursery of wickedness, a hot bed, in which is generated all kinds of profanity.

It must put the feelings of the Christian to the rack, to hear men without any apparent remorse, blaspheme the name of Jehovah, and indulge themselves in gambling and drunkenness, as is frequently the case in armies. Mr. Lee's mind was made to feel very acutely on this account.—" But, (says he,) though I was in the midst of profane swearers, I was the more on my guard; for I well knew that I could not withstand my enemies unless I was constantly supported by divine grace."

From Thomas' tavern, near the present town of Raleigh, the army moved on towards the South, passed through Chatham County, crossed How-River, at the Island-Ford and Deep-Creek. at Romney's Mill, crossed Drowning Creek at Coles' bridge, and the

4 *

next day entered the state of South Carolina ; and
then to the banks of the Pedee River, where they
encamped.   During the week they made forced
marches, and the soldiers could obtain but half rations
of meal.

In order to show that his zeal and ardour for the
cause of the Redeemer remained undiminished during the fatigues and trials of a soldier's life, we shall
lay before the reader a few extracts from his journal.

" Sunday 13th of August, we lay by and did not
march ; about 3 o'clock in the afternoon, I preached
to a large number of soldiers, from Isa. iii. 10, 11.
Say ye to the righteous, &c. Many of the hearers were
very solemn, and some of them wept freely under the
preaching of the word.   I was happy in God, and
thankful to him for that privilege of warning the
wicked once more.   It was a great cross for me to go
forward in matters of so much importance, where
there were few to encourage, and many to oppose ;
but I knew that I had to give an account to God for
my conduct in the world—I felt the responsibility laid
upon me, and was resolved to open my mouth for
God.   I often thought I had more cause to praise
and adore God for his goodness than any other person.
For some weeks I hardly ever prayed in public, or
preached, or reproved a sinner, without seeing some
good effects produced by my labours.

" Thursday 17th, about 10 o'clock in the morning,
we received the unexpected news of general Gates'
defeat, near Campden, which took place the day
before ; the news spread through the camp, and all
were called out on parade.   All appeared solemn ;
not an oath was heard for several hours.   The
mouths of the most profane swearers were shut.   We
hen commenced a retreat back to North Carolina.

"Monday 28th, we marched down to Romney's Mills, on Deep River. On the 29th, I was taken very sick. The next day I went to Mr. Crump's, about three miles from the camp. I was so sick that I could not return to camp that night. I was brought to examine my heart closely concerning my hope of heaven ; and was comforted to find that I had no doubt of my salvation ; for I believed that should the Lord see fit to remove me from this world, I should be called to join the armies of Heaven.

" Tuesday the 5th of September, the army marched from Deep River, and I joined them though quite unwell.

" On the following morning the Colonel told me, inasmuch as I was not willing to bear arms, I must join the pioneers. I was afterward appointed sergeant of the pioneers, which was a safe and easy birth ; there were but few in that company, and I had to direct them in their labours, which was not hard. The soldiers suffered much for the want of provision, for the greater part of the week. We crossed Harraway River, and came through Randolph County ; we were frequently alarmed at night, so that I was much fatigued by severe marches by day, and sleeping little at night. But the best of all was, my soul was kept in peace, and at times, I felt great fellowship with the Father and with the Son !

" On the 15th of September, at night, some of our men took a noted tory from under guard and carried him a little way off, and hung him up, without judge or jury. Some inquiry was made about it the next day, but no person would confess the fact, and it passed over. This circumstance took place near Salisbury, where we tarried four nights.

" Sunday the 24th, Mr. Green Hill preached in the
camp ; his text was 1 Thes. v. 19. ' Quench not
the Spirit.' The next morning before day we had
orders to prepare and leave the ground in ten minutes,
for the British were expected to be on us in a short
time. We left the ground before day, and the wa-
gons came on towards Salisbury about 16 miles, and
then had orders to turn back to the Cross-Roads,
which was about 9 miles ; we retreated about 7 miles,
and halted to get something to eat ; we then had orders
to march immediately. The enemy came to Charlotte, and had an engagement with our people, and
several men were killed. Some who overtook us,
who were with the baggage, were wounded and
bleeding. We marched about 18 miles that day, and
made it quite late in the night before we came to a
halt. We stayed two or three hours, and cooked
something, and eat a little; and then marched immediately, without taking time to sleep. We marched
again sometime before day, and the roads were
thronged with people, men, women and children,
with their property, flying from the face of the
enemy. The colonel rode up and said to me, ' Well,
Lee! don't you think you could fight now ?' I told
him I could fight with switches, but I could not kill a
man. We came to Salisbury and encamped in town
that night, expecting the enemy would be after us
every hour. The night was very cold.

" On Thursday, 28th of September, we crossed the
Yadkin, at Island Ford, on account of the water
being very high.

" On Sunday, the 8th of October, I was but poorly
employed ; we had no religious meeting.

"Tuesday the 10th, general Butler came into camp with a number of men, and took command of the whole army.

" At night the news arrived in camp that on Saturday last the Americans had a skirmish with the British and tories in Kings' Mountain, where our men gained a complete victory, and killed many of the enemy, and took the rest prisoners. We were all glad to hear the news ; but some rejoiced with horrid oaths, and others determined to get drunk for joy. For my part, I felt thankful to God, and humbled before him, knowing that the battle is not to the strong.

" October 13th, colonel Morgan joined us with a part of his regiment—some of our soldiers were very sick—I went among them where they lay in barns, at the point of death, and talked to them about their souls ; and begged them to prepare to meet their God. When convenient, I attended the funeral of those who died, and prayed at the grave.

" Wednesday the 18th, we had a sharp frost, which was a great advantage to those who were sick. In the evening Col. Washington, with his troop of horse joined us. The next day we crossed the Yadkin River to the South, and the day following, marched a small distance above Salisbury, and took up late at night. On Saturday we were up before day, and after some consultation among the officers, we were informed that we were not to march that day. We were in constant expectation of an attack from the enemy. I felt my mind calm and stayed on God ; but having my rest so much broken of late, I felt quite dull and heavy.

" In the evening, by general Butler's order, 500 men were despatched in search of the enemy. In

the evening I walked out into the woods alone to
pray and meditate; and it was to me a time of comfort and peace. I had such a deep sense of the love
of God, that I was humbled in his presence, and my
soul was filled with gratitude and love.

"Sunday 22d October, we continued in camp all
day and had no religious meeting. On Tuesday following, Gen. Jones came into our camp with his men.
Many of the militia officers and soldiers began to be
very uneasy about remaining any longer, as they supposed their time of service had expired, and several
had already deserted.

"Saturday 28th. They drummed out of camp two
captains and one ensign for deserting.

"Sunday Oct. 29th.—On this morning I obtained
my discharge. The general said as there were two
sergeants of the pioneers, and one was sufficient, it
would be best for me to resign, and as I was the oldest in office, I might have the privilege if I chose it.
I accepted the offer—took my discharge—settled some
business—took leave of many of my old acquaintances,
and left the army." And we may well imagine that
he did not quit it with much regret.

Here he ended his military career. It certainly sub-
jected him to many trials, and to much labour; but
he had an opportunity of benefitting the souls of his
fellow creatures by preaching Christ unto them. In
addition to this, God did not leave his soul without
comfort, but continued to supply him with grace to
enable him to bear hardness as a good soldier of
Christ. In the character of a soldier, we have seen
him determined to keep a conscience void of offence
towards God and man. True, he could not, consis-
tently with the dictates of his conscience, take the life

of an enemy, but let it be remembered that he considered himself not only a Christian, but a preacher of the
gospel of Christ ; believing that it was his duty to pro_
claim the glad tidings of salvation to dying men, he
could not violate the dictates of his conscience, in
shedding the blood of any man.

His discharge from military duty was a plain indi-
cation of the favourable interposition of Divine Providence towards him ; and affords an encouragement to
all to do their duty, in whatever circumstance of life
they may be placed.

CHAPTER IV.

—◦◦◦—

Exercises previous to his entering the Travelling Ministry—Attends the Virginia Conference at Ellis', but did not take an appointment—He finally consents to travel for a season.

We noticed in the preceding chapter that he obtained his discharge on the 29th of October, and after taking an affectionate leave of his friends, commenced his journey homeward.

The country had been so much desolated by the marching of a hostile army that he found it extremely difficult, on more than one occasion, to procure a little bread for his subsistence. He was, however, fortunate enough at other times to fall in with kind and hospitable friends, who freely administered to his necessities.

Saturday the 4th of November, he had the pleasure of saluting his dear relations at *home*, after an absence of three months and a half. We may easily imagine how grateful he was to God for bringing him once more to the enjoyment of domestic life.—He had now an opportunity of visiting his numerous friends and relations, some of whom, since his departure, had been brought to the knowledge of the truth as it is in Jesus: among whom were a sister and his brother, Nathaniel Lee; this to him was a matter of great comfort.

From this time until January 1781, he continued preaching at various appointments of his own, and

5

attending the ministry of others whenever an opportunity served. During the remaining part of the
year he experienced many severe exercises of mind.
owing principally to two causes. The first from an
expectation of being called again to perform a military
tour : from this apprehension he was, however, soon
relieved, although he had been drafted a second time.
But the danger passed over, and the horrors of a
protracted war began to subside, and the enemy retir-
ing from that section of the country, he was suffered
to remain in quiet. Notwithstanding his apprehen-
sions were relieved on that score, his mind was much
impressed from the belief that there was a greater
work to which he would be called.

It was frequently and forcibly impressed upon his
mind that it was his duty to devote himself more
entirely to the work of the ministry, or in other
words, to resign himself to the travelling ministry.

Mr. Lee had witnessed in some degree, the beneficial effects of the itinerating plan of spreading the
gospel. Though the Methodists had but recently visited the country, yet he had had an opportunity of hearing them, and of seeing the blessed effects of their ministry in the revivals of religion heretofore mentioned.
And by reading the scriptures he plainly saw that Christianity was first promulgated by means of a travelling
ministry. Under this view of things, and feeling his
mind powerfully impressed that it was his duty to
exert all his powers for the salvation of men, he was
led towards the Methodist itinerating ministry.

And who that reviews the last century but must be
forcibly struck with the blessed effects of this method
of spreading the knowledge of salvation by the remis-
sion of sin? Great Britain has arisen from a state

of moral darkness to become light in the Lord. And these United States have been equally favoured with the transforming power of Divine Truth. Had the predictions of the enemies of Methodism been verified, that "ridicule alone would put them down in a few years," thousands now in glory, would doubtless have been sunk in eternal wretchedness.

That the Methodist preachers have had enemies to encounter is well known ; but it is equally well known that they have been greatly owned of God, having been instrumental of reviving evangelical principles and holiness, not only among their own people, but also among the various denominations of Christians ; so that even their enemies have been constrained to acknowledge the finger of God. Piety to God and zeal in the cause of Christ have long since become so characteristic of the Methodists, that any person, manifesting any unusual zeal for religion, is immediately, by way of reproach, branded with the epithet of Methodist. May they long continue to exemplify in their conduct, the truth and the purity of the doctrines and precepts of Christ.

To these people Mr. Lee had already united himself. With them he found the fellowship of the saints. He believed their doctrine, and had commenced to enforce it upon the understandings and consciences of others. And he now began to feel that a dispensation of this gospel was committed unto him. But the thought of relinquishing the comforts of domestic life, and more especially of engaging in so important an undertaking, produced for a season, much anxiety and some hesitancy ; he therefore strove to content himself in a more limited sphere of action until his way should be made more plain. The following extracts from his journal will show the exercise of his mind at this time.

"I had for some time been deeply exercised about travelling and preaching the gospel ; and at times, it appeared that I could not with a clear conscience resist the thought, and still was unwilling to go, fearing that I should injure the work of God, which I loved as I did my own life. I finally concluded that I would change my state,* supposing that I should then be freed from these exercises ; but when I made the attempt, I continued to pray, and prayed in earnest that if it was the will of God that I should ever be called to the itinerant field, that I might not succeed : but by the intervention of some means, be prevented; I have often felt thankful to God that matters turned out for my spiritual advantage, and in this respect, believe that my prayers were answered.

"My exercises about travelling and preaching still continue. I have been often solicited by the preachers to take a circuit, but am afraid that I shall hurt the cause of God, which I wish with all my heart to promote. I feel willing to take up my cross and follow the Lord, but tremble at the thought of touching the ark of God too hastily."

But his mind was more and more weaned from the world, and seemed to be gradually preparing for the work he had to do. And often, while delivering his message to his fellow men, the power of the Lord was felt in the assembly, and his ministry blessed to the awakening of sinners, and the consolation of believers.

* At that stage of Methodism in the Virginia conference, a man incumbered with a family rarely ever moved out of a local sphere. This notion has prevailed from that time to the present, not for want of means, but for the want of an inclination. Thus age and talent are fairly driven out of the conference in too many instances.

The following extract will show that the Lord was graciously pleased to add some seals to his ministry.

"On Saturday 14th, I went to meeting at Robert Jones', but I did not get there till the sermon was over; but was in time to be in the class meeting; at the close of which a young man came to me, and taking me by the hand, told me that on the 12th of May last, he came to hear me preach, and was cut to the heart by my discourse; from which he went home and could neither eat, or drink, or sleep, in peace until the 4th of June; at which time the Lord turned his mourning into rejoicing. I felt humbled in the dust, and praised the Lord. Well, thought I, if the Lord has blessed my labours in the conversion of one soul, I will try again, and preach for the Lord."

Under these encouraging circumstances he discovered how amply the Lord rewarded him for his momentary toil, and felt resolved to trust all into his gracious hands.

Thus we perceive that men may be called and qualified to preach the gospel, independently of what is called a classical education. To turn sinners from darkness to light, and from the power of Satan to God, is the grand design of the Christian ministry. And although human learning may qualify men to defend the outports of religion, that alone is not sufficient to qualify them for teaching sinners the way to heaven We do not mean to deprecate learning; but in regard to the Christian ministry, it holds a secondary place to experimental and practical religion. Those who are *inwardly moved by the Holy Ghost* to take upon themselves this holy office, whether learned or unlearned, will give evidence of their divine mission.

by the success of their labours in bringing sinners to the knowledge of the truth as it is in Jesus.

In April 1782, he attended the annual conference, which was held at Ellis' Chapel, in Sussex County, Va. At this conference there were present about thirty preachers. He was permitted to sit in the room while the preachers were transacting their business, except in the examination of characters.

He was particularly struck with the spirit of harmony and brotherly affection which prevailed throughout the whole body present on that occasion. These amiable traits of the Christian character, have in every age of Christianity, done much for the advancement of pure and undefiled religion.

The spirit which prevailed at this conference cannot be better described than in his own words.

"The union and brotherly love which I saw among the preachers, exceeded every thing I had ever seen before, and caused me to wish that I was worthy to have a place amongst them. When they took leave of each other, I observed that they embraced each other in their arms, and wept as though they never expected to meet again. Had the heathens been there, they might have well said, 'see how these Christians love one another!' By reason of what I saw and heard during the four days that the conference sat, I found my heart truly humbled in the dust. and my desires greatly increased to love and serve God more perfectly than I had ever done before.

"At the close of the conference, Mr. Asbury came to me and asked me if I was willing to take a circuit; I told him that I could not well do it, but signified I was at a loss to know what was best for me to do. I was afraid of hurting the cause which I wished to pro-

mote ; for I was very sensible of my own weakness :
at last he called to some of the preachers standing in
the yard a little way off, and said, 'I am going to enlist
brother Lee :' one of them replied, 'what bounty do
you give ?' he answered, 'grace here, and glory here
after will be given if he is faithful!'

"Some of the preachers then talked to me and persuaded me to go, but I trembled at the thought, and
shuddered at the cross, and did not at that time consent."

From the time he attended the conference at Ellis
until November following, he employed his time in
preaching and attending to the arrangement of his
temporal concerns, in order that he might, at any time
be able to obey the will of God.

November 3d.—At a quarterly meeting, being much
persuaded by the preachers to travel a circuit, he
gave his consent to travel half a quarter, having now
determined to make a trial for a few weeks, and leave
all, to follow the Lord Jesus Christ.

Having attended a few appointments on what I suppose was then called Sussex Circuit, he received a
letter from the presiding elder, Caleb Peddicord,
requesting him to accompany E. Drumgoole to that
part of North Carolina which lies to the North and
West of Edenton, for the purpose of forming a new
circuit.

CHAPTER V.

—◦◦◦—

He goes in company with Mr. Drumgoole to form a new Circuit—Some trials and exercises about travelling—Quaker hospitality—Formed a Circuit called Campden—Concluding Remarks.

HAVING now given his consent to enter more fully into the work of the ministry, he concluded to embrace the openings of Providence, and if the Lord was with him to continue, and if not, to return home.

Some difficulties occuring at this time which, in after life would have appeared comparatively trifling, almost damped his ardour; and he was tempted to relinquish the undertaking, when he was barely upon the threshold. But meeting with his colleague, like Paul who met the brethren at the three taverns, he took courage and boldly resolved to prosecute his journey. Mr. Drumgoole and himself arrived in Edenton on the 1st of December. The first person with whom they formed an acquaintance was Parson Pettigrew. With him they attended church on that day, and after Mr. Pettigrew had read the morning service, Mr. Drumgoole gave an exhortation; and by permission, made an appointment to preach at the place the next day. That night they were comfortably entertained by the parson, who was thought by the people to be a pious man. The next day they attended the appointment which had been made the preceding day, and Mr. Drumgoole preached to an attentive congregation.

Leaving Edenton, they pursued their journey, in order to find some others who were willing to receive them as the messengers of Christ, and to hear the word of life dispensed. The adventures of that day were somewhat singular, and in the sequel served to give Mr. Lee some idea of that plainness of a dress which is characteristic of the people called Friends. After travelling all day, and night coming on apace, they stopped at the house of a Quaker, and asked him if they could be permitted to tarry with him that night, "If you choose to get down, (said the honest Quaker,) I will not turn you away." This blunt reply quite confounded young Lee, who for a while doubted whether he could trust his hospitality or not, but as it was no time for ceremony, they dismounted, went in, and strove to make themselves welcome, and indeed they found that he was not lacking in that hospitality for which their sect has ever been noted.

Before the guests retired to bed, they begged permission to pray in the family.—"If you have a mind to pray, (says the Quaker,) I will leave the room:" and accordingly went out and pulling the door after him, left them to enjoy their devotions in their own way.

The subjoined extracts will show more distinctly the success of their mission.

"Wednesday 4th of December, we rode early in the morning, crossed Pasquotank River, and came to Mr. Jones', at the Plank Bridge.

"A little after dark when the people, hearing that we were preachers, came and requested us to preach, and notice being given, we had about thirty people collected in the course of an hour, and E. Drumgoole preached to them. The people were solemn, and appeared to be desirous for us to come amongst them again, as they had but little opportunity of hearing preaching.

"Saturday 7th, we attended at brother Halstead's, Norfolk County, Virginia. E. Drumgoole preached, and I gave an exhortation. Some of these people had formerly been in society with the Methodists, and the circuit preachers came regularly among them; but during the revolutionary war, the preachers left them, and they were without preaching for about five years; but they waited and prayed for the preachers to come among them again, and for some time they have been favoured with regular preaching.

"Sunday 8th.—At the North-west Brick Church, E. Drumgoole preached to a large concourse of people, who were very attentive, and somewhat affected. —I was pleased with the congregation.

"Tuesday 10th, we came to an old church where E. Drumgoole preached, and I exhorted,—we had a profitable time together. We then went to Colonel William's and stayed all night. The Colonel is a man who fears God, and was well pleased at our calling to see him.

"Friday 13th, E. Drumgoole preached at a place called Indian Town, and I gave an exhortation—we had a large house full of attentive hearers—my soul was much comforted at that time, and I felt glad to be there.

"We then left Currituck County—crossed North River—dined at Mrs. Lamb's, who was a Baptist, who treated us kindly. We then came to General Gregory's, and at night in his dwelling house, we had a large congregation, although the weather was very cold.

"Saturday 14th, we came to Sawyer's and held meeting; we had a solemn time, and I believe good was done,

"Sunday 15th, at River Bridge, where we had a large company of well behaved people to hear the word of eternal life: it was a solemn and profitable time.

"Wednesday 18th, E. Drumgoole preached at Yeopin Church, to a large congregation of attentive hearers; we then rode home with the Rev. Mr. Pettigrew near Edenton, and spent the night with him. Our journey in the low lands from Edenton to Norfolk County in Virginia, and back again, has taken sixteen days, in which time we have had nineteen meetings, chiefly among people who were not acquainted with the Methodists; but the general wish was that we should return again; and we so far succeeded in our plan as to form a circuit, which was called Campden. I felt thankful to God for the privilege of visiting that strange people, and I had no doubt but our labours were acceptable to God, and profitable to the people."

After having formed the outlines of a circuit in a part of the world which had been so long destitute of the means of grace, they left it with the expectation that others would be sent to fill up the intermediate places.

Mr. Lee then proceeded to visit his father, and to spend a few days among those with whom he had passed the days of his childhood : and from that time until the setting of the Virginia conference he did not travel regularly. He continued at his father's about two months, during which time he was by no means idle. When he was not employed in preaching or attending the ministry of others, he was labouring with his own hands, or as he termed it, " was busy at work." He was frequently entreated both by word and letter to go into a circuit, and give himself entirely to the work of the ministry, but he was fear-

ful of undertaking in so important a work hastily.
He besought the Lord to teach and direct him in the
right way. He concluded finally that he would get all
things in readiness, and attend the conference, and
then if he should see his way clear, to go, and if not,
to give up the idea altogether. Suspense is always painful. And while the mind
hangs quivering in suspense upon a question involving
such important consequences as does that of engaging
in the work of the Christian ministry, it produces the
most exquisite sensations. " To go, or not to go," was
now the question to be decided in Mr. Lee's mind.
And all his hesitancy upon this subject evinces a mind
conscientiously desiring to do that which is lawful and
right in the sight of God. And those who mark the
result of his choice, will not doubt but that he was
ultimately directed by the wisdom which cometh from
above. We pretend not to decide on the motives of
those who may have declined their ministerial labour
for some more easy employment. Whether it was
owing to their want of zeal, or to the backwardness
of the people to afford them a competent support, it
is to be lamented that so many have forsaken the field
of labour, and devoted themselves to secular pursuits.
So did not Jesse Lee. His ardent soul, filled with
love to God and man, continually thirsted for the salvation of men. Of this he gave full proof in all the
subsequent acts of his life.

CHAPTER VI.

—⚬✦⚬—

He attends Conference at Ellis' Meeting House—Appointed to
Caswell—Goes to Amelia, from thence to Sussex Circuit—
He is blessed in his own soul, and his labours made a blessing
to others.

IN a work like the present, where brevity is one
important consideration with the compiler, it will not
be expected that every incident of the life of the subject of this memoir can be noticed. The principal
object of the writer is to exhibit those virtues which
adorned his life, and to follow him through his ministerial labours, if not step by step, yet in such a manner as always to keep him in view, without attempting
to deviate materially from the track. The daily occurrences of a man's life can hardly interest or edify the
public, when there is a sameness in the details ; there
must be some variety, or the narrative becomes tedious and dull, and the reader either hurries through
the pages, or lays aside the volume in disgust.

There is a fondness for the marvellous in most
readers which leads them to look for something of an
extraordinary nature in every work which they attempt
to peruse. It should be recollected, however, that in
following the track of an itinerating minister who
travelled so extensively as Jesse Lee did, that there
must necessarily be some diversity of incident, some
variation in the scenery, and some striking interposi-
tions of Divine Providence and grace. But it is not

necessary that there should be difficulties at every
step. Our materials are drawn from real life, and
therefore we are not allowed to make fiction appear
like truth, for the purpose of gratifying the vitiated
tastes of the admirers of novel and romance.

We shall find in the sequel, that the subject of this
memoir, after finding out what was his duty, never failed to perform it, however crossing to his inclinations :
that, although he did not court danger, yet he never
fled from it, but patient and persevering in the discharge of his duty, he looked to God as the great
arbiter of all his actions ; and expected a reward
from him, and him alone.

Every step taken by Mr. Lee, relative to his entering the itinerant field, was taken with due cautionand
circumspection, fearing lest he should "run before
he was sent." But having at length made up his
mind to make the trial, he accordingly attended the
conference held at Ellis' Meeting House in Sussex,
which commenced its sitting on the 7th of May, 1783.

At this conference he consented to take an appointment, " notwithstanding (says he,) I have had ten
years experience as a Christian, and have been a
public speaker more than five years, I trembled at
the thought of the station I was about to fill."

The business of conference was conducted in great
peace and harmony, and in three days it was brought
to a close, and all were ready to go to the places
assigned them—he was appointed to Caswell Circuit,
North Carolina. Caswell at this time was but a moral
wilderness : it had been but recently taken under
the superintendance of the Methodists, who were
resolved to take in as much ground as they could con-
veniently cultivate. This wilderness has since, in

many places, blossomed as the rose ; and many in
that section of the Lord's vineyard, have been brought
to the knowledge of the truth through the instrumentality of the Methodists, some of whom have gone to
receive the reward of their labours, in the church
triumphant.

We shall here take the liberty of noticing what
was to him a singular phenomenon.

On Sunday the 25th of May, he preached in
the morning at Mrs. Heath's, and in the afternoon at
Tatum's. On his way to the latter place he saw a
large meteor or ball of fire, shoot from the N. East
towards the S. West. It appeared to move slowly
in a horizontal direction for many miles, and then
passed out of his view below the horizon. What contributed to make it more remarkable was, that the sun
shone quite clear at the time. Several minutes after
the meteor disappeared, he heard a loud noise resem-
bling distant thunder.

The pious mind makes every occurrence of Providence, whether in the kingdom of nature or grace, a
lesson of instruction. And though many of the phe-
nomenæ of nature, as to their cause and ends, elude
the scrutinies of philosophy, they all proclaim, in the
ear of the scientific Christian, the majesty of the
Great Supreme. Even the meteors that shoot through
the air, by their evanescent appearance, may remind
us of the momentary enjoyments we derive from present objects ; while the fixed stars, " Those mighty
orbs," may serve to fix our attention upon those permanent and perpetual enjoyments which are at the
right-hand of God.

In a few weeks after Mr. Lee had received his
appointment from conference, he took leave of his

6 *

weeping relatives, and commenced his journey towards
his circuit : in travelling thither he had the satisfaction
of seeing one who professed to have obtained the forgiveness of her sins when only ten years of age.   At
the time he saw her, she had professed religion three
years, and still held to her integrity ; her mind was
more than ordinarily enlightened for one of her age ;
she prayed in the family when called upon, and was
happy in the enjoyment of religion.   How blessed are
they who are early taught in the school of Christ! and
before evil habits get an ascendency, receive the
impressions of the Holy Spirit, and grow up in the fear
and love of God.

He continued his journey, and on the 23d of June,
arrived within the bounds of his circuit.   Upon examination he found it only a part of a circuit taken
off from another ; and as there were two preachers
appointed to travel this remnant of a circuit, it was
necessary that they should enlarge their borders by
taking in new preaching places.

He commenced his appointments on the 26th, at the
widow Parker's; "where (says he,) I preached to a
few people, most of whom were called out of the harvest field." without having time to adjust either the
mind or the body, as we may suppose, "and the day
being warm and the people much fatigued, they were in
poor order for attending a place of worship."

The following day he was much exercised in mind
on account of some disorderly members, and was from
that, as well as from other circumstances, so much discouraged that he was almost inclined to return to his
father's again.   A step which, candour obliges me to
say, would have been very unjustifiable had he taken
it. Happy for him and for thousands that he got the

better of those unpleasant feelings, and was enabled to persevere in his work.

Sunday 29th, he preached at Parish's Meeting House, where he felt his soul quickened and his spirit much revived. The following Tuesday he preached at the same place, and enjoyed more inward satisfaction in speaking, than he had for some time ; the people were considerably affected under the word, and he believed that God had not forgotten to be gracious.

Upon trial it was found that the circuit was not large enough for two preachers, and it was thought most expedient for one to remove; and accordingly as Mr. Lee was the junior preacher, he was sent to travel Amelia Circuit ; he was by no means displeased with this arrangement, and left the circuit after having travelled it only three weeks.

We here subjoin some extracts from his journal.

"Sunday 20th of July, I preached at Whitaker's, (Roan Oak Circuit,) and the congregation wept under the word preached. When we met the class, the power and presence of the Lord was among us, and many cried aloud. I was so deeply affected that I could not speak, till I had stopped and wept for some time. I preached again at night, and the people wept greatly.

" Monday 21.—We had a very lively meeting at brother Young's in the day, and again at night, where there were about forty members in society, and none of them professed to be converted except the leader of the class, but many of the mourners were deeply distressed on account of their sins.

" Tuesday 22d, we had meeting at Low's, and the next day at John Clayton's, then went up into Warren County, where I met with John Easter, and held meet-

ing at Wm. Jean's ; the next day we came to Benjamin Doaie's in Halifax County, where John Easter
preached a profitable sermon.

"Sunday 27th, we held meeting at Jones' Chapel ;
the next day at brother Lock's ; the day following at
Richard Whitaker's, and the two following days at
Tar-River Church. We had a good deal of life among
us at these meetings.

"Saturday 16th, and Sunday 17th of August, I
attended a quarterly meeting at the Tabernacle, Roan
Oak Circuit. The first day we had two sermons, and
the next day we had a lively love feast. Then I
preached, J. O. Kelly preached and J. Easter exhorted.
It was indeed a day of the Lord's power, and many
souls were comforted. One young man was awakened
by the sermon which I preached, who afterwards
became a travelling preacher.*

"At this quarterly meeting the preachers concluded
that it would be best for me to go to Amelia Circuit in
Virginia, and fill the place of a preacher that could
not travel any longer. I willingly consented ; I crossed
Roan Oak River to T. Jones', and tarried all night.
The next day I parted with several of the preachers,
and set off to my father's, where I arrived safe on
Wednesday afternoon.

"Sunday 24.—I came to Amelia Circuit, and travelled on somewhat successfully until the middle of
February, 1784.

Thursday December 25th he has these remarks :

" This day the people came out at Thompson's, and
we had a comfortable meeting ; and my soul was much
comforted in preaching to a people who had but little
religion, and it was a solemn, profitable time to the
hearers.

* Mark Moore.

"At the close of the year I looked back on the many trials through which I had passed, and took a view of the many blessings conferred on my soul, and was truly thankful to God. The Lord give me grace to spend my strength, my talents and my life to his glory. Amen.

"Saturday 31st, I preached at Mr. Spain's with great liberty to a good congregation, and the Spirit of the Lord came upon us, and we were bathed in tears—I wept—and so loud were the people's cries, that I could scarcely be heard, though I spoke very loud. I met the class—most of the members expressed a great desire for holiness of heart and life, and said they were determined to seek for perfect love.

"Sunday 1st of February, I preached at Coleman's with life and liberty, to a weeping congregation. When I met the class, we were highly favoured of the Lord, with a comfortable sense of his love shed abroad in our hearts; the brethren wept, and praised God together; I was constrained to praise God aloud for his goodness towards me; I was indeed very happy.

"Saturday 14th.—We held our quarterly meeting for Amelia Circuit, at old father Patrick's—we had a good meeting for the first day. On Sunday morning we had a happy love feast; at which time I wept much, and prayed earnestly that the Lord would take every evil temper and every wrong desire out of my heart, and fill my soul with perfect love. I felt the pain of parting with my friends in that circuit, among whom I had been labouring for six months; I bade them farewell, and went to Sussex to travel the next quarter.

"Wednesday 18th, I took my place in Sussex Circuit, and preached at my father's house, from Luke xix. 10. *For the Son of man is come to seek and to save that which was lost.* It was a solemn day with me, and I felt a constant breathing after the Lord, and a longing desire to love him with all my heart. O Lord! hasten to my relief, and grant me the desire of my heart for thy mercies' sake.

" The next day I preached at the widow Heath's, and th day following, at a place called The College : the day after I preached at Howel's Chapel, where the Lord was pleased once more to visit my soul ; I spoke with many tears, and was very happy—the hearers wept greatly—it was a time of refreshing from the presence of the Lord. When I met the class, the people could hardly speak for weeping. It was a precious day to my soul. When I arose in the morning, I spent some time in walking about, meditating, and in earnest prayer. After a while I went into the woods and sat down, and began to reflect on what the Lord had done for my soul ; and then began to think what He was still willing to do for me, till I wept before him. My cry was, " glory to God for ever ;" he is the joy of my heart all the day long ; the cry of my soul was,

" I want no sharer of my heart,
To rob my Saviour of a part."

" Sunday 22d, I preached at Ellis' Meeting House to a few people, and felt my soul all on fire of love. The next day I held meeting at Bednefield's, and the day after at Mr. Warren's. In the afternoon as I was going home with one of the friends, he told me that the Lord had, not long since, sanctified his soul : his looks and his words satisfied me that he felt what he said : I was so deeply affected at the relation he gave me, that I wept heartily as I rode along the road. Glory to God for his goodness to my poor soul.

"Sunday 29th, I preached at Lane's Meeting House, and at night we held a watch night, at Evans'. I laboured hard that day, and was greatly blessed in my labours ; the people were lively in religion, and I was happy in God. I have had very few meetings of late that could be called barren ; for I have been much blessed in private, and in public ; and have had, generally, much communion with God.

"Sunday 7th of March, I preached at Robert Jones', to a serious congregation, and blessed be God, it was a happy time, and the Lord was among us of a truth. In the evening I went to Wm. Oliver's, to see Thomas Chew. a travelling preacher, who was sick.

"Friday 12th, was my birth-day. This day I was twenty-six years old, and have enjoyed religion about eleven years ; and I thank God for the peace and comfort I still find in my soul. I feel as much as ever determined to spend my life in the service of God, and to live and die a Christian.

"Saturday 20th, I preached at Howel's Chapel, from Ezek. xxxiii 11. "Say unto them, as I live, saith the Lord," &c. It was to me a time of uncommon comfort. When I came to the last part of the text, and to show what Christ had done for the people that they might not die, many of the hearers wept, and some of them cried aloud. I saw so clearly that the Lord was willing to bless the people, even while I was speaking, that I began to feel distressed for them, and at last I burst into tears, and could not speak for some moments ; after stopping and weeping for some time, I began again, but had spoken but a little while, before the cries of the people overcame me, and I wept with them, so that I could not speak ; I found that love had tears as well as grief. My full heart was constrained to cry,

> " No pain, no suffering I decline,
>   Only let all my heart be thine."

" I continued to preach with much liberty for a
few days after, but by exerting myself too much, and
travelling in the snow, and wet weather, I took a
severe cold, and was scarcely able to travel to my
appointments ; and for several days, I was not able
to preach, but would give a short exhortation,
meet the class, and dismiss the people.

" Friday 2d April, I preached at Jordon Richardson's, to a few people. I found it a considerable
cross to preach, as brother T. S. Chew was present ;
but I considered that Christ died on the *cross*, and
that I must die under the cross, if ever I get to
heaven. I felt much concerned for the salvation of
the people, and was happy among them. The next
day I preached at Wm. Richardson's, where the
Lord was pleased to communicate great grace to our
souls ; many of the society were in tears when I
met the class. Surely the Lord was in that place,
and I was truly happy ; and yet my cry was still,

> " 'Tis worse than death my God to love,
>   And not my God alone."

" Sunday 4th, I preached at Robert Jones', to a
serious company of people, and had liberty among
them ; but the severe cold I have laboured under for
some time, has bowed down my spirits, so that I can
neither read, nor write, nor meditate, with as much satisfaction as usual. I have lately found my soul much
blessed by reading the life of Mr. Walsh.

April 9th, being Good Friday, I preached at Perkin's ; and while I was speaking of the sufferings of
Christ, I had a comfortable view of him by faith, as
hanging on the cross, and bleeding and dying for me.

Glory be to God! that I did feel a sincere love to the Lord Jesus : O, that I may love him with all my heart ; and serve him all my days."

During the whole of this month he was able to attend his appointments, and preach to his hearers, in the power and demonstration of the Spirit.—He felt a continual hungering and thirsting after righteousness. One meeting which he attended on the 21st, deserves to be mentioned ; he preached at Rowls' :—" Here, (he observes,) while I was speaking, I was so sensible of its being the will of God that we should be sanctified, that I was ready to believe that God would destroy sin both root and branch. I lifted up my soul to God in prayer, and with tears in my eyes ; and blessed be God, I felt him near, very near to my soul ; my faith and confidence in God was much strengthened. The friends wept much, and some of them said they had been seeking perfect love by works, but they were determined now to seek it by faith, and by faith alone."

The spirit of piety, humility, and zeal, which is breathed in the preceding extracts, will not fail to make them acceptable to the truly pious. And who that reads them attentively, will not feel a desire to attain to that heavenly-mindedness which was in a good degree, acquired by the subject of this memoir? And who that preaches the gospel of the lowly Jesus, would not like him, feel for his congregation, and weep over them, while pointing to the Lamb of God, whose blood cleanseth from all sin ?

CHAPTER VII.

—◦✛◦—

THE Virginia Conference for the year 1784, was held at Ellis' Meeting House, and commenced the 30th of April. Three conferences had been sucessively held at this place; which circumstance reflected much credit upon the people of the neighbourhood at that time ; who spared no pains in aiding the cause of God, and opening their houses to the ministers of the gospel.

Among the ministers who attended the conference at Ellis', was the Rev. D. Jarratt, who, although a minister of the Protestant Episcopal Church, was disposed to assist the Methodists, both by his advice and by his zealous labours, at all times when convenient. His piety and humility, were such as to endear him to all the sincere followers of Christ. The power of the God of Elijah generally attended his ministry ; and at that time, the Methodists, having no ordained ministers, found the services of Mr. J. peculiarly acceptable ; as from him they could receive the ordinances of the Lord's Supper, and baptism. Often did the Methodists, in that day, listen with pleasure to the doctrine which fell from his lips, and joyfully assemble around the table of the Lord to receive from his hands the blessed memorials of the death of our Lord and Saviour Jesus Christ.

From this Conference Mr Lee received an appointment to Salisbury Circuit, North Carolina. After visiting his relations as usual, he set out on his journey, in order to enter upon the work assigned him.

On the 9th of June, he was enabled to reach his circuit, and on Saturday the 12th, met Isaac Smith, his colleague, at Salisbury, where they had an appointment to preach.—He observed, " that there was a society of truly affectionate Chi-tians in that town." While here, he was induced to visit the spot where the army encamped in 1780 ; at which period he was confined to the company of wicked men, but now by his own consent, on a very different errand, among religious friends, to teach them the way of the Lord more perfectly.

In entering upon his field of labour, he met with great encouragement ; first, inasmuch as he had an opportunity generally, of meeting large congregations, who appeared anxious to hear the word of eternal life. Secondly, the Lord graciously condescended to own the word preached, to the comfort of believers, and to the awakening of sinners. Thirdly, his own soul was frequently comforted and blessed, while striving to benefit others by his public labours. Under such encouraging circumstances, it is not to be supposed that he would faint or tire by the way.

The reader may judge by the following extracts, of the success of his ministry, and the dealings of God with his own soul.

"Sunday 13th, I preached at Hern's, to a large company of solemn hearers. While I was speaking

of the love of God, I felt so much of that love in my
own soul, that I burst into a flood of tears, and could
speak no more for some time, but stood and wept. I
then began again; but was so much overcome, that I
had to stop and weep several times before I finished
my subject.—There were very few dry eyes in the
house. O my God! what am I that thou art mindful
of me? It was a cross to me to come to this circuit,
but now I feel assured that the Lord will be with, and
support me.

"The next day I preached at brother Carter's,
where I spoke, with many tears, to a weeping congregation.

"Wednesday 16th, I preached at John Randall's,
with some liberty. The man of the house was always
deaf and dumb; yet can pronounce the name of his
wife, and the name of his brother very distinctly : but
I could not learn that he ever uttered any other word.
He is esteemed a pious man, and by signs, will give a
good experience of grace, both of his conviction, conversion, and of his progress in the service of the Lord ;
of the pleasing hope he has of heaven when he leaves
this world.

"Thusday 17th I preached at C. Leadbetter's on
Amos iv. 12. 'Prepare to meet thy God, O Israel!'
I bless God for that meeting, my heart was greatly
affected, and my eyes overflowed with tears. Towards
the end of my discourse, the hearers were so much
wrought upon, that I was in hopes of seeing some of
them converted before the close of the meeting.

"Sunday 20th, I preached at Coles, but the congregation was so large, that the house would not hold
them, of course we had to look for another place ;
we got under the shade of some trees, where I spoke
7 *

with great freedom, and with a heart drawn out iu
love to the souls of the people ; and I felt a longing
desire to be instrumental in bringing their souls to
God. When I met the class, the friends wept greatly, while they heard each other tell of the goodness
of God to their souls. The comfort I felt on serving
God that day would make amends for the sufferings
of a thousand troubles—let the people praise thee, O
God ! let all the people praise thee.

"The day following I was sent for by Mrs. Parks ;
I went over to see her, and found her very ill, and
as I thought near her end ; but she was not prepared
to die. I talked to her about her soul's welfare, and
she wept and said she was not prepared for death—
she continued to cry, and pray for near an hour ; and
we prayed with her : after which she began to ex-
claim against herself saying ' I was once near death,
and I promised God that if he would raise me up, I
would serve him, but as soon as I recovered my
health I became as careless as ever.' In a short time
her hands, and feet, became cold. She then talked
to her husband, and said, ' don't grieve for me we cannot stay together always, and I am going first ; don't do
as I have done, by putting off repentance for a death
bed.'—She then desired some one to call in one of
her near neighbours, who quickly came in, she said,
' I wanted to see you, I have thought there was some
coldness between us, and I want to die in peace with
all persons.' They soon made friends : she then
charged her husband to bring up her children in the
fear of the Lord, and be sure to keep them from
breaking the sabbath. Her words were so affecting
that I believe there was not one in the house that
could refrain from tears. I could not bear the thoughts

of her dying unprepared : I therefore knelt down and prayed for her again, and wept before the Lord, and besought him to pardon her sins, before she was taken out of the world. After prayer she looked more lively, and from that time, began to revive, although a little before her hands and feet were cold and stiff, and she appeared to be in the agonies of death."—

From the foregoing we may learn, First, how dangerous it is to put off repentance to a sick bed Secondly, that after having made a solemn promise to serve God, we should never violate that promise : God will not be mocked, although he may bear long with us. Thirdly, we see the power and efficacy of prayer, and the mercy of God extended in bringing one from the gates of death, prolonging the day of probation, and giving time and space to repent.— Surely God is merciful and gracious, long suffering, plenteous in goodness and truth, and willeth not that we should perish, but that all should come to repentence and live.

" Wednesday, 23d, (he observed) I preached at what is called Jersey Meeting House ; we had a good meeting, and I was happy in God while I was speaking. When I had finished Colonel G—s' wife came to me and began to cry, and said ' I am the worst creature in the world ; my heart is so hard I don't know what to do,' and begged me to pray for her. I hope she is not far from the kingdom of God."

Although he was generally blessed with a great degree of liberty, in preaching, yet sometimes his mind was somewhat beclouded, and to use his own words " put to it to get along with his subject." Does not God for wise purposes suffer this, to bring his ministers to a sense of their own weakness, to prevent

them from trusting in their own strength, or the abilities which they possess ? But these clouds, were not
suffered long to hover over his mind ; they were
dispelled by the Spirit of God which giveth light, and
liberty to the humble, who feel willing to acknowledge their weakness and rely on him for strength.

"Tuesday, August 10th. I preached at Tillman's,
and felt an ardent desire to be of some service to the
souls of the people. There was a gracious move
among the hearers, and before I got through my discourse, I wept over my audience for some time ;
none but God knows what I felt at that time; my
heart was ready to break with grief on the account of
poor sinners, who were perishing in their sins. In
many cases, it appeared as if I could preach till I
dropped dead in the pulpit, if it would be the means
of bringing souls to the knowledge of God : my heart
cried out, ' O Lord ! revive thy work in the midst
of the year.'

" Sunday, September 5th, I preached at a new
meeting house to a large company of attentive hearers, and continued to speak for an hour and a half,
although in a weak and feeble state ; the people wept
greatly, and one woman professed to be converted.

" Monday October 4th, I preached at Costus ;
where, after sermon, we held a love feast, and were
greatly blessed together: all eyes were bathed in
tears. An old man present, who was seeking the
Lord, but had never been converted, rose up and
spoke, in a most melting manner, and with tears
streaming from his eyes observed. ' I am almost
ready to depart this life, and am not prepared to die.
and you may judge how I feel!' Blessed be God it
was a day of comfort to my soul : the language of

my heart was, O my God! let me die, rather than grieve thy Spirit, or wound thy cause, but may I be for God."

A few days after the date of the above extract he experienced a very singular display of providence. in the preservation of his life. Crossing Yadkin River, it being deep, the current strong, and he not being well acquainted with the ford, he presently found himself among cragged rocks which were concealed from his view by the darkness of the waters : this was a critical juncture ; for one moment his horse was swimming, then plunging over the points of rugged rocks ; while Mr. Lee, was incumbered with a great coat, with his saddle bags on his arm, and being but an indifferent swimmer, he had but little expection of being delivered from the danger which then threatened him ; but through the good providence of God he was brought through unhurt, and his life preserved for future usefulness.

Shortly after this he visited his relations in Virginia and North Carolina, and then returned to his circuit again.

Some time previous to his visit to Virginia, he had experienced considerable affliction of body, which rendered his travelling painful, and in many instances dangerous. On one occasion he was taken so violently ill on the road that some of the company despaired of his life, but under these afflictions he still retained strong faith in Christ ; believing that they were sanctified for his good.

On the 12th of December, he received an official note informing him that Messrs. Coke, Whatcoat, and Vasey, had arrived on the American shores, delegated with powers from Mr. Wesley to call a conference for the purpose of transacting business of great importance to the societies in this country. This conference was appointed to be held in Baltimore, to commence its sitting the 25th of December.

In consequence of the very short notice given to some of the preachers in the more remote parts of the work, they were unable to attend at the time appointed. This was the situation in which Mr. Lee was placed at this time. He received the notice only twelve days before the commencement of the session, and it was then in a season of the year, the most unfavourable for travelling ; and being at the distance of five hundred miles he could not, in his poor state of health, possibly attend. He concluded therefore, that it would be most prudent for him to remain on his circuit, and labour for the good of souls, as much as the state of his health would admit. He commenced the first day of the year 1785, with new resolutions of soul to dedicate himself more entirely to the service of God. Upon retrospecting his life, he found by blessed experience that he had made some progress in the knowledge and love of God. And yet he desired more than ever to be dedicated to his service. While soliciting divine assistance he was enabled to discover how much he stood in need of it ; for the frequent affliction to which he was then subject warned him of the necessity of being always ready.

About the first of February he had the satisfaction of meeting with Mr. Asbury, who, at the late conference held in Baltimore, had been ordained General Superintendant in conjunction with Dr. Coke, who had received that appointment from Mr. Wesley. This may properly be considered an important era in the annals of Methodism. Hitherto the

Methodists had been considered only as Societies, destitute of the orders, and of course of the ordinances of the Church ; but at this memorable conference, they were constituted under the title of "The Methodist Episcopal Church."

The first interview which he had with Mr. Asbury after he had received episcopal ordination, gave rise to some incidents which may, perhaps, interest the reader, and which go to show that good men may often differ in sentiment.

Experience is not only necessary for the perfection of every system, but also to correct the prejudices arising either from education or from want of mature reflection.

The subject of this memoir attended an appointment with Mr. Asbury, at a Col. Hendron's. Just before the commencement of divine service, Mr. Asbury made his appearance, having on his black gown, cassock, and band. Mr. Lee, so far from being pleased at seeing the superintendant of the Methodist Episcopal Church in this attire, that he absolutely felt himself grieved, on account of what he deemed an innovation upon that plainness and simplicity which had always been characteristic of the Methodists in America.

He concluded that these appendages would have an appearance too imposing upon the people generally ; not perhaps, recollecting at that time, that Mr. Asbury, in this respect, only followed the example of Wesley himself. No doubt he was sincere in his motives, in opposing so warmly the wearing of cassocks, and bands, by the Methodist clergy ; but as this was not a matter of conscience but only of opinion, every one had a right to think for himself on the subject.

These badges of ministerial profession were soon laid aside, and the use of them has never been revived among us.

Mr. Asbury being now appointed to a high and responsible station, had an increased weight of business on his hands, not only in travelling from conference to conference, and superintending the work generally, but also in administering the ordinances of the church.

At that time Mr. Henry Willis was in company with Mr. Asbury, for the purpose of assisting him in his labours : Mr. Lee also continued with him for some time ; and at Mr. Asbury's request, accompanied him as far south as Charleston, S. Carolina.

Travelling with Mr. Asbury, they passed through a place called Charaws, where they were kindly received and entertained by a merchant of that place. Here Mr. Lee became acquainted, and entered into conversation with a young man, who was clerk to the merchant, at whose house they put up. This young gentleman was a native of Massachusetts, and entertained him with an account of the customs, and religion of his native state. Mr. Lee immediately felt a strong impression on his mind, that he ought to go and preach the gospel to that people.

This impression was not a bare impulse of the moment, but continued from that time until he was enabled to realize his wishes. He frequently conversed with Mr. Asbury on the subject, and expressed his ardent wish to be permitted to go upon a mission among the people of the New England States. But Mr. Asbury, at that time, thought it best to progress gradually, and go where they were invited ; calculating, probably, that it was best to acquire a greater

number of preachers before they extended their
labours so far; and that it would require the exertions of more than one, to give a permanent footing
in those territories.

Mr. Lee, after this, made very zealous exertions
in order to enlist preachers to go with him on this
missionary expedition; but was very unsuccessful for
several years in gaining recruits, and it was not until
nearly five years had elapsed from the time he first
felt an impression on this subject, before his wishes
were realized. We will close this chapter with
extracts from his journal.

"Wednesday 23d, February, we rode down to
Georgetown, in South Carolina, and put up at a Mr.
Smith's; the next night Mr. Asbury preached in
town to a large congregation of people, who were
quite serious and attentive. Just before we set out
for preaching in the evening, the gentleman of the
house informed us that he could not attend preaching,
as it was his turn to superintend a ball that night. I
had been praying earnestly that if the Lord had sent
us to that place, that he would open the heart, and
house, of some other person to receive us; and after
meeting, Mr. Waine invited us to call upon him.—
From that time his house became a home for our
preachers whenever they came that way. The next
day we rode to Mr. Scott's tavern, where we stayed
without expense.

"Saturday 26th, we set out pretty early and met
brother Willis, who had gone before us to Charleston,
and now came back to meet us. We arrived in
Charleston that day, and put up at Mr. Edgar Willis',
who was a merchant, and a friendly gentleman. We
went and obtained leave to preach in an old meeting
house, formerly occupied by the Baptists. We then

had notice published in the newspaper, that the
Methodists would preach the next day in the old
house, forenoon and afternoon. I felt my heart
much engaged in prayer to the Lord for a blessing
on our labours in that city.

"Sunday 27th, I preached the first sermon in the
old meeting house, at 9 o'clock A. M. from Isa. liii. 5,
6. *Seek ye the Lord while he may be found, &c.* I
preached with some faith and liberty, and the people
appeared to be quite amazed. I had only about
twenty hearers, who attended to the whole discourse;
but there were many who came in and looked on
awhile, and then went off quietly. This may be considered as the first permanent stand that was made in
that city by the Methodists. The Messrs. John and
Charles Wesley, had preached there in 1736 ; and
Mr Joseph Pilmore in 1773 ; but did not continue
long amongst them. We came with a view to continue preaching in the city, if our labours should be
owned of the Lord. Mr. Edgar Wells, at whose
house we put up, attended preaching, and was, he
afterwards confessed, awakened ; and from that time
sought the Lord in earnest, and within a few weeks
time, he was happily converted."

Thus we see that God owns the faithful labour of
his servants, and gives them souls for their hire ; and
is not this the highest reward they can ask ?

Mr. Asbury continued in the city a few days, and
left Mr. Willis as the stationed minister of the place,
by whose indefatigable labours a society was formed,
which has continued until the present day.*

After continuing with Mr. Asbury about twenty-six
days, he left him in Charleston, and returned to his
circuit.

* See Lee's History of Methodism in America, page 112.

CHAPTER VIII.

—◦✦◦—

MR. Lee returned to his Circuit just in time to go around and take an affectionate leave of those with whom he had laboured during the year.

"By this (says Christ,) shall all men know that ye are my disciples, if ye have love one to another." And again, St. John, writing to the believers— "Beloved let us love one another ; for love is of God ; and every one that loveth is born of God, and knoweth God." It is surely a true mark of our discipleship if we love God, and love one another. Heathens themselves have been astonished at this noble trait' in the Christian character, and although ignorant of the cause, yet were constrained to say ; "See how these Christians love one another."

Sharing the same toils, bound upon the same pilgrimage, and sons of the same heavenly parent, and partakers of the same grace ; can it be a subject of wonder, that Christians should be endeared to each other, or that Christians should love their ministers who faithfully labour with them, and bear them up before a throne of grace, in their fervent and unceasing prayers?—It was this attachment which the believers at Ephesus had for the Apostle Paul, after having been benefitted by his labours for the space of three years, and which caused them at the hour of parting, to fall on the neck of their beloved pastor, and weep, " sorrowing, most of all, for the words which he spake, that they should see his face no more."—We cannot better apply the above remarks, than by making a few extracts from Mr. Lee's Manuscript Journal.

" Saturday, April 9th, Salisbury. The Lord was sensibly present, many of the people had cause to bless God for this meeting. One woman professed to find the Lord. My grief was greatly encreased at leaving these affectionate people. I believe they were as much grieved at parting with me, as I was at leaving them. We had many tears together.—

" In the Evening I preached at Hickman's from Ephesians v. 1. *Be ye therefore followers of God as dear children.* I felt what I said, and I hope the people felt it too.—I wept while preaching, and they wept while hearing. But the thought of going away would hardly suffer me to speak. They wept, and some aloud when they took their leave of me.

" Sunday 10th. Hearn's. 2 Peter iii. 18. *But grow in grace.* I had liberty in speaking to-day ; the hearers were much affected.—After preaching we held a love feast, and I bless God I was greatly comforted, I found it to be a time of love to my soul. Many of the friends were powerfully wrought upon. I believe there were but few dry eyes in the house. When I made mention of leaving them, they wept aloud as if unable to bear the parting scene.

"Monday 11th. Leadbetters. I had to settle a dispute between some of our friends, which had been
in agitation for some months. I undertook it with
great reluctancy; but I had reason to be thankful
for our meeting in the end. We first went to prayer;
then I exhorted a while; and asked some of the
friends to pray. Then I got them to speak one at a
time. When we first began most of us fell a weeping;
and I believe there was not a dry eye in the house.
All seemed agreed to drop it, and say no more about
it; but I told them they must say all then, what was
to be said, that there might be no more of it
hereafter; but there was so much crying that it was
some time before we could hear all they had to
say; but in the end they all seemed to ask pardon, and each one freely forgave the other, and
promised to be as though the dispute had never
been.—I am well convinced I never saw the like
before. After we had settled this point we set off;
but I had a sorrowful parting with my dear friends.
When I bade them farewell there was scarcely one
that was able to speak, being all in tears. My grief
was almost more than I could bear.

"Wednesday 13th, At the new meeting house I
preached from 2 Corinthians xiii. 11. *Finally,
brethren, farewell. Be perfect, be of good comfort, &c.*
After I had concluded and told them I was going to
leave them, and begged they would pray for me,
immediately they began to weep, and I could say no
more: I set down and wept several minutes. I then
left the house, but before I could get far, they came
around me weeping. I began to bid them farewell,
and to speak a few words to them; but my grief was
so great, that I was soon forced to stop. I never

saw, or felt such a parting scene before. At times it seemed that I would as soon have died, as to be parted from this people : but upon due reflection I could say the will of the Lord be done."

Who that has experienced, in some degree the grief of parting with Christian friends, does not look forward with pleasure to that world of rest, where the redeemed of the Lord shall meet, to part and sorrow no more ?—

He left his charge in Salisbury on the 14th, and attended the setting of the Annual Conference at Green Hills, which commenced the 20th of April. Among those present at the conference was Doctor Coke, who took an active part in the deliberations of that body ; and among other subjects which were introduced, that of slavery claimed no small part of his attention. Ever since his arrival in America his thoughts had been intensely fixed, in finding out some method, for the extirpation of this evil rom amongst the Methodists.

He had viewed this evil, which he found existing in the southern department of the work, in an abstract form, not perhaps duly considering that thousands were involved in it, not through choice but necessity, and possessing a zeal which would bow to no difficulty, he went on enforcing the necessity of an immediate and unconditional emancipation of that unhappy portion of the human race.

Mr. Lee's notions on this subject were somewhat different from the Doctor's ; he, with every friend of humanity, deplored the condition of this portion of Adam's family, and felt the most sincere regret for their situation ; but at the same time he anticipated what in reality was brought to pass some years after, that the spirit of the people would be roused by pressing the subject too closely ; and that it would be the means of closing the door effectually against their future emancipation. He therefore thought it best to pursue a more calm and deliberate course, and that every step in a question of so much importance should be taken with the utmost prudence.

From the manner in which he expressed his sentiments on this topic, the Doctor concluded that he was unfriendly to a cause, which he conceived every friend of religion was bound to support with all his might ; and during the examination of characters he urged this as an exceptionable part of Mr. Lee's character, with his usual warmth and energy. To this Mr. Lee replied with suitable promptness, and being interrupted by the Doctor, while attempting to vindicate himself against this allegation, a spirit was produced and words elicited, which perhaps were improper at that time. The Doctor soon discovered, that his words had wounded the feelings of Mr. Lee ; and with true nobleness of soul made an apology which was satisfactory ; and the breach was effectually healed.

The subject of American slavery has long agitated the minds of philanthropists, both in the church and in the state ; and it is generally found much easier to find arguments to condemn the practice than it is to apply a corrective to the existing evil. Every friend to humanity would rejoice to see the day when these descendants of Ham should be liberated from their bondage, if it could be done without endangering the peace of society, and without detriment to the slaves themselves. As the case now is, there is some consolation in reflecting that many of these depressed

sons and daughters of Africa, have the blessings of
the Gospel conveyed to them ; and that, through
this medium, their condition is somewhat amelio-
rated by the Christian conduct of their masters. How
long they might have remained destitute of the
moralizing and comforting influence of Christianity in
their own country, who can tell?

From this conference, he attended one held in
Brunswick Circuit, at a place called Mason's ; here
much agitation was excited on the question of slavery, the particulars of which we shall pass over ;
believing that the public mind is becoming daily
more enlightened on a subject which involves the
vital happiness of thousands, we shall confide in the
wisdom of our legislators, to bring matters to a
favourable issue.

In the mean time the desires of the benevolent
who are engaged in the amelioration of the condition
of many, by establishing a Colony on the African
shores, we trust will be fully realized.

From the conference at Mason's, Mr. Lee, either
at his own request, or that of the superintendant,
went on to the Maryland Conference, which commenced in Baltimore the 1st of June.

While in Baltimore he enjoyed much of the presence of God, both while attending public worship,
and also in his closet. At evening he observed, " I
say to myself, soul where hast thou gleaned to day ?
thy labours how bestowed ? what hast thou rightly
said or done ? what grace obtained or knowledge
won, in following after God ?"

About this time he was innoculated with the small
pox, which turned out as favourably as could be
wished. This prudent precaution exempted him

from future exposure to the disease which, before the introduction of vaccination, prevailed in large towns and cities, at some periods, to an alarming extent.

After recovering from his indisposition he left Baltimore, and on the first of July arrived within the bounds of the circuit of Carolina which he was appointed to travel.

The following extracts, I trust, will be acceptable to the reader.

"Monday, July 4th. This evening I enjoyed the presence of the Lord, and could but bless his Name that ever he called me to seek his face: for two days I have felt willing to undergo any thing for the Lord, that he shall permit. I have been reading Madam Guion's Life ; and seeing what she suffered, and how patiently she bore all things for the sake of Christ, it has caused me to pray fervently that I might be brought also to suffer cheerfully and joyfully whatever cross I might have to bear."

Tuesday 5th. He preached at Charles'. While telling of the goodness of God to others, he felt the inward testimony of the indwelling of the Spirit of God in his own soul.

"Blessed be God, (says he,) that he does look upon the low estate of his servant. I have little to say to any one of late, except on religious matters. I feel my heart much detatched from the world, and a constant breathing after holiness. O when will the time arrive, when I shall be filled with all the fulness of God!

"Wednesday 6th. This evening while walking in the fields and meditating it appeared to me that I was almost ready and willing to leave the world. O my soul! bless the Lord : and all that is within me

magnify his name for ever : I would not be without
my Lord one day for all the world. I had rather
suffer affliction, nay, death itself, with the people
of God, than enjoy the pleasures of sin for a season.
Though I am well convinced there is no pleasure to
be found in sin; the pleasure which the wicked seem
to enjoy proceeds only from the gratification of the
senses, and is always more in appearance than in
reality. The Lord pity such people, who are in
danger of loosing their precious souls every moment,
and yet are crying ' peace, peace,' to themselves,
when God has not spoken peace to them.

"Sunday 10th. At the Fork Meeting House, I
preached with a good deal of life and liberty from Col.
iii. 3, 4. I felt very much for the people ; and some of
them I hope felt for themselves ; their tears proved
that they felt the word. When I preach and can see
that the people are affected, then I am contented; but
how hard it is for me to be satisfied, when I see no visible stir among the hearers. For several days, I have
felt much deadness to the world. This morning I
met the coloured class, and was greatly comforted
among them : I was astonished to hear them speak as
much to the purpose as they did ; they were dressed
very decently. I could not doubt but they were
seeking the things which are above.

"Saturday October 1st. At Smith's I preached
from Gal. v. 1. *Stand fast in the liberty wherewith
Christ hath made you free.* I bless the Lord this
was a day of liberty to me ; while I was speaking my
soul was lost in wonder, love, and praise, and could
but call upon my soul to bless the Lord. I seemed
to be swallowed up in the will of the Lord. I hope
the word reached the hearts of the hearers. I know

that my care of the people does not lie altogether in
preaching to them ; I have now began to press home
family duties, the necessity of family religion. I
desire to teach the people all things necessary for
life and salvation. O my God! if thou hast sent me
among this people, bless my labours, and let me
see the work of the Lord revive ; and feel it revive
in my own heart. Lord answer my request!

" Sunday 2. Fork Meeting House. My text was
Colossians. iv. 2. *Continue in prayer, and watch in
the same with thanksgiving.* This was a time of
refreshing from the Lord. O my soul! bless the
name of the Lord, for he has dealt bountifully with
me. I spoke almost two hours, and the hearers
were dissolved in tears. I now see that the Lord
does not cast off for ever. Though heaviness endures
for a night, yet joy comes in the morning. Then I
met the class and gave them an exhortation with
respect to bringing up their families, and how to
live and act one with another.

" Sunday 16th. I rose this morning very unwell,
and set out to town which was a mile off, before the
stars withdrew their shining. I preached at the
Court House at sun rising, 1 John iii. 1. 2. *Behold,
what manner of love the father hath bestowed upon us,
that we should be called the sons of God! &c.* Though
I was unwell this morning, I spoke with a good deal
of comfort, to many hearers. I had reason to believe that the word reached some of their hearts.
As this was an unusual hour for preaching in this part
of the world, some expected to see or hear great
things, and for fear of being too late, they hardly
slept any on the preceding night."

Thus he continued during his stay upon this circuit,
much devoted to God ; and although we hear him

speak frequently of weeping congregations, and of feeling the power and presence of God, yet he was not unfrequently assailed with temptations by the grand adversary, but he was resolved not to yield to the contest, and tamely submit. He set a resolution to resist the devil in the name of the Lord, and immediately found the power of the tempter weakened.

Sometimes he felt his mind so much oppressed with heaviness and fears that he concluded more than once that he would return home, and give over the arduous duties in which he had engaged. But perhaps the very next appointment which he attended, a ray of divine light would break upon his soul, his darkness was scattered, his mental embarrassment removed, and his spirit so much refreshed and strengthened, that he felt more than ever determined to continue labouring and suffering in the kingdom of Christ.

He that comforted his disciples, by saying, ' Lo I am with you to the end of the world,' gave success also to the labours of his servant, for he had the satisfaction of seeing the work of the Lord measurably revive ; some seals were added to his ministry, some to the Church, and peace and harmony prevailed amongst its members.

Towards the middle of March 1786, he left his circuit with considerable regret, and set out for Virginia, visited his father and relatives, and proceeded to Lane's Meeting House in Sussex, where the Virginia Conference commenced on the 10th of April.— It was at this place that he received the mournful intelligence that the Rev. John Fletcher, that truly pious, learned, and highly respectable and useful servant of Christ, was no more—that he had gone to receive the reward of his labours, in the Church Triumphant. The death of Mr. Fletcher was a cause of deep sorrow, not only among the pious followers of Christ in England, but also in America. His works of faith and labour of love, will never be forgotten.

From this conference, which continued its session not more than two days, he returned to Maryland preaching at various appointments on the way ; and attended a conference at Abingdon, which commenced the 8th of May. Although he was eligible to deacons orders, yet after solemnly weighing the matter in his own mind, he thought proper to defer it until some future period. From this conference he was sent to travel Kent Circuit ; and by the 12th of May was able to take his appointments.

So voluminous are the journals of Mr. Lee, and they contain so much valuable and useful matter, that the compiler sometimes feels at a loss what portion to select. He will endeavour, however, to make such selections as he considers most interesting and useful. There is a sort of uniformity in the daily exercises of a mind undeviatingly devoted to God, which, by being often repeated, become monotonous to the reader ; but when accounts of these exercises are intermixed with remarks upon passing events, and connected with public labours which go to benefit mankind in the most important matters, they assume an interesting aspect, which arrests the attention of the pious and intelligent reader. Such, it is humbly hoped, will be found the character of most of the extracts which follow.

" Sunday 14th. At Chester-Town, I preached from 1 Thes. v. 19. " *Quench not the Spirit.*"—1. Showed

9

the many ways in which the Spirit of God operates
upon the hearts of the people. 2. How the Spirit
may be quenched. 3. The consequence of quench-
ing the Spirit. 4. The blessed effects which will
ensue if we quench it not.

"I feel my soul quickened while speaking to the
people—I find my heart much drawn out in prayer to
God in their behalf. O! may I have cause to bless
God that my lot was cast amongst this people. There
is nothing in the world that I want to see so much as
a revival of religion—O may I feel it as well as see it.

" Monday 29th. At Plumer's I preached from Dan.
vi. 16. "*Thy God whom thou servest continually, he
will deliver thee.*" As soon as I began to sing, I felt
my soul happy in the Lord, and while I was praying,
the power of the Lord was sensibly felt in the midst ;
but while I was speaking from the text, the Lord was
more powerfully present. There was a weeping on
every side, both among saints and sinners. Blessed
be God, it was a precious time to me ; I can truly say,
that I did sow in hope this day.—This was the most
powerful day I have seen in the circuit.

"Sunday, June 11. Chester-Town, 10 o'clock, I
endeavoured to show the nature, necessity, and effects
of prayer, from 1 Thes. v. 17. The people were
very attentive all the time of sermon. Towards the
latter part of the discourse, the poor hearers were
quite overcome, and weeping was heard in every
part of the house. I felt such a love for the people,
and such a desire for their salvation, that my heart
seemed ready to break. At length my tears prevented utterance, and I stopped for a few moments,
and then resumed my discourse. O what a time it
was among the people ! There was scarcely a dry

eye in the house : some of the most dressy people
shook, being deeply affected with the word which
reached their hearts. If I never have the comfort
of seeing these people brought to the Lord, I think
I have had the comfort of seeing them cut to the
heart under the word. The Lord has been good to
me this day, and the language of my heart is,

"Dearest Jesus, though unseen,
    My believing heart must love Thee ;
Poor, despised Nazarene,
    A true and constant friend I prove Thee :
Sinking in thy balmy name,
    O! how I love my dearest Lomb."

I felt great peace in my soul after meeting was over.

"This morning I met the black class, visited
a sick person, and then went and visited the prisoners
before preaching. I know my moments are very
precious, and it is a great pity that I should let so
many pass away unimproved. After dinner we rode
down to the Old Chapel, and at 4 o'clock I preached
from 1 Tim. ii. 4. "Who will have all men to be saved,
and come to the knowledge of the truth." I felt a.
degree of liberty in speaking. The people were
much affected. I had a pleasing view while I was
speaking of the willingness of God to save all men.
I am sure I felt willing to spare no pains in teaching
them the way to be saved. I bless the Lord that he
does not leave me without some comfort. I feel still
determined to pursue my course, though death and
hell obstruct my way. This night I went to bed in
peace.

"Saturday, 8th July, I met the children in Chester-
Town for the first time. I have been convinced, in

my own mind ever since I came to this circuit, that it
would be of great advantage to the children to meet
them here as well as in other places : I had no cause
to doubt it after our first meeting. At 3 o'clock I
met the women's class ; and I believe they could all
say it was goo' to be there. I felt my soul happy
amongst them ; and the greater part of the class was
melted into tears. This is the first time the men and
women have been met apart since I divided the class.
I do think that the class increases in grace as well as
in number.

"Thursday 12th October," he thus writes :—
"We had a melting time in class-meeting, at Wood-
land's. It was a time of great comfort ; some, when
spoken to, could only answer with their tears. There
was an elderly woman with her two daughters who
stayed in, and desired to join society. When they
made the offer, many of the friends wept aloud for
joy ; for joy hath tears as well as grief. I opened
the hymn-book and gave out the following words :

    ' Who are these who come from far ?
      Swifter than the flying cloud ;
      Thick as flocking doves they are.
      Eager in pursuit of God.

      Trembling as the storm draws nigh.
      Hast'ning to their place of rest ;
      See them to the windows fly,
      To the ark of Jesus' breast.'

"I think this day I felt a resolution to give my all
to God ; I have but two mites, and I now cast them
into the Lord's treasury. O my God! I have no
better sacrifice to make—wilt thou accept my soul
and my body ?—they are thine—thou hast given them

to me, and now I render them back to thee, and keep
back no part of the price.—O my soul! bless God ;
and forget not all his benefits.

Upon reviewing the labours of this year, it may be
truly said that he was instant in season and out of
season. At one time, he speaks of getting out of his
bed, with a high fever, to attend an appointment and
form a new class. At other times, riding through
the rain while it fell in torrents, to meet his congregations, or at least, to attend at the place appointed.
In all these duties he felt an inexpressible peace, to
which the slothful and indolent are utter strangers.

On the 30th of March, he took his leave of Kent
Circuit, which included within its bounds, Kent,
Cœcil, Caroline, and Queen Ann counties. This
being amongst the first circuits formed on the continent, and containing large societies of lively and
steady members, made it pleasant to the preacher
who travelled it. There were, during the time Mr.
Lee travelled it, three hundred added to the societies
He observed that in four weeks, he had to preach
thirty-one times, and meet fifty-two classes. Though
he had laboured among them with comfort, and left
them with a mixture of sorrow and joy, yet his heart
cried out, "Not my will, but thine be done, O God!"

CHAPTER IX.

—◦✦◦—

Attends Conference in Baltimore—Appointed to Baltimore City Circuit—Preaches on the Commons in Baltimore—A great Revival of Religion in Virginia—The flame spreads to Maryland—Makes a visit to Virginia—1788 Attends Conference at Baltimore and Philadelphia—Refuses Ordination—Appointed to Flanders—Visits Virginia again.

THE conference which Mr, Lee attended this year. and from which he received his appointment, was held in the city of Baltimore the 1st of May 1787, After the business of conference was over, he went to visit his friends in Kent, to whom he was much attached, and continued several days, preaching at various appointments.

It afforded him particular pleasure to visit one who, although lying upon a sick bed, was rejoicing in the love of God. As soon as he entered the room where she was laying, she began to weep and praise God, and to tell what the Lord had done for her soul. She said, addressing herself to Mr. Lee, "Last Sunday week, when I took my leave of you at the meeting house, you spoke to me about the welfare of my soul, and it had such weight with me that I promised the Lord that I would not eat, drink, or sleep, till he pardoned my sins ; and all that night I did not sleep. The next day about 4 o'clock, the Lord set my soul at liberty, and I wanted to see you ; I knew you would help me to praise the Lord."

A word in season, how good it is! Those who
remain unmoved under the most searching and energetic ministry of the word, are often awakened to a
sense of their danger, and excited to seek the Lord,
by a word addressed to them personally. Such
appears to have been the case in the present instance.
And this, with thousands of other instances of the
like nature, should teach us to be instant in season
and out of season, to exhort and rebuke with all
authority and long-suffering. "In the morning sow
thy seed, and in the evening withhold not thy hand ;
for thou knowest not which shall prosper, this or that."

From visiting his friends in Kent, he went to travel
a circuit adjoining the city of Baltimore, where he
laboured with good success, until the latter part of
August, at which time he took his appointment in the
city of Baltimore.

On this station, he diligently attended to the duties
of a pastor ; such as visiting the poor, instructing the
children, preaching in public, teaching from house
to house, and attending the sick, and meeting classes ;
besides the various other duties, requisite for a minister to attend to with constancy and punctuality. He
not only performed the stated duties generally expected
of a minister of Christ, but he *sought* for opportunities of doing good to all who were willing to be
benefitted by his labours : knowing that in a large and
populous city like Baltimore, there must necessarily
be many who seldom, if ever, entered a Methodist
meeting-house, he resolved to give all an opportunity
of hearing, who would hear ; and accordingly he made
an appointment for preaching on the commons. The
following extracts will show how much encouragement he had in this undertaking.

"Sunday August 26, on the Commons at 6 o'clock I preached on Isa. lv. 7. *Let the wicked forsake his way, and the unrighteous man his thoughts: and let him return unto the Lord, and he will have mercy upon him; and to our God, and he will abundantly pardon.* I was greatly comforted in speaking from first to last ; and, glory be to God! it was a time of power. Toward the end of the meeting, it appeared to me that the Lord was about to visit every soul with his love.—It was a melting time, and many silent tears were dropped—some of the finely dressed people could not forbear weeping—we had an amazing large congregation, of all ranks, and of many persuasions.—When we broke up and parted, I was greatly pleased to see the company walk away so quietly. I came away rejoicing in the Lord, and praising God for his presence with us. It appeared to me that God was about to revive his work in the town."

After preaching on the commons for six or eight sabbaths, having in every instance, large and attentive congregations, he then went to the market on the point, and preached to a vast assembly. Among others who attended upon these occasions, there were numbers of sailors, who but for field and market preaching, might never have heard the gospel. All were serious and solemn, and uncovered their heads, as though they had entered a house of worship.

He also preached several times in the market on Howard's Hill, with such favourable appearances of success, that he could not doubt but that the fruits of his labours would be seen in days to come.

While he was labouring in Baltimore the Lord was pleased, in a good degree, to own and bless his efforts.

Monday, September 3d, he observes, "I met the class and was much comforted. I joined two in class. and both of them professed to have lately found the Lord. I have observed of late that the greater part of the stir has been among the young men and boys : several of them have been awakened and joined society."

This year was remarkable for a great and almost unprecedented revival of religion in Virginia. Mr. Lee frequently received letters from that quarter. informing him of the progress of the work. It seemed indeed like the commencement of the millenial reign of Christ gradually dispelling the darkness of the world.

In March 1788, he resolved to visit his native place, as well to see his relations as to share in the glorious work still progressing in that part of the Lord's vineyard.

This visit was a source of more than ordinary pleasure, as the following extracts will show.

" Sunday, 30th of March. Petersburg. At 11 o'clock I preached on Mark viii. 36. *For what shall it profit a man, if he shall gain the whole world, and lose his own soul ?* I had a pretty large company, and felt great liberty in speaking, and the hearers were much affected ; and from the beginning there were many silent tears shed—I felt my soul drawn out in love to God and man ; and before I was done the power of God was manifested among us. One woman dropped down from her seat like a person struck dead ; but in a little while she was enabled to rise and praise a sin pardoning God aloud, and many shouted for joy. I observed a woman finely dressed, just at my right-hand, who trembled and shook as though she had an ague ; at length she stood up, and I expected every moment to have seen her drop down in the place where she stood. In a little time a young woman came and took hold of her, and they both fell down on their knees together. The young woman began to pray aloud for the mourner : in a little time another young woman came, and kneeling down, prayed with all her might. By this time there were several cry-ing aloud, and the house rung with the cries of the people, both men and women. I began to weep myself, and was forced to stop preaching. In a litttle time the woman near me, for whom the young women were praying, was enabled to arise and praise God for having pardoned her sins. Cries and groans were heard in every part of the house. I could not help praising God aloud among the people. Here were two who professed openly that God had pardoned their sins; and many careless sinners were cut to the heart. Such a powerful meeting I have not seen for a long time ; and blessed be God, I not only saw it, but I felt it also."

In the afternoon, 4 o'clock, at the same place, he preached to about twelve hundred hearers, who were remarkably solemn. It was an unusual thing to see so large a religious assembly in Petersburg.

On visiting his father's family, what must have been his feelings, when he heard that all his brothers and sisters had professed to have found the pearl of great price !

Indeed, the work seemed to be general, throughout the circuits on the south side of James' River. The young were the principal subjects who professed faith in Christ ; but not confined exclusively to them. But may we not pause a moment, and inquire, where are all those who were gathered in during these great revivals ? To this it may be answered, that many

since have fallen asleep in Jesus, after having witnessed a good profession before many witnesses.
Others remain to this day ornaments to the church,
who have been enabled to keep their garments
unspotted from the world. We should be happy
could we stop here, and say such is the situation of
all. Truth, however, compels us to make a different
statement, and to say with regret, that not a few who
professed to be cleansed, have become again polluted.
The cup of joy and peace, from whence they could
once drink with pleasure, they have dashed from their
lips; and the tongue once employed in the praises of
God, is now employed in speaking evil of that cause
which they once loved. Some of those very persons
who could feel no pleasure in any company but the
people of God, are now the companions of the wicked,
and no longer have fellowship with the followers of
Christ.

This manifest departure from faith and a good conscience, is no new thing under the sun. At one time,
in the days of our Lord's personal ministry, so many
of his disciples forsook him, that he turned to the
apostles and said, *Will ye also go away?* And even
among the distinguished Twelve, a treacherous Judas
was found. The same depravity of heart, the same
viciousness of conduct, and the same proneness to
depart from a life of holiness and devotion to God,
may be found in every age of the world, not excepting the days of apostolic purity and simplicity. But
it would betray either a want of mature thought, or an
invidious discrimination, to draw an inference unfavourable to the doctrine taught, or to the whole community, on account of the defection of some of its
members from rectitude of conduct.

Respecting the revival in Virginia, we will make one more extract.

"I surely have cause to bless and praise God, that I came to Virginia this spring, to see my old friends. But such a change in any people I never saw.—There are many of the young converts that are as bold, zealous, and as solemn as old Christians. There are but few, either men or women, boys or girls, but what will pray when called upon, and sometimes without being asked.

"They told me instances of persons who were quite careless in the morning, and perhaps laughing at religion, but going to meeting, they were cut to the heart, and dropped down as if dead; and after lying awhile, some perhaps for hours and others not so long, have leaped up, and praised God, from a sense of his forgiving love; and it has been quite common for Christians, when they have been much comforted, to praise God aloud; and while in an ecstacy of joy have gone to the wicked, and taken hold of them, and exhorted them with tears to seek the Lord. Others have gone to their wicked relations, parents to their children, children to their parents, the husband to the wife, and the wife to the husband, and wept over them and prayed for them till the power of God has laid hold of them, and they have been made subjects of converting grace. So mightily has the Lord blessed the labours of his people in this place. I have never seen any thing more like taking the kingdom by violence than this. I have no doubt but many will say this is not of God, for God is not the author of confusion. But I answer, it must be of God; for the people are justified, and many are sanctified, and the devil cannot do this. But some will say, so much noise

10

cannot be of God ; but the Lord has by this means,
awakened and converted many, that were careless
before. Let the Lord work his own way. It is clear
that the Lord has his way in the whirlwind. If we
could have all the good without the confusion, if such
there be, it would be desirable, but if not, Lord send
the good, though it should be with double the confusion. We are too apt to say ' Lord prosper thy work
by this or that means.' But if we pray for the work
to revive, let this be our cry, Lord make use of some
means to save the people, and let him work his own
way. If souls can but be converted, I will be contented."

Toward the latter part of April he left Virginia, in
order to return to his work in Maryland. It would
have been very pleasing to him to have stayed a little
longer, had it been consistent with other engagements,
to enjoy the company of those Christians who seemed
all alive to God, and whose only pleasure was his
service. But on returning to his circuit he discovered that God was not confined to time nor place ;
his power being every where the same.

The flame which had been spreading in Virginia,
had began to kindle in the vicinity of Baltimore, and
in almost every meeting which he attended there was
some display of the power of God.

In September, when about to give up his charge,
he makes these remarks.

" I have been in this circuit for fifteen months,
and though I met with many troubles in the beginning, and but little outward encouragement, for sometime, yet I have cause to bless God for his great
goodness to me in the end.

" There has been great love and union between the people and myself, from first to last, and many souls have been awakened and converted in the circuit this year. I suppose there has not been so great a work among the people for eight or ten years, as there has been this year. And in many places the work is still progressing ; there have been much pain and sorrow, and many tears shed at our parting. I have often thought, that I should obtain power to refrain from weeping at leaving a circuit; but as yet I have not. I have seen such a gracious work in several places in this circuit, and have been present where so many of them have been converted, that I shall never be able to think of those times and seasons without feeling a degree of comfort."

It would be well to remark that a part of these fifteen months were spent in the city of Baltimore, but the far greater part were spent in the circuit.

September 9th, 1788. The conference set in Baltimore, where there was much good done by the preaching of the Gospel. He was here much importuned to receive ordination, but could not feel his mind reconciled to receive it.

On the 25th, of the same month, he attended conference in the city of Philadelphia. Mr. Asbury feeling the want of ordained ministers who might be competent to administer the ordinances, undertook to remonstrate with Mr. Lee for his backwardness in this respect, but still he persisted that it was best to remain as he was.

There is not the least shadow of reason to believe hat he at all doubted the validity of our ordination. He was not among that number who contended for a succession of Episcopal ordination from the Bishop of Rome, or that believed it could only be validly done by a bishop of the Established Church of England. He believed in none of these unsupported and antiquated doctrines. Neither did he censure others for receiving the holy office, because he was willing 'that every one should be fully persuaded in his own mind,' as this was the course which he was determined to pursue himself. And although his refusal to receive orders might have the appearance of obstinacy, to those who were not acquainted with his real motives, yet we are by no means disposed to attribute it to this cause. Motives of interest alone might have had some influence on the minds of individuals, to induce them to step into orders, when so repeatedly solicited by the Church, but motives like these weighed nothing with Mr. Lee; for even when it was proposed in the conference at Philadelphia, that ministers should receive a small compensation for celebrating the rites of matrimony, he opposed it with all his might. In this respect he might have erred, but judging from the tenor of his life, we are bold to say that it was his most decided opinion at that time, that such a course should be pursued.

He received an appointment to travel Flanders Circuit. Unfortunately among the people with whom he laboured this year, Calvanism* had taken deep root.

* By *Calvanism* is to be understood the doctrine of unconditional decrees, by which a part of mankind are doomed to inevitable ruin, who only do according to such decrees, and the rest eternally secured in the covenant of Redemption. This doctrine stands directly opposed to that part of Methodism, which asserts that Christ died for *all* men, and that those who are lost, are lost because they *refused* to be saved when they might have been saved.

A more formidable barrier could not have been placed in his way.

It was here that he received an account of a singular conversion, which, for the sake of its novelty, I will give in his own words.

" An Indian squaw, who was awakened some years past, when there was a great work among the Presbyterians in this part of the world, concluded that God would not hear her, because she could not pray in English; but in the depth of her distress she recollected that she could say ' January, February,' and she immediately begin to pray ' January, February,' ' January, February,' and repeated the words till her soul was happily converted."

He continued to travel this circuit several months before he could be gratified with the prospect of seeing much good result from his labours ; and it was not until January 1789. that his hopes began to revive, as the following extracts will show.

" Sunday January 25, At Newborough I preached on Col. iii. 3, 4. *For ye are dead, and your life is hid with Christ in God. When Christ, who is our life, shall appear, then shall ye also appear with him in glory.* I had a company of attentive and affected hearers; and my heart panted for more grace, and for the welfare of the people. It was indeed a time of comfort to my soul : and I had great liberty in speaking. I was led to believe, that there would be some revival of religion among the people. O Lord! hasten the happy time. We had a happy class meeting, and most part of the class said their hearts were engaged with the Lord."

" Foster Town, 4 o'clock. We had a large congregation, and though the house was much crowded, yet

the people were very attentive. And the Lord
blessed me with great liberty while declaring the
necessity of the new birth.   I sensibly felt that the
power of God was among the people ; some of them
were cut to the heart and wept freely, and some of
them wept so as to be heard at a distance.   O; my
soul, praise the Lord, and forget not any of his benefits.   When we broke up, several people came to
me and begged that I would come and preach in
their neighbourhood, as no Methodist had ever
preached among them.   I agreed to give them regular preaching."

"Allen's. Watch night. I preached on 1 Cor. xvi.
13. *Watch ye.* I found great liberty in speaking from
these words, and was blessed in my own soul ; I spoke
very long and loud ; and the power of God came
down among the people, and many of them wept
greatly ; many groaned and wept aloud.   O my soul
praise the Lord, and let the remembrance of this meeting make me ever thankful.   I spoke with tears in
my eyes, and comfort in my soul.   If I may judge
from my own feelings or the looks of the people, I
should conclude that a revival of religion is about to
take place in the neighbourhood.   I have not seen so
melting a time among them before.   I knew not how
to give over speaking, and continued speaking for an
hour and three quarters."

At another time he observed, "I spoke freely and
fully against unconditional election and reprobation,
and I found great liberty in speaking, and the power
of God attended the word : many of the people wept
greatly, and some cried out aloud. I really expected
that the Lord would make bare his arm in the conviction of some soul at that meeting. I told them at last

that God had taken his oath against Calvinism, because
he had declared by the mouth of his holy prophet,
' As I live saith the Lord God, I have no pleasure in
the death of the wicked, but that the wicked turn from
his way and live ' On uttering these words, I felt so
much of the power of God, that it appeared to me as
if the truth of the doctrine was sealed to the hearts
of the hearers.   Many of those who were careless in
the beginning, were forced to weep and mourn in the
congregation, and could not conceal their tears, before
we were done.

" Thursday, March 12th.   This is the day of my
birth, and I am now thirty-one years old,   O my soul,
praise the Lord, that he spares me from year to year.
I felt a heart thankful to God for his great goodness to
me ; and I felt a desire to be more than ever devoted
to God.

" This day I preached at Samuel Arthur's, on
Zech. viii. 23.   We will go with you, for we have
heard that God is with you.   I was about to form a
new class, and made choice of this text in order to
show the necessity of going with those who walk with
God, or with whom the Lord is.   In the end I joined
four persons in society.   I hope the Lord will take
care of this little flock, and make their number large,
their faith strong, their hearts pure, and their lives
blameless.

" Wednesday, 6th of May, I preached at Wm. Gar-
retson's, on 1 Cor. xiii. 13.   And now abideth faith, hope,
charity, &c.   There were many serious at this meeting, though apparently not much wrought on until
towards the close of the meeting.   We had a comfortable class meeting, and three persons joined society.
One woman gave a particular account of the manner

in which she had been brought to the knowledge ot
the truth a little before, and the manner in which she
spoke, left no room to doubt of the sincerity of her
heart. I lodged at brother Mapes' that night, who
informed me that he had been an enemy to the Methodists, till he heard me preach a few months before : he
and his wife are now in society, and bid fair for heaven."

After travelling Flanders Circuit until the middle
of May 1789, which, upon the whole, was by no means
the most agreeable circuit he had travelled, he took
his leave of many to whom he had been endeared by
the ties of Christian affection.

He had devoted nine months labour in a part of the
world inhabited by the natives of almost every clime,
and possessing almost as many different creeds. Among
materials so heterogeneous, it is not surprising that
little apparent success should attend his labours. He
was the first Methodist missionary who went into that
part of the country.

During his visit to Virginia, he had the satisfaction
of finding that a brother, John Lee, who had been
made a subject of converting grace during the revival
in that part of the world, felt a desire to engage in
the work of the ministry. He accordingly accompanied
the subject of this memoir to the north, and assisted
him in his labours on his circuit; he afterwards
became a member of the conference travelled successfully for several years, then located through infirm-
ity of body, and finally died much devoted to God, in
the full assurance of a glorious immortality.

CHAPTER X.

—◦◦◦—

Attends the Conference in New-York—Appointed to Stanford —Commences his labours in Connecticut—Cool reception in Norwalk—Mr. Davenport, a New-Light—Opposed in Strat-field—Inscription on Robert Sandeman's Tomb—Gets among the Free-Will Baptists in Rhode-Island—The woman's account of an Arminian—Some fruits of his labour in Read-ing—Preaches at Hartford—Undergoes an examination at New-Windsor—Visited Mr. Whitefield's Tomb—Concluding Remarks.

THERE are periods in a person's life, which, on account of some occurrences which have taken place, are more interesting than others. If we take a retro-spect of our past lives, we shall, probably, recollect events which seemed to transpire fortuitously, and yet those very events, trivial as they might appear, were connected with important eras in the future his-tory of our days. These are no inconsiderable proofs of a wise superintending Providence, which continu-ally guards and directs all our steps.

Those who have read the preceding pages, have perhaps borne in memory the circumstance of Mr. Lee's meeting with a young gentleman in the south, who was a native of the state of Massachusetts, and with whom he conversed freely on the religious state of the people of New-England; and also the solicitude which he expressed of visiting that part of the world. Since then we have seen him gradually moving on towards the very place which he desired to visit; and

by a regular progress in labour and in suffering, as well
as in experience, his mind became more and more
prepared for the arduous undertaking.

He attended the conference in New-York in May,
1789, and received an appointment to Stanford Circuit,
but we may easily judge that in giving his consent to
this appointment, he did not consult his ease or temporal aggrandizement.

In attempting to pourtray the religious views and
feelings of the people in the New-England States at
that period, it will be necessary to apprize the reader
that the revolutionary war, which had changed the
civil administration of the United States, did not produce any material change with regard to the ground
which was occupied by the standing order of the Eastern States. It is true that the powers of ecclesiastical
courts were circumscribed, and the right guaranteed
to every one that he should worship God according to
the dictates of his own conscience. But though this
was the case, their ecclesiastical and civil regulations
were so interwoven that the one derived support from,
the other. All who could not produce a certificate
that they attended worship and paid for its support in
some dissenting congregation, were obliged, by law, to
pay in proportion to their income, to the standing and
privileged order, the Presbyterians and Congregationalists. All were born of these orders. Thus was
their religion supported by law. And having long
maintained these exclusive rights and immunities, and
being exceedingly tenacious of their privileges, and
the peculiarities of their theological tenets, they
were prepared to resist any innovations which might
be attempted. And as Methodism, in several respects,
presented points directly at variance with their esta-

blished doctrines, it required no little intrepidity to enter their enclosure, and present, as must be done, a hostile attitude. A less resolute mind would have shrunk from so arduous an undertaking. But Jesse Lee moved under an impression that he was called of God, especially to this work ; and the result fully justified his pretensions, and evinced the purity of his motives, and the rectitude of his conduct. Neither the terror of an established ministry, arrayed in all the armour of human learning, and supported as it was, by the civil authority, nor the anticipated opposition of the majority of the people, who were known to be strongly attached to all their peculiarities, could intimidate or in the least dishearten the soul of Jesse Lee. In the name of God, therefore, he set forward, and on the 11th of June arrived in the state of Connecticut.

The first sermon which he preached in the state of Connecticut was in Norwalk. Here he found congenial spirits who had drank at the same fountain with himself. For it must be remembered, that although from long custom the inhabitants had become generally confirmed in the principles which had been taught them by their fathers, yet there were many exceptions to the general rule, who were willing, like the noble Bereans, to search, "and see, whether these things were so."

I have thought proper to make the preceding remarks, in order to prepare the mind of the reader for the extracts which it is intended to make from Mr. Lee's Manuscript Journal.

"Wednesday, June 17th, I set off to take a tour further in Connecticut than ever any of our preachers has been. I am the first that has been appointed to this state, by the Methodist conference. I set off with prayer to God for a blessing on my endeavours, and with an expectation of many oppositions. At 4 o'clock, I arrived in Norwalk, and went to one Mr. Rogers', where one of our friends had asked the liberty for me to preach. When I came, Mrs. R. told me her husband was from home, and was not willing for me to preach in his house. I told her we would hold meeting in the road rather than give any uneasiness. We proposed speaking in an old house, that stood just by, but she was not willing. I then spoke to an old lady about speaking in her orchard, but she would not consent, but said we would tread the grass down. So the other friend went and gave notice to some of the people, and they soon began to collect, and we went to the road, where we had an apple tree to shade us. When the woman saw that I was determined to preach, she said I might preach in the old house; but I told her I thought it would be better to remain where we were. So I began on the side of the road with about twenty hearers. After singing and praying, I preached on John iii. 7. *Ye must be born again.* I felt happy that we were favoured with so comfortable a place. Most part of the congregation paid particular attention to what I said, and two or three women seemed to hang down their heads, as if they understood something of the new birth. After preaching I told the people that I intended to be with them again in two weeks, and if any of them would open their houses to receive me, I should be glad, and if they were not willing, we would meet at the same place; some of them came, and desired that I should meet at the town-house, the next time; so I gave consent.

Who knows but I shall yet have a place in this town where I may lay my head ?

"Thursday, 18th, I rode about sixteen miles to Fairfield, and put up at Mr. Penfield's tavern, near the court-house, and soon told them who I was, and what was my errand ; the woman of the house asked me a few questions, and in a little time wished to know if I had a liberal education. I told her I had just education enough to carry me through the country. I got a man to go with me to see two of the principal men of the town, in order to get permission to preach in the court-house ; the first said he had no objection, the other said he was very willing. However, he asked me if I had a liberal education. I told him I had nothing to boast of, though I had education enough to carry me through the country : then I went to the court-house, and desired the school-master to send word by his scholars, that I was to preach at 6 o'clock ; he said he would, but he did not think that many would attend. I waited till after the time and no one came ; at last I went and opened the door and sat down. At length the school-master and three or four women came ; I began to sing, and in a little time thirty or forty collected ; then I preached on Rom. vi. 23. *For the wages of sin is death: but the gift of God is eternal life, through Jesus Christ our Lord.* I felt a good deal of satisfaction in speaking. My soul was happy in the Lord ; and I could but bless God, that he gave me to feel for the souls of those that heard me. The people were very solemn toward the end of the sermon, and several of them afterwards expressed, in my hearing, their great satisfaction in hearing the discourse. After Mrs. Penfield came back to the tavern, she pressed me much to call the

11

next day and preach at her sister's, who, she said, was much engaged in religion, and would be much pleased with my manner of preaching. This appeared to be an opening of the Lord : so I told her I would. I stayed all night, and prayed with the family, who were very kind, and would not charge me any thing, but asked me to call again.

"Friday, 19th, I rode to Timothy Wheeler's, about four miles, and after delivering a letter to the woman of the house from her sister, Mrs. Penfield, she read it, and seemed much rejoiced that I had come. She then began to tell me how it had been with them, and said there were a few of them that met once a week to sing and pray together ; but they were much discouraged by their elder friends, and that they had been wishing and praying for some one to come and instruct them, and seemed to believe that God had sent me. At length she said she was so rejoiced that her strength had almost left her, and setting down she began to weep. Mr. Black, one of our preachers, had been there a few years before, and some of the people had been wishing for the Methodists ever since. They spread the news as much as they could, and at 7 o'clock the people met, and I preached to an attentive congregation. After meeting, some of the people stayed to talk to me about religion, and wished to be instructed in the ways of the Lord. I think five or six of them are truly awakened ; one, I think, has experienced a change of heart ; but those under distress would be often saying, they were afraid they had never been awakened. I told them, if they saw that they were in danger of hell, and felt a desire to be born again, they might know that they were truly awakened."

"Saturday, 20th, I called at a house on the road at the request of the man of the house, and had been there but a little while before an elderly woman came in and says to me, ' And you are a man going about to do good. I told her I tryed to do good, and so began to ask her some questions about the state of her soul I came on to New-Haven, nine or ten miles from Milford ; I put up at Parmley's tavern. In this city they have a Church and two Congregational meeting-houses, beside the Chapel at the College."

"Sunday, 21st, at 5 o'clock, P. M. I preached in the court-house, Amos v. 6 *Seek ye the Lord, and ye shall live.* I had a considerable number of men at meeting, among whom was the President of the College, and many of the students, and one Congregational minister. We had not many women by reason of the storm that came up just as we were assembling together. I spoke as if I had no doubt but God would reach the hearts of the hearers by the discourse. The people paid great attention to what I said, and several expressed their satisfaction. Mr. Jones asked me to go to tea with him, which invitation I accepted. While together, I told him much of our plan.

"Wednesday 24th, I travelled a stony road to Reading, and according to direction, called on Esq. Benedict, but he was not at home ; so I got my horse and rode to Mr. Rogers', to consult him about the matter, and while I was talking to him, Mr. Bartlett, a Congregational minister came by, and being informed who I was, asked me home with him ; and after I had been there a while, he asked me some questions relative to doctrines, and I endeavoured to inform him what kind of doctrines we preached : he said he could not invite me into the meeting-house, because I held what he thought was contrary to the gospel. I told him I did not expect an invitation to preach in the meeting-house, but if I was asked, I should not refuse: however, Mr. Rogers sent his son down in a little time to let me know that there was a school-house that I could preach in, so I made the appointment that I could preach for the people at 6 o'clock. Having met at that hour, I preached on Isa. lv. 6. *Seek ye the Lord while he may be found.* &c. I bless God that I had some liberty in preaching. The old minister at whose house I lodged, is a great advocate for dancing, although he does not prac- tice it himself."

From thence he rode to Danbury, and obtained permission to preach in the court-house, twice on the same day. From Danbury he went to Ridgefield, where he was permitted to preach in the town-house. He also visited Rockwell in Wilton Parish, Canaan, Middlesex, Norwalk. Fairfield; and had some hope that the Lord owned the word preached at each of these places.

The following extracts will give information of the further success of his mission.

"Friday, July 3d. I preached at Stratfield, at the house of deacon Hawley: the house was filled with hearers. I had great satisfaction in preaching: and some of the people were melted into tears. I felt my soul transported with joy: and it appear- ed to me that God was about to do great things for the neighbourhood. There are about a dozen in the place that meet every week for the purpose of conversing on the subject of religion, and of spend- ing some time in prayer; some of them belong to the Church of England, and others are Congregationalists; they desired me to meet with them in the evening, to which I consented, and I spoke to them just as I would at one of our class meetings, and it was a very comfortable time. The greater part of them kneeled down when we went to prayer, a thing that I expect some of them never did before in public. They all seemed exceedingly pleased with the manner of the meeting; and several thanked me for my advice, and, and desired me to remember them in my prayers. The deacon's wife told me, that some of them had an intention of joining us; I told her if they desired it, I could not object, though I did not intend to persuade them. I hope the Lord will direct, bless, and save them.

"Saturday 4th, I set off about the middle of the day and was much exercised about calling to preach at Stratford, sometimes I seemed to have no faith, but at other times I had a little hope that good might be done. At last I determined to take up my cross and make the trial. So I went and put up at a tavern, and went to the man that kept the key of the town house, and obtained his consent to preach in the house. But he said he did not know much about the Methodists, they might be like the New Lights. I told him, I did not know much about them, but some people said we favoured them in our preaching 'Well, (says he,) 'if you are like them, I would not wish to have any thing to do with you.' I asked him what objection he had to the New Lights. 'Why, (said he,) 'they went on like mad-men : there was one Davenport that would preach and hollow, and beat the pulpit with both his hands, and cry out 'come away, come away to the Lord Jesus Christ,

11 *

why don't you come to the Lord! till he would foam
at the mouth, and sometimes continued it, till the
congregation would be praying in companies about
the house :' for my part I wished that the like work
was among the people again. I let a man have my
horse to ride through town, and give the people
notice of meeting. At sunset, they rung the church
bell, and the people collected. The Congregationalists
insisted on my going into the meeting-house, but I
begged off for that time. I had a large company in
the town-house. I preached on Eph. v. 1. *Be ye
therefore followers of God, as dear children.* I was
much assisted in speaking, I felt happy in the Lord,
and comforted to see the people so attentive. When
I was done Mr. Solomon Curtis came to me, and
askèd me to go and lodge with him, and wished me to
make it my home. Another said he would conduct
me to the house, and taking me by the hand, he
walked all the way by my side. I don't know that I
have had so much kindness showed me in a new
place, since I came to the state.

" Sunday 5th, I rode to New-Haven. At 5 o'clock
we met at the state-house, at the ringing of the bell ;
but some of the influential men insisted on my going
into the meeting-house, so I gave consent. I preached
on Job xxii. 21. *Acquaint now thyself with him, and be
at peace, &c.* At first I did not feel very well satisfied, being raised in a high pulpit with a soft cushion
under my hands, but in a little time I felt the fire from
above ; my heart was warmed, and drawn out in love
to my hearers ; I felt great liberty toward the last,
and some of the people dropped several silent tears,
and the countenances of many showed that the word
reached their hearts. I had two of the Congrega-

tional ministers to hear me ; Mr. Austin, the minister
of the house, and Dr. Edwards, son of the former
president of Princeton College. After meeting I
came out, and some told me they were much pleased
with the discourse ; but no man asked me home with
him. I went back to the tavern and retired into a
room and went to prayer, and felt the Lord precious
to my soul. I did believe the Lord had sent me
there ; if so, I was sure I should find favour in the
eyes of some of the people. In a little time Mr.
David Beacher came and asked me to go home with
him, and said he would be willing to entertain me
when I came to town again. I went home with him,
and his wife was very kind ; but his wife is not a friend
to Calvinism. After dark, a young woman got her
work and sat down to knitting ; I was, indeed, much
astonished at this, it being Sunday evening, and spoke
to her about it : they told me it was customary for
the Congregationalists throughout the state, to commence the Sabbath on Saturday evening, and continue it until sunset on Sunday.

"Tuesday 7th, at New-Town, at the request of
the people, I preached in the meeting-house. At
the appointed time they rang the bell. A little after
sunset I preached on Mark viii. 36. *For what shall it
profit a man, if he should gain the whole world, and
lose his own soul?* I had quite a large congregation,
I suppose more than is common to be seen there on
a Sabbath day. I spoke quite loud and very plain.
I felt happy, and my soul did rejoice in the God of
my salvation. I spoke of the loss of the soul, and
the torments of the damned, for some time ; I did not
give them velvet-mouth preaching, though I had a
large velvet cushion under my hands,

" Wednesday 8th, I rode to Reading, and dined at
Mr. Rogers' ; and after resting a while, I walked
down to Mr. Bartlett's. The minister and a few
people came in, and wanted to enter into a conversation about principles, and inquired what kind of
doctrines we held ; but I said but little to them. At
length the minister came in, and the people requested
him to give me leave to preach in the meeting-house,
but he said he was not willing, and should not give
his consent ; but if the people chose it, he should
not stop it. Then he asked me, if I would be willing
to take a text and preach my principles fully, for the
people wanted to know them ? I told him, I was not
willing to do it at that time ; and intimated to him
that what I preached, I would wish to preach on a
subject that I thought would be most for the glory of
God, and the good of the hearers ; and told him that
I did not believe a sermon on principles would be
for the glory of God at that time. He then wanted
to talk about Christian perfection, and said there was
no perfection in this life. I told him, after a little time,
that certainly no man of religion could say there is
no perfection in this life, for, to deny perfection was
to deny the Bible, and all revealed religion. I then
made mention of a few texts of Scripture, which put
him to a stand. The room was by that time, quite
full of people, and he asked me again before them all,
if I would preach upon my principles ? I looked
upon it, that he asked me before so many people that
he might have it to say that I refused to let my principles be known, because they were too bad to be
heard; so I told him if I found freedom, I would on a
future day appoint a time for the purpose, and preach
fully on the subject. He observed that some of the

people would come to hear me out of curiosity.—
Here some was offended because I preached the possibility of being suddenly changed, from a state of
sin to a state of grace.

"Wednesday 29th, I rode to Fairfield, and at 6
o'clock, I preached on John v. 40. *And ye will
not come to me, that ye might have life.* I had a larger
company than I ever had before, and felt pleased and
comforted while speaking. The minister of the place
had been complaining of our coming amongst them,
and I suppose will complain more. Some of the
people began to have their fears that I intended to
draw away a part of their church. Mr. Penfield
asked me if my particular view was not to form a
society in that part of the country? I told him my
particular view was to call sinners to repentance;
but if the Lord blessed my labours among the people,
and they desired to join with us, I could not forbid
them. As soon as I came out of meeting I mounted
my horse and rode four or five miles, to Mr. I.
Hall's, a little above Stratfield. I found the people
waiting for me, for it was then quite dark; to whom
I preached. During the first prayer some of the
sleepers of the house gave way, and the people were
somewhat affrightened, but after prayer I moved to
the passage, or entry of the house, and addressed the
people. Both rooms and the entry were crowded with
hearers; and many stood in the yard; all heard with
attention. When meeting was over several remained,
and talked a while. One who was a stranger, came
and began to speak very much in praise of the sermon, and told how glad he was to see me. I began
to tell him I was a stranger in the place, and wished
to see religion prosper. I find in this part of the

world, as well as in other new places, if the people
are pleased with a strange preacher, they do not hesitate to praise him to his face. Alas! they little
know how liable we are to be tempted, if not
overcome, by pride. When the company was
gone, I was informed that the Sunday before, the
Church minister gave his people a lecture about
going to hear strange preachers, and they knew he
meant the Methodists. The Congregational minister
gave his flock a little *beating* on the same subject,
which I suppose was one reason why so many came
out. This is often the case when one minister speaks
against another : it causes many to desire to hear
him for themselves.

"Thursday 30th, I rode through Greenfield, a few
miles to the west of Fairfield, and called to see
Doctor Dwight at his school, and conversed with him
upon the expediency of coming to the place, and
whether or not a house could be obtained for me to
preach in : he said he had no house to dispose of
but the school-house ; but he did not find freedom to
encourage our plan at all ; yet he said if we came to
preach in the place, he would come to hear us, that
if there were any thing wrong he might know how to
oppose it. He kindly invited me to call at his house
and take dinner, but I had not time.

"Wednesday, August 5th.—Rode to New-Field,
and at deacon Hawley's, 4 o'clock, I preached on 1
Pet. ii. 9. *But ye are a chosen generation, a royal
priesthood, an holy nation, &c.* I felt my soul much
quickened while I was speaking, and the hearers
were very solemn ; some of them affected, so that
others might behold it. I had a large company
together, and by reason of a heavy rain, many of them

did not leave the place till near 9 o'clock P. M. We
had a kind of conference meeting at night, and several
questions were asked and answered. There has
been a great deal said against us since I was here last
week. The people are much alarmed with a fear
that I will break up the society. One of their ministers told the people in public, that the Methodists
held *damnable principles, &c.* All their fears of the
large society being broken up, proceed from no
other circumstance than this :—two women talk of
joining our society, but they are unable to tell when.
Surely, if these people knew that God was on their
side, they would not fear so much.

"Thursday 6th, I went to Mr. Well's, and a Cal-
vanist came to converse with me for a while, and
after talking over our different sentiments, we joined
in prayer, and parted. Then I rode to Reading,
about sixteen or seventeen miles. I have seldom
travelled so bad a road on dry ground, as that was.
The day was uncommonly warm, sometimes I could
hardly bear the steam that arose from my horse ; and,
poor creature, he sweated till my great coat, four
double, and my saddle-bags were wet through. When
I got to Mr. Sandford's, I felt very weary, but had
only a little time to rest. In a few minutes I walked
to Mr. Rogers', and preached to a large number of
people, within and without doors. The people in
this place can bear to hear any vice spoken against,
except dancing.

"Thursday 13th, we rode to Fairfield, at an hour
by sun. I preached on Prov. xxviii. 13. *He that
covereth his sins shall not prosper: but whoso con-
fesseth and forsaketh them shall have mercy.* I had
some satisfaction in speaking to the people, and they

were attentive to the word. But some of the inhabitants seemed to be afraid to hear, because the minister did not like my coming amongst them. Even the
tavern keeper and his wife, where I always put up,
made an excuse to leave home before I came; and
the reason, I understood, was because the minister
complained of them for entertaining me. After meeting was over, a man came to me and said the women
complained that I preached so loud that it made their
heads ache, and they wished me to speak a little
lower the next time I came: but I hope God will
help me to speak hereafter, so as to make their hearts
ache. I rode to Mr. Well's and stayed all night.

"Friday 14th. Stratfield, Well's New-House. At
4 o'clock I preached on 1 Pet iii. 12. *For the eyes of the
Lord are over the righteous, and his ears are open to
their prayers.* I felt an humbling sense of the
goodness of God while I was speaking; some of the
people heard with watery eyes. I hope God will
soon revive his work in this place, for the devil
begins to roar. After meeting I observed that some
of the people that always came and spoke to me,
went away and took no notice of me ; and no person
gave me an invitation to his house, which was an
uncommon thing, for formerly I had various invitations ; but I understood that the poor things had been
buffetted by the ministers from the pulpit, and by their
acquaintance in private, till they hardly knew what
to do. One minister had been trying for two or three
times in his sermons, to prove that a man could not
fall from grace ; and another turned loose upon us,
and said, from the pulpit, that there were six hundred of us going about the country, preaching damnable doctrines, and picking men's pockets. One of

the deacons of the meeting did not like it, and went
and advertised the minister in the public paper, and
informed the public how he persecuted us. This
noise is not without a cause. I hardly ever knew
much persecution where the people were at case in
Zion.

"Sunday 16th, we rode to Milford, and preached in
the town-house, and endeavoured to show the necessity of a preparation to meet God. The house was
crowded with people, and some of them appeared to
be persons of note ; and they were very attentive
to what was spoken, and tears stole down from several eyes, while solemnity sat upon their countenances.
I felt great liberty in telling the people what it was
to be prepared to meet God, and the comfortable
consequence of such a preparation. I hope my
labours will not be in vain in the Lord at this place.
When I was done, I came through the crowd,
mounted my horse, and set off without having any
invitation to call at any man's house. This is the third
time I have preached at this place, and have not
yet become acquainted with any person. If I can
but be useful, I am willing to remain unknown among
men. We then rode to Mr. Gilbert's, in New-Haven.
He and his wife appear to be God-fearing people.

"Monday 17th, I rode to Derby, and at night I
preached on Rom. xiv. 17. I had a good company
of hearers, which is more than I ever had before at
this place. I felt happy in God, in declaring his
word. O! that God would revive his work in this
place. I bless God that he yet keeps my spirits up
under all my discouragements. If the Lord did not
comfort me in hoping against hope, or believing
against appearances, I should depart from the work in

this part of the world; but I still wait to see the salvation of the Lord.

"Thursday 20th. As I passed through Danbury, I stopped and took the following account from a large stone, fixed at the head of a grave.

"Here lies until the resurrection, the body of Robert Sandeman, a native of Perth, North Britain, who, in the face of continual opposition, from all sorts of men, long and boldly contended for the ancient faith ; that the bare work of Jesus Christ, without a deed, or thought, on the part of man, is sufficient to present the chief of sinners, spotless before God : to declare this blessed truth, as testified in the Holy Scriptures, he left his country, he left his friends, and after much patient suffering, finished his labours at Danbury, 2d April 1771, aged 53 years.

'Deign'd Christ to come so nigh us
    As not to count it shame,
To call us brethren.   Shall we blush
    At aught that bears his name ?
Nay; let us boast in his reproach,
    And glory in his cross ;
When he appears, one smile from him
    Shall far o'er pay our loss.'

"Monday 31st, I set out on a tour for Rhode-Island state, and it was my fervent prayer to God that if my undertaking was not according to his will, that the houses of the people might be shut against me ; but if my journey was right, that God would open the houses and hearts of the people to receive me at my coming.

"I left New-Haven after dinner, and had got but a little way from town before I fell in with a man that was riding nine or ten miles on my way.   He appeared to be a religious man, and encouraged me to go on to

Guilford, and call on Lieutenant Hopson. I did so, and Mr. Hopson met me at the gate, and as soon as I dismounted, he said to me, ' I hope you are a brother in Christ.' I told him who I was, what I was, and whither I was going. It was then about sunset ; but he sent word to his neighbours, and soon collected a room full of people, to whom I preached. I felt my soul alive to God among these strangers, and some of them wept freely. Of a truth I perceive God is no respecter of persons. I found some lively Christians in Guilford, of the Baptist persuasion, and could bless God that I came amongst them.

"Tuesday, September 1st, I set out pretty early in the morning, and rode to Killingsworth, and called on Adam Staunton, and stayed till after dinner. I had hard work to get him to give his consent for me to preach in his house on my return, however, he submitted at last. Then I rode to Saybrook, and obtained leave to preach in the school-house on my return. Then I crossed Connecticut River, and rode to Jason Lee's, in Lyme. I got there a little after dark, and was very kindly received. He is an old man, and a Baptist preacher ; esteemed for his gifts and piety, and much beloved among his people.

" Wednesday 2d, it rained in the forenoon, and I tarried till the middle of the day ; and then making two appointments for my return, I came to New-London, and put up at Jonathan Brooks. I told him who I was, and that I had a desire to preach in the city at night. He immediately sent word among the people, and at night they collected at the state-house. My heart was much drawn out to God while I was declaring the necessity of 'the new-birth. Deep solemnity rested upon the audience, and some of the dear hearers wept greatly : I felt as if I was among the faithful followers of the Lord Jesus. My cry was, surely God is in this place. I had a large company of people, of different ranks and professions. Every thing seems to prove that my journey is of God. O! Lord, never let me blush to own thy name :

"Thursday 3d, I passed through Stonington, and crossed Pawtucket, into Rhode-Island state, and went to Mr. Stanton's, who kept the coffee-house in Charleston, Washington County. He was not at home, but his wife being a religious woman, I entered into conversation with her, and soon informed her that my business in coming, was to preach to the people ; so she sent word to her neighbours, and gathered a large room full ; to whom I preached, on Rev. iii. 20. *Behold, I stand at the door, and knock : &c.* I felt some liberty in speaking to them, and some were melted into tears under the word. After the discourse was finished, they began according to their custom ; and after singing, one said, ' where the Spirit of the Lord is there is liberty !' and now, you are all at liberty to speak. So they began to speak, one at a time, and several spoke, both men and women, during the evening. In the first place, they generally gave an account of their feelings, and state of their souls ; and would then express their sentiments respecting the sermon ; and observed that they believed God had sent me to preach to them : and exhorted all the people, as well as the preacher, to go on in the ways of the Lord ; and sometimes they would call aloud, ' O my neighbour, (calling the person by his name,) come to the Lord Jesus Christ.' And at other times, ' O brother, such a one, don't you feel for poor sinners.' All this they sung out in such a tone, that I could scarcely refrain from weeping. There has been a great revival of religion amongst them a few years past; some call them ' New-Lights,' by others, they are styled *Separates*, some *Seventh-day Baptists*, because they keep the seventh day instead of the first, or the Christian Sabbath. They hold with baptising none but believers, and their mode is plunging.

"Monday, 7th. I have found great assistance from the Lord of late : sometimes I have had no doubt, but that the word was owned and blessed of the Lord? To-day I have preached four times, and felt better at the conclusion of my labour than I did when I first arose in the morning. I have found a great many Baptists in this part of the country, who are lively in religion. They are mostly different from those I have formerly been acquainted with ; for these will let men of all persuasions commune with them, if they believe they are in favour with the Lord. I think the way is now open for our preachers to visit this part of the land. It is the wish of many that I should stay, and beg that I would return again as soon as possible, although they never saw a Methodist before. I am the first preacher of our way, that has ever visited this part of the country. The roads are very stony from Connecticut River to Rhode-Island, as far as I went."

"Saturday, 12th. I rode to Wallingford, about 13 miles from New-Haven, and went to Atwater Cook's, who went and obtained leave for me to preach in a meeting-house, that is vacant for the present. At night the people came together, and I preached on Acts xxiv. 25. *And as he reasoned of righteousness, temperance, and judgment to come, Felix trembled, &c.*

12 *

I found hard work to preach to the people, and was led to fear that they were not engaged with God for themselves; but the fault might lie in me. They have two meeting-houses and a church in this place, and one of the congregations has a minister, which a young woman told me was an *Arminian*. I asked her what principles an Arminian held—'Why,' says she, 'they hold, that if a man does his part, Christ would not be wanting on his; and she thought that was making Christ half a Saviour.' I told her my principle was, that Christ would not be wanting on his part. provided we performed what he required of us.

"Wednesday, 16th. Reading. At 3 o'clock, I preached on Amos iv. 12. *Prepare to meet thy God, O Israel.* I felt assistance from the Lord, and spoke with assurance in his name. I did not spare Calvinism, but bore a solemn testimony against the doctrine which so generally prevails in this part of the world, which in substance is this : 'The sinner must repent, and he can't repent; and he will go to hell if he don't repent:' or, as a lawyer expressed it in my hearing, 'you must believe or be damned; and you can't believe if you are to be damned.' But some of these people begin to see that something must be done before justification; though some of the preachers in these parts, are on the new divinity plan, i. e. a man can't repent till he is born again. From this doctrine, good Lord deliver me!

"Friday, 25th. I preached in Weston township, on Matt. xxii. 14. *For many are called, but few are chosen.* I had a very large congregation ; the house and yard were filled. I felt much liberty in speaking. and continued just two hours from the time I began. The people were affected under the word. I laboured to prove that all men were called to leave their sins, and that power was given with that call, to obey it: and that man was called before he was chosen. I had a Congregational minister sitting just before me, and a Baptist minister close to my left-hand, and while I was drawing the bow at a venture, and letting the arrows of truth fly, I found the ministers were greatly frightened at the noise of them, or else wounded by their barbed points, for they would turn and twist, and writhe, during the discourse, which proved that their feelings were not of the most pleasant kind. When I was done, the Baptist minister came and spoke to me, and said if he took my ideas, either he or I was in some very great errors, &c. An aged man told him he thought it was very ill usage, to speak in that manner before the people, for he believed that the people were well satisfied with what they had heard ; and his speaking might prevent them from being bene-fitted, and that if he had any fault to find with the dis-course, he should have taken me out and told me privately wherein I was wrong. The preacher under-took to speak a little more, but another old man began, and they soon silenced him. The other minister set off, and when he got to the door he turned round and said, ' he should set himself in order against the next sabbath-day, to expose the errors which his people had heard that day.' The hornet's nest is stirred up, and if they sting me or persecute me, I must bear it as they bore the arrows; but if I am shielded, they cannot hurt me.

"Then I rode down to Stratfield, and at night I preached on John x. 27. *My sheep hear my voice, and I know them, and they follow me.* I thought, when I began, that I would touch upon the danger of falling

from grace; for the people had often said that I was
afraid to preach my principles. I began, and spoke
quite long on the subject, and with much satisfaction.
The people heard very attentively, and some of them
seemed to believe what was spoken. Then I had a
kind of class-meeting, and spoke to about twenty persons. I then told them that if any desired to join the
Methodists, I would receive them. The next morning three women joined in class, and appeared willing
to bear the cross, and to have their names cast out as
evil for the Lord's sake. This is the first class I have
formed in my little circuit.

"Saturday, October 10th. Old Mills. At 2 o'clock,
I preached on 1 Tim. i. 15. *This is a faithful saying,
and worthy of all acceptation, &c.* I felt some comfort in my own soul, and the people were very attentive to the word; and one woman kneeled down when
I prayed, which is an uncommon thing in such a new
place. Several persons asked me to go home with
them after preaching, and spoke in a very familiar
manner. I went home with a man of the place, and
took tea; and then rode to Stratford, and put up with
Solomon Curtis, as usual. When I went in, his wife
did not ask me to sit down; however, I took a seat.
In a little time she asked me to drink tea, but I had
no need. Her husband came in and spoke to me, but
did not appear so friendly as formerly. At dark, I
asked Mrs. Curtis, if her husband was going to meeting? she said, '*she guessed not,*' so I went to the town-
house alone, and was hard put to it to get a candle.
but I bless God, I felt quite resigned, and not ashamed
to own my Lord. After preaching, I returned to Mr.
Curtis', and found he had but little to say. He went
to prayer without saying any thing to me, and then I

waited to see if he would ask me to go to bed. After some time he got up and asked me to cover up the .ire when I went to bed. I told him I would go to bed then, if it were agreeable. I suppose the whole complaint was owing to my telling him, when I was there before, that I believed a man, after being converted, might fall away and be lost: for he is a stiff Antinomian. The next morning he lay in bed till late, and soon after he arose, I set out, without family prayer or breakfast. I often wonder that I am not turned out of doors.

"Monday 19th, I preached at Greenwich, but made no appointment to come again, for no one desired it. The priest and deacon of the place have taken much pains to convince the people of the evil of letting me preach in the parish; and withal, they told the people that if the society is broken up, they must bear the blame. Poor priests! they seem like frightened sheep when I come near them. There are about forty-five of them in the bounds of my two weeks circuit, and the general cry is, 'the societies will be broken up!'

"Friday 23d. At David Olds', in Weston, I preached to a large congregation: the house was much crowded, though it was very large. I suppose the reason why I had so many to hear me, was owing to their minister's preaching against me two sabbaths in succession. The people heard me with great attention, and many tears were shed. I had reason to praise God, that I felt my soul happy in his love. I generally find, in this state, when I am most opposed, I have the most hearers. The Lord seems to bring good out of evil. If my sufferings will tend to the furtherence of the gospel, I think I feel willing to suffer; but if I had no confidence in God, and as many to oppose me, I believe I should soon leave these parts. But once in a while I meet with something to encourage me, and by means of the grace of God, I stand.

"Monday, December 21st, we rode to General Waterbury's, where I received several letters from the south, which informed me of hundreds, if not thousands, that have been lately brought to the knowledge of God, in Maryland and Delaware states. Several of our preachers, Mr. Asbury among the rest, expressed a great desire for the welfare of myself, and my dear New-England hearers. My soul rejoiced in God while I perused these letters. O what am I! that I should be noticed by my superior brethren, and favoured by my gracious God? Why am I not every moment devoted to the Lord? Surely, if any creature in the world has cause to love the Lord, I have.

"Thursday, 24th. I preached in Fairfield to a good company of people. I hope my Lord will yet give me some seals to my ministry in Fairfield, a poor hardened place! To-night, thanks be to God, I was invited by a widow woman to put up at her house; this is the first invitation I have had since I first came to the place; which is between six and seven months. I did not accept the offer, though engaged to accept in a future day, if all should be well; but at present, had to ride about three miles to Mr. Jennings' to visit a sick woman, who seemed determined to seek the Lord. More preaching places are opened for me; nay, more than I can attend. O my Lord! send more labourers into this part of thy vineyard. I love to break up new ground, and hunt the lost souls in New-England, though

it is hard work; but when Christ is with me, hard
things are made easy, and rough ways are made
smooth.

"Saturday, 26th. At night I preached in Stratford,
with much satisfaction, to an attentive people; but I
fear that I shall offend some of them by urging the
necessity of being up and doing. These people don't
like to hear that there is something for men to do;
they had rather be told to sit still, and wait for Christ
to call them with an irresistable call; they complain,
and say they can do nothing. I complain of them and
say, they might do more than they do. To-night the
people were surprised at my speaking so clear and
fast without notes.

Monday, 28th. I preached in Reading, and found
great assistance from the Lord in speaking: I felt that
God was amongst the people, one or two kneeled down
with me when we prayed. The Lion begins to roar
very loud, in this place, a sure sign that he is about to
lose some of his subjects. I joined two in society
for a beginning; a man who has lately received a witness of his being in favour with the Lord, led the
way; and a woman, who I hope was lately converted,
followed. Glory be to God that I now begin to see
some fruit of my labour in this barren part of the
world; several in this place feel the want of a Saviour.
O my God! favour this part of thy vineyard with
ceaseless showers of grace.

"1790—Friday, 1st of January, I rode to Wilton,
and at night, at John Rockwell's, I preached on 2
Pet. iii. 18. *But grow in grace.* I felt some freedom
in striving to stir up the people's pure mind by putting
them in remembrance, and to urge them to go forward in the narrow way to heaven. Glory be to God,

that he ever called me to work in his vineyard, and
sent me to seek, and to feed the sheep of his fold in
New-England. I am permitted to see another new
year ; and, blessed be God, I find new desires to
spend it to the glory of his name, and that in a more
acceptable way than I ever did a year, in all my life
Sometimes I feel my heart so much drawn out in warm
desires for the people, that I forget my dear friends
and relations ; and if it were not for the duty I owe
my parents, and the great desire they have to see me,
I think I could live and die in this part of the world.
The Lord only knows the difficulties I have had to
wade through, yet his grace is sufficient for me ; and
when I pass through the fire and the water, he is with
me ; and rough ways are smooth, when Jesus bears
me in his arms.

" Saturday 23d I visited several families, and
then rode to Stratford and at night preached in the
town-house, which was well crowded with attentive
hearers. I believe I never had so many together in
this place before. I did not spare Antinomianism ; and
the word seemed to have free course to the hearts of
the hearers. Oh that some precious souls may date
their conversion from this meeting. I anxiously wished to get hold of the two pillars of Antinomianism, and
like Sampson shake down the building in which many
thousands of souls are lodged, and sporting themselves
in their wickedness : and if I were to die with the
fall of that doctrine, I should think my death as ho-
nourable as was Sampson's. Mr. Peck, asked me to
his house, and I went. After I had been there a while
two women came in, and one of them soon began to
talk about inward religion, and told me that God had
converted her soul a few weeks before, and she ap-

peared to have a very clear witness of the happy change. Blessed be God for one witness for Jesus in this town.

"Sunday 24th. At half after 10 o'clock, I preached at the Old Mill, to a large congregation. I love to have the house filled with hearers, let it be great or small. I believe generally that the word has more weight, when the people sit thick than when thinly scattered about the house. After meeting I sat out, and my soul was transported with joy, the snow falling, the wind blowing, prayer ascending, faith increasing, grace descending, heaven smiling, and love abounding. If there were no other comfort promised, than such as I then felt, I should think it my duty to serve God, and my chief happiness to live in such a frame as this. But, glory to God, this is only a foretaste of what is promised.

"I rode to David Oldes', Weston, And at 3 o'clock, I preached on Acts xvii. 30. *And the times of this ignorance God winked at; but now commandeth all men every where to repent.* I insisted much on the willingness of God to save the world ; and that he never commanded any man to do, what he could not do. The Lord was with us of a truth, several hundreds were together : the house was large, but scarcely sufficient to hold the people, and some of them stood outside of the house with their hats off, and the snow falling on them, yet they seemed contented to hear the word. Most part of the assembly were very solemn, and many heard with tears in their eyes. Surely the Lord will not let his word fall to the ground or return void.

"In this neighbourhood there are many real friends to the Methodists ; and a little below they are

13

engaged in building a preaching house for me, without consulting me on the subject. O what a mercy it is that God gives such a creature as I am, favour in the eyes of so many people i. this part of the world. I understand by a friend of mine, that a tinker was among them a little time past, and inquired where he could get some work, and one told him that the Methodists were likely to beat a hole through the Saybrook platform, and if he could mend that, and wait long enough, he might be employed. I think we shall soon get such a hole in it, that neither tinker nor minister, will be able to stop it, so as to keep the people from seeing its flaws. Here I had more invitations to preach in new places ; but could not engage, for I had not time to spare.

" Monday 25th. I rode to Reading, and at 2 o'clock, I preached to a large congregation, the hearts and eyes of the people were touched while I prayed them to be reconciled to God. I hope the fruit of this meeting will be seen in a future day. I suppose one reason why I had so many to hear me, was owing to the minister's speaking against the Methodists the day before. I was informed he talked to his people for some time, and told them, ' to take care how they heard other preachers, and particularly the Methodists,' but the people did not take his advice. I thought I would let them know my mind freely, and therefore told them, that I intended to form a society as soon as possible, and that I would give certificates to any one that applied, and receive into society any that were awakened, if they desired it. I suppose I shall not be forgiven for this shortly. We had a little meeting at brother Sanford's at night, and one man obtained a certificate to clear him from paying rates to his minister.

" Thursday 28th. I preached at Jacob Wheeler's, in Limestone, and after meeting formed a class, two men and two women; perhaps these may be like the leaven hid in three measures of meal, that may leaven the whole neighbourhood, and many may be brought to say, I will go with this people, because we have heard that God is with them.

" Friday, February 5th. The day was extremely cold, but I set out and rode about sixteen miles to Fairfield woods. At 1 o'clock, I preached on 1 Tim. i. 5. *Now the end of the commandment is charity, out of a pure heart, and of a good conscience, and faith unfeigned.* The house was a good deal crowded with people, and the Lord was amongst us, and the hearts of some were touched, while they were constrained to hang their heads and weep. An old man said, that I preached just as their ministers used to preach, when they were lively in religion; another said, I preached his mind exactly, for he could not believe in the doctrine of election; and said that I need not be afraid, but what I would have hearers enough if I continued to preach as I did; another said, he never heard a man that preached his mind so fully, till he heard me. I hope my God will keep me humble when esteemed, and faithful when despised.

" Saturday 6th, I rode to Putney, four miles above Stratford, and put up with Captain Daniel Boothe, and at 2 o'clock at his brothers, I preached with great liberty and much comfort to my soul; some of the strange hearers were much affected, and tears run down their cheeks. I was never in this place before, and now I am not alone, for God is with me. I feel as if I should be willing to spend my days in going before my brethren, like John the Baptist, and prepare the way for them.

" After meeting an old man came and spoke to me,
and asked me why I did not go into the back settlements, and preach to the people that were not favoured with the Gospel, as they were in Putney : I told
him my call was to sinners, and that I found many of
them wherever I went. I then asked him, if all the
people in that neighbourhood were converted ? He
said, they had the means ; I asked him if any of them
preached in Putney ? He said no, but they preached
near enough for all to go and hear. I told him he put
me in mind of the dog in the manger, who would not
eat the hay himself, nor suffer the ox to eat it ; they
would not come to preach in the place, and was not
willing that I should ; at which many present could
not refrain from laughing heartily. He said, ' a busy
body about other men's matters', according to the original, was one that preached in another's parish without his consent. I told him the words might be well
applied to him, in *meddling* himself with my preaching. He still insisted on the necessity of my going
where there was no regular preaching, and where the
people were suffering for the want of it. I told him
if he thought that some ought to go to the new settled
parts of the country, that he was the very man to go.
He said he was too old : I replied, that a person was
never too old to do good. We then parted, and he bid
me adieu. When I came away, I asked what old gentleman that was ; they told me, it was Mr. Birdseye, a worn-
out priest, that preaches once in a while, and was but
little admired by the people. I wist not that he was a
priest, and no wonder that the people laughed, when I
compared him to the dog in the manger, though I
knew nothing of him.

" Saturday 13th. I set off early in the morning, and
had more than 20 miles to ride, to a quarterly meeting,

On the road, I was advised to cross a large pond on the ice, which, they said, would save me nearly a mile's riding. I suppose the pond was a mile and a half over: I saw the footsteps of other horses, that had gone before me, and had an old man's word withal, for my safety. Sometimes the ice would crack and split under my horse, as if he were going through ; at which he, as well as myself, were often frightened. It brought me seriously to meditate on the goodness of God, and his repeated promises to those who put their trust in him. O! thought I, if I can trust myself and horse on this ice, at one man's word, and by seeing the tracks of those that have gone before, surely, I may trust my soul on the Lord Jesus, who has promised not to leave me, or suffer me to be tempted more than I am able to bear; especially, when I trace the footsteps of those holy men who have gone before, and borne the cross till death. Though the ice would crack as if ready to swallow me up, yet there was no danger, for it was very strong. Then I would cry out, O my soul, fear not, though thou art pursued by men and devils, thou canst not be hurt, while stayed upon the Lord Jesus Christ.

"Monday 22d. Reading, at 3 o'clock, I preached on Luke xv. 32. *For this thy brother was dead, and is alive again; and was lost, and is found.* The Lord was among the people of a truth ; and, blessed be his name, my soul was quickened, and some of my hearers melted under the word. O! that their tears may be noticed by the Lord, and all their wants supplied. At night, we held a class-meeting at A. Sanford's, which is the first they have ever had in the place. About thirty people attended, and I spoke to

13 *

a part of them, and found some that seemed to be truly awakened.

" Tuesday 23d. We sent for one of the neighbouring women to come over; she came, and I talked to her about her soul : she was much distressed, and said she could find no peace to her soul. I prayed with her, and for her, and she wept freely. Surely, there is a great prospect of a revival in this place. O that the flame may catch from house to house.

"Saturday 27th. We had our quarterly meeting at Dan-Town. Just before the time of meeting, a friend informed me, that there were three preachers coming from a distance to labour with me in New-England. I was greatly pleased at the report, and my heart seemed to reply, 'blessed is he that cometh in the name of the Lord.' When I saw them riding up, I stood and looked at them, and could say from my heart, 'thou hast well done, that thou art come.' Brother Jacob Brush, an elder, and George Roberts, and Daniel Smith, two young preachers, came from Maryland state, to assist me in this part of the world. No one knows, but God and myself, what comfort and joy I felt at their arrival. Surely, the Lord has had respect unto my prayers, and granted my request.

" Wednesday, March 3d. Brother Brush went to see brother Roberts, whom we had left behind sick, and brother Smith and myself set out to the eastward, leaving brother Brush to supply my two weeks circuit. We rode to Joseph Hall's in Stratfield, and tarried all night.

"Sunday 14th. Weathersfield, in the North Brick School-House, I preached on 2 Cor. viii. 9. I enlarged on the sufferings of Christ, and showed the people how they, through his poverty might be made rich. Some of the people sensibly felt what I said, and tears ran down from the eyes of my hearers. Glory be to God, that we were favoured with the presence of him who walked in the fiery furnace with his children. O that the Lord may revive his work in this place! Here we met with a couple of old friends from Hartford,* Mr. Thomas Hildrup and Mr. Coop, who rejoiced to see us on our way to their city. They informed us, that the Lord was reviving his work in Hartford. My soul rejoiced at the glad tidings, and I was ready to say, Lord, we are well able to go up and possess the land.' I left brother Smith behind, to preach to the same congregation in the afternoon. I went on to Hartford, and put up at Mr. Winship's, a private lodging prepared for me, by my two old friends. Here I was informed that several persons were awakened by my preaching, when I was here before. The hearing of this, seemed to humble my soul in the dust, and to strengthen my faith. Ah! Lord, what am I, that thou shouldest own my labours, and comfort my soul! Not unto me, not unto me, O Lord! but unto thy name give glory. At 2 o'clock they rang the bell, and we met in the statehouse. I preached on 1 Thes. v. 19. I had a large company of hearers to speak to ; and glory be to God for his goodness to me in speaking his word. I felt

* Mr. Lee visited Hartford on the 9th of December, and continued in the city two days; during which time he preached twice or thrice, to large and attentive congregations. He was much pleased with the visit, and was encouraged to hope that God was about to open an effectual door for the preaching of the gospel by the Methodists in that place His hopes were fully realized, for many were stirred up to inquire the way of the Lord more perfectly. and to see that there was something in religion which they had never experienced,

my soul happy in the Lord, and the people heard with
great attention, and with many tears. I felt as if the
word had taken hold of the hearts of the hearers ;
and was greatly in hopes, that God would awaken some
of the sleepy sinners. The comfort I felt at this
meeting, was worth more than all the pleasures of
this poor world. I hope this place will be famous
for vital religion.

" At dark we met again in the state-house, at which
time I preached on 1 Tim. vi, 12. I felt a strong
confidence in God, and had no doubt but what he
would bless my well meant endeavours, and own my
labours. Paul may plant, and Apollos may water, but
thou alone, O God ! canst give the increase. Some
of the people were willing to give us the right-hand
of fellowship, and bid us God speed in our undertaking. I left the people with a heart to pray for
them, and to entreat God, for Christ's sake, to bless
the word preached, to their souls' salvation.

"Monday 15th. We spent the day in visiting the
sick and the well, who desired our company. In the
afternoon, I spent a few hours very agreeably with
some persons who came to see us, in talking of the
form and power of godliness ; but, according to the
New-England custom, we spent a little time in talking
about principles ; especially, the probability of men's
being lost after they are converted to God. We met
again at night in the state-house, where I preached
on John xvi. 20. I felt great freedom in preaching
from first to last ; my eyes were often filled with
tears, and sometimes I could hardly keep from weeping aloud ; my soul fed upon the word, while I was
endeavouring to feed the flock of God. We had
more people in the state-house this night, than had

ever been seen there on any occasion. They were very solemn and attentive, and many of them were deeply affected, and wept bitterly under the word. It appeared to me that God was opening the way for us to be received by, and greatly blessed to the people. After we broke up, several persons came and spoke to me, and begged my prayers. It has often been my prayer of late, that if our undertaking in visiting these parts, were according to the will of God, that he would open the houses of the people to receive us, and their hearts to receive our instructions. Here my prayer is visibly answered. We have repeated invitations to call upon, and lodge with the people ; and they earnestly request our prayers, attend our ministry, and desire our advice. My heart is drawn towards the people in the eastern states. If the Lord opens my way before me, I think I shall visit them shortly.

"Tuesday 16th. We obtained directions, and rode to Farmington, ten miles from Hartford, and was advised to call on old Mr. Woodruff, who lives at the edge of the town. We had been there but a little time before the old man began to talk about principles, and the old lady to fix dinner. We continued the discourse till we had dined. When the old man found out that we believed a person might fall from grace and be lost, he discovered a good deal of anger, and said, if David had died in the act of adultery, and Peter while swearing, they would have been saved. Then, said I, 'after a man is converted he is obliged to be saved, he can't help it?' Yes, says he, he is obliged to be saved whether he will no, for it is impossible for him to help it. He said, he would as soon hear us curse God at once, as to hear us say

that God would give his love to a person and then
take it away again.   I told him, God never would take
it from them, but they might cast it away.   He said,
if God sent the leprosy on a man, no one but God
could take it away.   So, says I, you think religion
and leprosy are much what, sent as a judgment upon
a person?   He did not know how to get clear, but
seeing he was much ruffled in his temper, I thought it
best to be moving; so we asked him the way to Mr.
Coles', but he would not tell us, for he said, Mr.
Coles would not like his sending such men to his
house.   However, we got directions from his wife,
and then set out.   I shook hands with the old man,
and told him I hoped God would reward him for his
kindness.

" Friday 19th.   Brother Smith left me and went to
Dan-Town after his horse.   I rode down to Derby,
and sent for the bell-man, and hired him to ring the
bell, and inform the people that I was going to preach.
A man of my former acquaintance came to the tavern
where I was, and said he was glad to see me as a friend,
but not as a preacher.   I told him I had come to preach
once more ; and that I had been visiting some new
places.   He said he wished well to religion, but did
not like so many parties ; I told him there were three
preachers sent to my assistance, and we had written
for three more, and that I was in hopes we should
spread all over New-England in a little time.   He
said he was sorry to hear it.   Now says he, ' I am
in earnest, I am sorry to hear it.'   He refuses to hear
me preach, and for no other reason than this, he is
afraid it will cause divisions.   At night I preached, and
after meeting, I rode home with Captain Baldwin, and
tarried all night.

"Sunday 21st. After preaching in Milford, I rode
to New Haven, and after the other meetings were out,
they rang the bell for me ; and I preached on 2 Cor.
v. 17. It was a very pleasant day, and a large congregation to preach to ; and they paid great attention to
the word. The number of people that attended, and
the liberty I felt amongst them, caused me to hope
that God would own the Methodists in New Heaven,
Lord hasten the happy time, I beseech Thee, and let
these people be brought to a knowledge of themselves, and of Thee !

At night, met at Mrs. Gilbert's for a conference
meeting, and being often asked, I exhorted with much
comfort in my soul, and some of the little number
appeared to be much engaged with God. I have now
formed New Haven circuit, for one preacher ; the distance which the preacher has to travel in going round
once in two weeks, is 120 miles. For this circuit we
have to preach in three cities, five towns pretty
thickly settled, and several country places. I have
now gone around it, and made my own appointments, and have preached seventeen times within
the last fourteen days. Oftimes while riding in this
part of the world, I have been brought to cry out, O !
that I had Whitefield's spirit, and could be as successful as he was. But immediately I hear an inward
voice say, ' you have need of a better spirit, than
Whitefield's : then I am brought to say, ' O that I may
have the Spirit of God for my guide and comforter.'
If I have this it is enough.

" Thursday 25th. Middlefield meeting, I preache d
on John iii. 17. I felt great comfort in declaring the
willingness of God to save the whole world. And in
showing what he had done in order to save all mankind, many of the hearers gazed at me, and seemed

to say by their looks, ' thou bringest certain strange
things to our ears.' They paid great attention, but
I suppose they could not believe it all; for many in
these parts think, that Christ only died for a few : I
hope truth will hew down Agag, and every Antinomian
error.

" 31st. I set out for Bolton, and I had rode but a little
way before I fell in company with a man that began
to talk about the times in Hartford. I told him, the
Hartford people wanted but two things to make them
comfortable, a little more money, and more grace :
this was an introduction to a religious discourse. I
told him there appeared to be a religious stir in Hartford. He said, there were two preachers who
preached in town on Monday night, that had come up
from the south, but they brought no new thing. I
knew that he had been to hear brother Smith and
myself. I told him a preacher's business was not to
teach any new thing, but to teach the people what
was written in the Gospel. Ah! says he, these
preachers speak louder than our ministers, and raise
their heads, and spread their hands, and hollow, as
though they were going to frighten the people. I
told him it would be well if they could frighten the
people out of their sins. I parted with the man, and
never told him who I was. I went to Captain Cone's
and stayed all night.

" Thursday, April 1st. I talked to Captain Cone,
about preaching, but could get no encouragement : an
old man that lived just by came in, and expressed a
great desire to hear me preach ; I told him if he desired it, I would preach in his house. He then excused
the matter, and said he had appointed to settle some
accounts with a man that day, so that it would not suit
very well. I thought it would never do, to delay my

time in that way, so I got ready and rode off, and Captain Cone went with me : when we had gone about two miles, we came to a large school-house, and many families lived in sight, so I concluded to stop and try to preach there. I went to the man who kept the key of the school-house, but he was not at home, however, I obtained liberty of the woman of the house to preach at night. They told me that there was an old man in the place that said he was ready to starve for the want of preaching ; well thought I, that is the place for me, for I am ready to starve, for the want of people to whom I may preach. I went into his house and was kindly received. At night I preached in the school-house to a few solemn hearers ; this place is in Bolton township, Tolland county.

" Saturday 3d. I rode to East Windsor, and was advised to call upon Timothy Strong; being a friend to religion, I inquired for him, and called at his house, and introduced myself to him after my common manner in this part of the country, by saying, ' I am a travelling preacher of the Methodist persuasion, and have come in order to preach in this place.' The old man began after the New England custom to inquire about principles. I passed a long and close examination, and after all, he could not give consent for me to preach in his house, though he had generally made all denominations welcome that applied. He said he would go with me to a Baptist's house about a mile off, and see what he would do ; so we rode up to Noah Bissell's, and there I passed another long examination before him, but he did not like all my principles, and therefore, could not open his doors. . I told him I generally made it a point to take no denial with respect to preaching, and if I could not get in

14

at one place, I made trial of another. The sun was
then about an hour high, I told them I would go and
try to get liberty to preach in the school-house. When
I was about to go, Mr. Bissell said he would keep my
horse, so I thanked him, and went to the man who had
care of the school-room, but he was not at home. I asked
his wife, respecting the matter, and got the key, and
went and opened the door, and returned the key. I
came back and told them what I had done, and they
condescended to spread the news. At dark, we met,
and the house was quite full of people, and I preached
on John iii. 7. The people paid great attention to
what I said. I suppose some of them were as attentive, as though they had been jury men upon a case
of life and death. But I was afraid they did not pray
for a blessing on what they heard. Some of the
women appeared to be melted into tears. I found it
to be a profitable time to me. O! how often do I
dread the cross ; and yet it never hurt me. I very
frequently find that after a heavy cross, I meet with
great satisfaction. If I could have the comfort without the cross, I should often be glad, but if the comfort is equal to the cross, as it often is with me, I
wish for a heavy cross ; for I do sincerely long for
great comfort. When I came from meeting, I felt
happy in God, and resolved to make another appointment to preach there the next morning at 8 o'clock.
When I returned to Mr Bissell's, he told me he would
then open his doors for me, if I chose to come again
and preach. He entertained me kindly.

    " Sunday 4th. East Windsor. Again, at 8 o'clock, I
preached on Matt. vi. 10. *Thy kingdom come.* I felt
some encouragament to hope that my coming would not
be in vain. O Lord! own the labours of thy unworthy

servant, and bless these people, to whom I have spoken. I rode down to Hartford, and ate dinner in a great hurry, and at half past 3 o'clock, I went to the court-house, and preached to a house full of serious hearers. It seemed to give springs to my faith, when I beheld the tears stealing down the cheeks of many of my hearers. I still believe God will abundantly revive his work in this place before long.

"Thursday 8th, was a fast day throughout the state, for in this state they keep an annual fast in the spring. The manner of fasting in general is to eat a hearty breakfast, as usual, then attend public worship in the forenoon and afternoon, without eating any dinner, and then have supper before night, so those that keep the fast eat but two meals between sun-rise and sun-set.

"Friday 9th. I preached in Suffield; while I was preaching a Baptist preacher came in, and after I was done, began to talk to me, by asking me, if I had a liberal education; I told him, I could speak the English language, but was not perfect in it. He said he supposed I understood what he meant by a liberal education; it was speaking the different tongues. I told him I could talk a little High Dutch. He then desired me to give him some account of my conversion, and call to the ministry. I told him that it would be too tedious for me to tell the whole, but I could tell a part. So I began, 'I sought the Lord and I found him.' The old man broke out immediately without letting me speak any further, and insisted on it, that no man ever sought the Lord, before he was regenerated, and that God is always found of those that seek him *not*. The poor man soon showed that his nature was too much like his name, his name is Hastings, and his nature *hasty*. Some of the com-

pany spoke to him about getting so high: he soon
stopped and said, ' well we have got too warm.'   ' O
come, (says I,) don't persecute me, if you have got too
warm own it ; as for my part, I feel very calm.'   ' Well,
(he said,) he would bear the blame.'   I told him when
I talked with people, I expected half the time to speak
in, but he wished to take the whole ; but still he
insisted on it, that no man ever had a desire to be
religious, till after he was born again ; for a desire
to serve God, was serving him.   I talked a little to
him, but could not say much, for the old man has not
much of what people call good manners, but would
begin to talk while I was in the middle of a sentence.
I would then stop and let him go on.   I told the people, I would preach in town next day, if they would
meet me, and then we parted.

" Saturday, 17th.   I set out and rode a few miles
into the state of Vermont, Windham County, and
being directed, called upon an old gentleman, who
appeared to be very kind, and willing to entertain me,
but had no hay for my horse.   He directed me to one
of his neighbours, where they were to have meeting
the next day.   So I rode to Benjamin Lee's, who was
very poor, but very kind.

" Monday, 19th.   I crossed Connecticut river to
the east side, into New Hampshire, and came through
a little corner of it, and so into Massachusetts again.
I came to Northfield, which has about fifty dwelling
houses in it.   The day was very rainy, but I kept on
to a town, called Montague, and put up at Lieutenant
Gunn's tavern.   They were very kind and friendly
to me when they understood I was a preacher.   Here
they knew nothing of the Methodists only by vague
report, and some accounts which they had seen in the

public papers, of the wonderful work of God among the Methodists in Virginia, between two and three years ago.

"Saturday, 24th. I felt some inward comfort, and my heart was moved with love to God, when I took a view of his past favours to me. In my late journey I have met with many discouragements, and have not found so much satisfaction in Massachusetts, as I have generally found in Connecticut.

"Monday, 10th of May, I met with brother Roberts, in Middletown. We then went to South Farms, and at 2 o'clock, I preached on 1 Cor. xiii. 13. I felt much satisfaction in speaking, and hope our meeting was to the glory of God. Some of the people in this place are a little set against me on account of my speaking favourably of infants, and saying, that all who die in infancy will be saved. Some of the Separates have spoken against me, both in private and in public; therefore I thought it necessary to give them a little reproof. I told them that people had a great deal to say against me, and one charge was, that I denied original sin. I told them that man was a fallen creature, and one argument was sufficient to prove it, which was this: When the Papist began to persecute the Church of England, they ran out from amongst them, and brought the same spirit with them, and then began to persecute the Presbyterians, who came over to New-England, and brought the same spirit with them, and turned upon the Quakers and hung them; and began to persecute the Separates; and now let the Separates take care lest they turn upon some body else. At these words many of the people smiled, and appeared well pleased.

14 *

"Tuesday 11th. I parted with brother Roberts. Then I came down to Haddam, and made an appointment to preach in the court-house. The people behaved pretty well, and some of them were free in asking me to their houses. The Methodists were never in this town before. Some of the people wish to have them. O Lord! send more of them into this part of thy vineyard, and send them speedily, if consistent with thy will.

"Monday 17th, I rode to Milford and dined, and then came to Stratford. When I got in sight of the town I felt comforted. As soon as I crossed the ferry, I called at a house, and the people appeared as glad to see me as if they had been my own relations. I gave out word that I would preach at night, and then came up to Mr. Peck's. When I got there, I found matters better still, and I was informed that some, in that place, had determined to join the Methodists. This caused me to rejoice that ever I came amongst them. I felt determined to go on, and brake up more New-England ground if possible, and then leave it for my better and abler brethren to cultivate.

"Tuesday 18th. I rode to Joseph Hall's in Stratfield, and there I met with brother Smith. At 5 o'clock, I preached on Rev. xvii. 14. I felt much comforted in my own soul while speaking. The people appeared much more engaged in religion than what they were when I was among them last. Brother Smith exhorted, afterwards I met the class, and found a sweet sense of the love of God in my soul, while the people were telling of the goodness of God to them. O! how I love the Methodists! I have not seen a class-meeting before for near three months; I often feel a wish to be always amongst the Metho-

dists, and yet am content to go before, and try and
open the way for others to follow. Lord Jesus, go
with me to the ends of the earth, and save me from
sin to the end of my life.   Amen and Amen!

"Wednesday 19th.   Rode back to Stratford, and at
night I preached, and brother Smith exhorted.   We
had a large company of solemn hearers.   Then we
went to Captain Peck's, and had a class-meeting, and
joined a small class together, which is the first beginning of a class in this place.

" Wednesday, June the 9th.   We rode to E. Ward's,
near Moose-Hill, in North Stratford Parish.   We
sent out and gathered a congregation, and at 5 o'clock,
I preached on Mal. iii. 18.   I was much assisted in
teaching the people, and had cause to bless God for a
sense of his love to my soul.   The hearers were
pretty solemn.   Then brother John Lee exhorted
with a considerable degree of liberty.   When meeting was over, Mr. Clark, a young Church minister,
came and sat down by me, and said he supposed, by
my preaching. that I did not believe that baptism was
regeneration, I told him, I did not.   But he looked
upon it, that baptism was regeneration, and that when
the child was baptized, it was born again.   I told him
if that were the case, then every unbaptized child must
go to hell ; and then asked him how it could be otherwise.   He tried to show how they might be saved by
Christ without baptism, but could not make both ends
of his argument meet.   He then began about the
power of ordination, and observed that all that were
ordained by the bishop, were sent of the Lord to
preach the gospel.   I argued that many who were
ordained by the bishop, were wicked men, and I was
convinced that the Lord never sent a wicked man to

preach the gospel ; and that Christ, as a good shep-
herd, never set a wolf over his sheep to guard them ;
and that a man, in order to preach the gospel, must
first be called to the knowledge of the truth, and then
to the work of the ministry. He said, if a man was
called by the Spirit of the Lord to preach the gospel,
then it would follow, that he would have power to
work miracles as formerly, &c. O ! what a pity that
any man should preach an unknown God.

"Friday 18th. At Middlefield, at 7 o'clock, I
preached on Eph. v. 1. It was a gracious season to
my soul, and I believe to the souls of many of my
hearers. I felt a longing desire for Christians of
every denomination to be united together. I ardently
wish for bigotry and party zeal to be done away. The
Lord begins to own the Methodists in this parish.
One young woman spoke with me, who appeared to
be very happy in God, and said, the Lord had sent me
to wake up her mind, and that the first time I preached
in the place, she was awakened ; and after a few weeks
of severe conviction, the Lord graciously pardoned
her sins, and enabled her to rejoice in God. Bless
the Lord, O my soul ! that he has given me one seal
to my ministry in this place."

The writer fears that he should swell this volume
beyond designed limits, were he to continue to indulge
his own inclination. As far as possible, the journal
shall speak for itself ; but we shall content ourselves
to finish this chapter with rather an abridged view of
his travels for the remainder of this year.

During the month of June. he resolved to extend
his travels further than he had heretofore done, and,
particularly, he had Boston in his mind as one place,
in which he intended to unfurl the standard of the

cross, He therefore, toward the end of the month, set out on his tour, visited Hartford again, and preached several times; then he directed his course to Bolton, and warned the wicked to flee the wrath to come. He was then at some loss how to direct his course; however, upon making some inquiries relative to the rout which he wished to pursue, he resolved to take Windham in his way. Here he preached to a solemn assembly, with much comfort to his own soul, and was earnestly requested by many, to tarry in the place several days; but finding it inconvenient to comply with their request, he hastened on to Norwich, and preached twice, but not without some fears that "the word was not received in faith by them that heard."

He then visited New-London. Here he could but thank God for bringing him among a people, once more, whom he dearly loved, and could own as brethren in the Lord. Though they were not called Methodists, yet he could claim them as his Father's children. After preaching in New-London several times with much comfort, he proceeded to Stonington Point, a place which had never been visited by a Methodist before. But here he was comforted in meeting with some who were "the dear people of God." He then went to Newport, and found some willing to give him the right-hand of fellowship; a sure sign that they were profited by his ministry.

From Newport, he went to Bristol, and preached; and from there to Warren; here he was invited by the ministers of other denominations to preach in their pulpits, and was treated kindly by the people generally. He then visited Providence, and preached five times in one private house, beside several sermons, which he preached in the court-house. He then direct-

ed his course to Boston, praying that if his journey to
the east, was of God, that the houses and hearts of
the people, might be open to receive him. On the
9th of July he reached the city of Boston, and immediately on his arrival, endeavoured to find out some
place where he might preach, but although he conversed with many on the subject, yet every expedient
failed. He could get none to encourage him in his
benevolent design ; none would put themselves to the
trouble of finding a suitable place where he might
deliver his message to the people. Finding the
persons whom he addressed on the subject, quite
indifferent, he finally concluded that he would preach
on the commons the day following. At the time appointed, which was 6 o'clock, sabbath afternoon, he
found a large assembly, which listened with more
attention and solemnity, than he had any reason to
expect, considering the novelty of the scene.

On Monday morning, he left Boston, not however, without a resolution of visiting the place again.
the ensuing sabbath. He rode to Salem, and preached in Mr. Joshua Spalding's pulpit, to a large company of attentive hearers. From thence he passed
through Ipswich, and went to Newburyport, and
according to direction called on Mr. Murry, a Presbyterian minister. When Mr. Murry found out that
he belonged to Mr. Wesley's party, he very politely
offered to treat Mr. Lee as a gentleman, and as a
Christian, but not as a preacher, viz. that he could
not let him preach in his pulpit. His apology was,
that he had been informed by letter, that a preacher
of the Wesleyan party, had lately been up the Connecticut river, and that he had held meetings in four different places, in one day. Mr. Lee informed him

that he was the man who had been guilty of the crime of preaching in four different places, in one day. But although not successful in getting Mr. Murry's pulpit, he after much exertion, succeeded in getting the court-house ; at which place he appointed to preach on his return. From Newburyport, he proceeded to Portsmouth, which was then the metropolis of New-Hampshire Here he preached to a solemn and attentive congregation, and some were truly thankful that he had visited that place. He then left Portsmouth, and returned to Newburyport. Here he found, that although he had obtained leave of the select men to preach in the court-house, when he was there before, yet, even in a few days, three of them had changed their minds, and were inclined to keep him out of it. However, in the evening the congregation assembled at the place, and one of the select men being present, opened the door, and Mr. Lee preached to a company of well behaved people ; some of whom were melted into tears before the conclusion of the sermon. Fearing lest they should form some objection to his preaching there in future, he resolved to make sure of one more time, and so appointed to preach at the same place the next morning at 6 o'clock. Morning preaching was a new thing in the place, but he had a great many to hear, and had reason to hope that many were profited by hearing, while he was blessed in speaking. After preaching, he called to see Mr. Murry, where he found Mr. Marshall, the Separate minister, and all agreed to go to the meeting-house and take a view of the remains of Mr. George Whitefield, which had been sleeping in silence for near twenty years, under the communion table, and just before the pulpit of the meeting-house. Having pre-

vided themselves with a candle, they descended into
the vault, and upon opening the coffin, they were enabled to witness the fearful change which the king of
terrors makes upon the most perfect forms.   On taking
a particular view, they discovered his ears, hair, and a
part of his nose had fallen off.   His face was nearly
in the common shape, though much contracted, and
appeared quite destitute of moisture, and very hard.
His teeth were white, and fast in their sockets.
His breast bone had parted, and his bowels disrobed.
His wig and clothes, in which he was buried, were all
decayed, except in a few places.   Parts of his gown
in which he was buried, still remained ; and were
quite hard to tear.   His flesh was black ; and, as might
be supposed, destitute of comeliness ; yet it is said, that
any person who once knew him, might discover some
traces of his former likeness.   After visiting this
dreary mansion, which contains the mortal part of one
'of the greatest missionaries that ever lived.   Mr. Lee
contented himself by bringing away a small relic of the
gown in which he was buried ; and prayed that he
might be endued with the same zeal which once
inspired the breast of its wearer.

Leaving Newburyport, he went to the New Mills,
and preached in the Baptist meeting-house.   Here he
received a letter from Mr. Spalding of Salem, informing him that he had made an appointment for him to
preach in his meeting-house that evening.   He accordingly went to Salem, and fulfilled the appointment,
and gave them a plain Methodist sermon.   Here he
was solicited by a man from Marblehead to visit that
place.   He hesitated at first, not knowing that an
opportunity would be presented ; but upon second
thought, he concluded to go and see them the next

day, which he accordingly did. Here he had cause
to believe that his preaching was made a great blessing to the people; for, says he, "some of them complain of being almost starved for the word."

From Marblehead, he rode to Boston, and preached
to about three thousand people, on the commons.
"Blessed be God, (says he,) he made his quickening
presence known, and met us in the fields."

During the past week, he had travelled at least
one hundred and thirty miles; made his own appointments, and preached ten times. But he found that not
only public duties were important, but that private
duties equally demanded his attention; to discharge
which, he found it needful that all his time should be
employed.

In this, his second visit to Boston, he not only
preached on the commons, but also in a private house;
and on one occasion, in a meeting-house belonging to
the Baptists, which was vacant. He also went to
Charleston, to see if any there were willing to receive
him as the messenger of Christ. Here he preached
in a private house, and had reason to believe that
many felt the weight of what was spoken. On the
ensuing sabbath, he preached upon the commons in
Boston again, to a much greater multitude than he
had seen on the two former occasions. Although
there had been a considerable fall of rain that day,
and the earth was rendered quite wet; he calculated
that there were not less than five thousand present.

From Boston, he directed his course back to the
state of Connecticut; and the first place in which
he preached, after leaving Boston, was in Enfield;
here he was much comforted with the presence of the
Lord. Hartford was the next place which called his

attention ; and accordingly, he delivered a message to
the people of that city : and went on to Middlefield,
where a quarterly-meeting was held the 23d of
July, within the bounds of the New-Haven circuit.
Although, in this place, the Methodists had preached
but a few times, yet the word had taken such hold
upon the minds of some, that when an offer was made
at this meeting, to receive members into society, six
came forward, and boldly resolved to be Methodists.

After travelling throughout many of the towns and
cities, both of Connecticut and Massachusetts, and in
the states of Vermont and New-Hampshire, and
preaching day and night, labouring indefatigably for
the good of souls, in a part of the country where the
Methodists were either not known at all, or merely
from distant rumor ; encountering with difficulties,
which nothing but the most undaunted resolution
could withstand, he makes these remarks :

"Here I may stop and look back on the year that
is past. But when I consider on the many dangers
I have passed through, the many mercies I have
received, and the many moments I have not improved,
I stand amazed at myself, and astonished at the goodness of God to me. It is now sixteen months and
eigth days, since our last conference, and in this time,
I have travelled several thousand miles, and preached
in six states, and in chief part of the large towns in
New-England. In most places, I have met with a
much kinder reception than I could have expected,
among persons holding principles so different from
mine; but yet I have been much opposed, and have been
under the disagreeable necessity of spending much of
my time in talking on controverted points, sometimes
in public and oftimes in private. When I was opposed,

if I discovered an inclination to wave the discourse,
they would immediately conclude that my principles
were so bad that I was afraid to let them be known ;
and if I were silent, all would go for the truth. For
these reasons, I have been led to debate the matter
with the principal part of those who have spoken to
me with a calm spirit. I have generally quietness of
mind while conversing on doctrinal points, and oftimes
seemed to be immediately assisted from heaven ; and
answers have been put in my mouth, that were not
familiar to me, when strange questions have been
asked. I was enabled to go through all my hardships
with great satisfaction, and was much blessed in
preaching to the people ; and the Lord gave me to
see some visible fruit of my labours, in the awakening
and conversion of some precious souls."

CHAPTER XI.

—◦✦◦—

He attends the Conference at New-York.—Receives Ordination.—Is appointed to Boston.—Hears of the death of his mother.—The affliction which his mind sustained on receiving this melancholy intelligence.—Receives a friendly letter from Lynn.—Difficulties in Boston.—His finances get low.—Raises a Society in Lynn.

IN the month of October 1790, Mr. Lee attended the conference held in the city of New-York. When taking leave of his friends in the New-England states, he was not fully resolved in his mind, whether or not he should immediately return to them again. This contingency always attends those who are engaged in the itinerant field. Those whose business it is to assign to the preachers their respective stations, find it necessary to change them, according as the expediency or necessity of the case may be. To this feature in our economy we are indebted, under God, for much of our success, in building up the church of Christ. When Mr. Lee attended the conference, he did not forget to intercede for the people of New-England. In a private interview with Mr. Asbury, which lasted three hours, he endeavoured to set forth, with all the arguments he could use on the occasion, the necessity of sending a supply of labourers into that section of the work. The bishop listened to his appeal with a candid ear, and a heart ever ready to feel for the state of Zion, and a disposition to use every effort for the spread of the Gospel, and to promote the inte-

15 *

rests of the church, granted his request, and sent several active and zealous men to the New-England states, and the subject of this Memoir was appointed to Boston.

At this conference he gave his consent to receive ordination. He accordingly was first ordained deacon in private, and the day following was ordained elder, publicly, with others.

He had frequently expressed a wish that if ever he were ordained, that it might be in a plain manner, that the Bishop might not have on his gown or band. Every thing was according to his wish, his prayer was, " That the preachers might ever labour for a plain dress, and a humble heart."

It may appear strange to some, why he refused to receive ordination until this period, having been eligible five years previous to the time of his' being ordained. The only answer which can be made to this inquiry is, that he did not feel his mind free to it; not that he called in question the validity of the ordination of the Methodist Episcopal Church. This, I believe, was foreign to his mind. Feeling his own unworthiness, he was cautious in treading on such holy ground. It was a matter, with him, which required the most mature deliberation.

We may safely conclude that he gave his consent at a very seasonable period. Travelling in a place, and among a people who had been strangers to the Methodists ; engaged in forming new societies, to whom it was necessary to dispense the ordinances of the Lord's house ; those who should be raised up under his ministry would naturally look up to him for the full exercise of ministerial functions, which might be the means of strengthening their confidence in the

minister, and confirming them in the faith of the gospel.

Novices in the ministry, not unfrequently abuse
their trust, and their inexperience betrays them into
errors ; but the man whose judgment is matured, having learned in the school of experience, improved in
knowledge and refined by grace; we may expect
from him a careful attendence to the important duties
incumbent on him.

Wednesday, 13th, of October, he received the
mournful intelligence, that his mother was no more
among mortals ; having departed this life on the 14th,
of September. He now found himself bereft of an
affectionate parent, whom he was never to behold
again in time. The effect which this intelligence had
upon his mind cannot be more feelingly expressed
than in his own words.

" This account drew tears from my eyes, and caused
me many a heavy sigh, but I could not doubt of the
happiness of my mother: she has professed to know
the Lord to the pardon of her sins upwards of seventeen years, and has proved by her life, that she possessed that religion which she professed. When I
was at home last, which was about two years and a
half ago, she appeared to be a mother in Israel, and
much alive to God. She was quite willing to give up
my brother John and myself to go and preach the
gospel, though it caused her many a bitter tear at
parting with us. O! may I always be ready for death,
though it should come at an unexpected hour. I was
much confused in my mind, scarcely knowing whether
it would be best for me to return to New-England,
or to go home. I tried to give myself to God in prayer,
and to beg for instruction ; at last I concluded that

it would be best for my brother John to go to Virginia,
and for me to go to Boston, according to appointment.

" Friday, 15th.   Brother John left the city and
set off for home. I went with him to the ferry, and
stood and looked after him for awhile, and then
returned with a sorrowful heart : the parting with
him appeared to be almost as distressin g as the news
of my mother's death."

On Tuesday the 19th, he left the city, and set out
on his journey, to the north.   That day at 4 o'clock,
P. M, he preached at New-Rochelle.   The next day
he travelled as far as North Castle, and preached at
3 o'clock.   The day after, he rode to Bedford, and
preached at 12 o'clock ; and at 4 o'clock he preached
in Dan-Town, where he was enabled to meet with
some of his old friends, who were much pleased at
his return.   Here for the first time he baptized a child,
and administered the Lord's Supper to a few communicants ; he also visited Stanford, Middlesex, Wilton,
Reading, New-Town, New-Stratford, Putney, Milford, Wallingford and Middlefield.   At the latter place
he baptized one woman and twelve children, and had
a solemn time in the ordinance.   From Middlefield,
he went to Middletown, to South-Farms, Weathersfield,
and Hartford.   At the last of which places he formed
a society.   From Hartford he set out for Boston, and
arrived there the 13th of November ; the next day
being Sunday, and having no place in which he could
preach during the day, he went to hear a Universalist,
but was far from being benefitted by his discourse.
At night he preached to a small company in a private
house.

" The following part of the week, (says he,) I met
with great and heavy trials. I took much pains in

trying to get a house to preach in ; but all in vain. A
few of the friendly people, made a little move also,
but did not succeed. One of the greatest friends that
I had in town when I was here before, did not come
to see me now, and when I went to see him, would
scarcely take any notice of me. I met with difficulties and troubles daily, yet I put my trust in God, and
in general, was confirmed in the opinion that God
would bless my coming to Boston. I spent one evening with Mr. John Carnes, merchant, who treated me
with great politeness, and said he would assist me in
any thing that he could. The greater part of the
week was wet, so that I could go out but little. My
cry was ' Lord help me.'

"Monday, 22d. I felt determined to try every
prudent means to procure a place to preach in, but
I was quite disappointed. Perhaps the Lord sees it
best for me to be tried in this manner, though it is
painful to me to be so idle.

"Monday, 29th. We had a letter from a gentleman in Lynn, who desired me to come and see him,
and gave me some encouragement, for he said, he had
a desire to hear some of the Methodists preach. I then
began to think that the Lord was about opening a way
for me to preach in that place. I made some inquiry
about a place in Boston ; and told some of my best
friends, that if they could not get a place, I would go
myself and try and do the best that I could. I began
to think the Lord would grant me my request, and
provide me a place to preach in.

"Tuesday, 30th. A man went with me to the
high sheriff, and we asked for liberty to preach in the
court-house. He said he could not give leave himself, but that the Clerk of the Court had the disposing

of the house, and we must apply to him. So we went to the Clerk, and told him what we wanted, but he very abruptly refused. After hearing him talk awhile, we left him, and I felt more discouraged than ever ; yet if I am right the Lord will provide for me.

"Thursday, 2d of December. At night one of my friends came home with me, and told me, he had used every means he could, to get a particular school-house for me to preach in, but had at last received a plain denial, and it was given up. This with all the other denials, bore pretty heavy on my mind, and I began to doubt again whether I ought to be in this place or not.

"Monday, 13th. About 2 o'clock, I left Boston and went in the stage to Benjamin Johnson's, in Lynn, about twelve miles. I got there a little after dark, and was very gladly received by him and his family. I felt as though I was at home, as soon as I arrived. I had not been there long, before he expressed a desire of having a Methodist society set up in the town, though he had not heard a Methodist preach for nearly twenty years. In this place I found several persons that had heard some of our preachers in the south, in past years. Some of the people consider it as a very favourable providence, that I have come to Lynn at this time, and they bid me welcome with a cheerful heart.

"Tuesday, 14th. At night, at Mr. Johnson's, I preached on John iii. 17. *For God sent not his Son into the world to condemn the world; but that the world, through him, might be saved.* I had a good many hearers, and great freedom in preaching, I bore a public testimony against unconditional election and reprobation ; and maintained that Christ died for all

men, without respect to persons. I felt much of the
power and love of God, and earnestly begged the
people to turn from their sins, and come to Christ.
The hearers were very attentive, and a few of them,
seemed to be somewhat affected. Bless the Lord O
my soul ! for bringing me among this people.

"Monday, 10th. I spent the day at Mr. Johnson's,
and in the evening, rode to Mr. Lye's, at Wood-End,
about one mile ; and at dark I preached on Gal. vi. 7.
The house was well filled with people and a considerable number of aged persons were present, and several
of the Quakers were there. I felt a great enlarge-
ment of heart, and much of the divine presence,
whilst I was warning the people not to be deceived.
The presence of God was in the assembly; some of the
hearers appeared to be greatly lifted up with love and
thankfulness. O ! that God may continue these serious impressions, on their minds, till they are brought
to the knowledge of God. I have not met with a
company of people for a long time that had so much
the appearance of a Methodist congregation as this.

"Wednesday, 22d. I was much pressed by some
persons, to stay longer, and when they found that I
could not, they earnestly begged me to come among
them again as soon as possible. Several talked strongly
of forming a Methodist society. I let them have our
rules, and left them to think further about it. We
then set out in a sleigh, and had a very cold, disagreeable ride to Boston. When I arrived in Boston, every
thing appeared as dark as when I left it, respecting
my preaching. I had to get a new boarding place.
When I settled my past boarding I had two shillings
and a penny left, which was all that I had. Some
days before, I felt concerned about my purse, not

knowing that there was enough in it to discharge the
debt due for my board. I was unwilling to let the
people know that my money was just gone, for fear
they should think it was money only that I was after.
But I soon felt confidence in God, that he would provide for me, though I knew not how. However, a
man in Lynn offered to buy a Magazine that I had for
my own use. I very willingly parted with it, and by
that means, was enabled to discharge the debt. And
if I can always have two shillings by me, beside paying
all I owe, I think I shall be satisfied."

· The remaining part of this year, and the year fol-
ing, until the latter part of the month of May, his
labours were principally in the following places, viz.
Boston, Lynn. Marblehead, Danvers, Manchester,
Beverly, Cape Ann Harbour, Ipswich, Hamlet, and
Salem.

Who would have anticipated such serious impedi-
ments as Mr. Lee found in the city of Boston ? Pre-
judice and bigotry, held such dominion over the
minds of these good Christian people, that no house
of worship, not even a school-house, could be procured for a Methodist preacher. He solicited, and
was repulsed. But under all these discouraging circumstances, reduced, in the midst of strangers, to
only two shillings in money, he resolved not to leave
the place. Here he lingered until he bore his testimony for Jesus. His preaching was not in vain in
the Lord. Some were touched under the word, and
brought to feel the force of divine truth. And let
the Methodists of Boston, who now enjoy such distinguished privileges, recollect that they are indebted,
under the blessing of God, to the indefatigable perseverance of Jesse Lee, amidst neglect and insults,
for their first establishment.

In Lynn, only twelve miles distant from Boston, how different the prospect! Here he was received with affection and cordiality. Many received the word with gladness, and like the noble Berian's were willing to ' search and see whether these things were so,' It will be seen from an extract from his Journal, that several persons in Lynn had formed a resolution, to become members of the Methodist church as soon as a convenient opportunity should be offered. Mr. Lee having given them sufficient time to become acquainted with our doctrines, and to make up their minds fully on the subject, he opened the door for their admission, and organized them into a society. This was on the 20th of February, 1791, and on the 27th of the same month an acquisition of several others was made to their numbers.*

In Marblehead, Ipswich and other places he with much difficulty made out to preach ; but he could scarcely move a step without being entangled in a

* While speaking of Lynn, we take the liberty of subjoining a short history of the progress of Methodism in that place. On the 14th day of December 1790, Mr. Lee visited Lynn and preached. He providentially arrived at a most seasonable period, and the word preached was singularly blessed. In a little more than two months, a Methodist society was formed, which within one week amounted to more than thirty members, and in the course of the ensuing May, upwards of seventy persons took certificates showing that they attended the ministry of the Methodists. This was necessary to free them from paying their regular quota to the ministers of the standing order.

The society, resolved to provide a place for public worship, in the building of which there was more dispatch used than is common on such occasions. According to Mr Lee's own account it was began on the 14th of June, raised on the 21st, and dedicated on the 26th of the same month. This was the first Methodist Meeting-House ever built in the state of Massachusetts.

It was not until July, 1792, that a society was formed in Boston For a more particular account, see Lee's History of the Methodist in America.

16

knot of committee men. These guardians of the town laws and privileges, constantly watched the movements of other ministers. Mr. Lee scarcely ever found them in a humour to give their unanimous consent for him to preach in the houses over which they had the guardianship ; but very frequently while they were deliberating upon the expediency, or inexpediency of his preaching, some friendly person would open his doors, and Mr Lee preached to numbers who flocked from every direction to hear the word.

The following extracts from his journal will give the reader some idea of his difficulties, as well as the success of his ministry.

"Saturday, April 16th. I rode to Salem and called upon Mr. Hopkins, in whose meeting-house I had frequently preached. He told me that some of the people were uneasy about my preaching, and thought it would not do to encourage me, by letting me preach in their meeting-house. He said he could not find any thing particularly, that they had against me, but he was forced to comply with their desires. He said, as to himself he wanted me to preach, and was very sorry that I could not; assuring me that for his own part he had not objection and he hoped I would not take it amiss. So I thanked him for the use of his pulpit till then, and he thanked me for my preaching amongst them; so we parted in friendship. I went to two of the select men, and asked for the court-house, to preach in. They gave their consent, but said, they could not determine on the matter till they all got together : so I left them to determine the next time they met. Then I rode to Lynn.

" Sunday, 17th. At Benjamin Johnson's, 10 o'clock, I preached on Psa. cxxvi. 5, 6. We had a

weeping time, and a very solemn meeting. Then at
2 o'clock, 1 Tim. v. 22. *Keep thyself pure.*
I found much satisfaction in speaking on this subject.
After preaching I met the women's class, and had reason to hope that their desires were increasing to do
the will of heaven. Then at night I preached in the
meeting-house for the first time, on Isa. lv. 7. I had
a very full house, and spoke with a great deal of freedom. I had many to hear me that seldom come to
our meetings. Yesterday I was denied the use of a
pulpit in which I had frequently preached; and
to day, I have obtained liberty to preach in a pulpit,
where I have never preached before ; so it is, I
pass through good and evil report, I have prosperity
enough to keep my spirits from sinking, and adversity
sufficient to keep me from being exalted above
measure.

"Monday, 18th. I rode to Boston, and at night, in
a private house at the north end, I preached on 1
Cor. xv. 33. I had more hearers than I commonly
have at this place, and they were very attentive. I
believe the word reached some of their hearts.

"Tuesday, 19th. I tarried in town, and at night at
the same place, I preached on Gal. iii. 9. *The just
shall live by faith.* We had much of the Divine presence amongst us, and I felt much inward peace, and
an increase of faith. The people were more affected
than they have generally been in this house ; and
they expressed a greater regard for me, and appeared
to be more friendly than usual. I am still led to hope
that the Lord will open the hearts of these people to
attend the word spoken by the Methodists, but let the
Lord work by whom he will. .

"Monday, 9th of May. I met the men's class in Lynn, in the morning, and they seemed lively and very humble. We had a sorrowful parting. It is not quite five months since I first preached in this place, and there are now in society fifty-eight members. About 10 o'clock, the men who generally attend on my preaching, came to me and obtained certificates, to show that they attended public worship with the Methodists, and contributed to the support of their ministry. After dinner I prayed with those that were present, and then bid them all farewell, and set out for conference at New-York."

CHAPTER XII,

—◦✦◦—

Attends Conference in New-York—Is appointed Elder of the New-England District—1792, Conference in Lynn—General Conference in Baltimore—James O'Kelly withdrew—Conference in Alexandria—Visits his friends in Virginia—Makes collections for building a Meeting-House in Boston—Returns to Lynn.

AFTER taking leave of those places which he considered as under his immediate charge, Mr. Lee repaired to New-York, taking on this tour many of the places where he had been accustomed to preach the preceding year. To his no small comfort, he found that things wore a more favourable aspect than formerly. In proportion as labour and diligence had been used, the cause of religion prospered.

On the 26th of June, 1791, conference set in New-York ; from which he received the appointment as presiding elder over several newly formed circuits in New-England. Litchfield, Fairfield, Middlefield, Hartford, Stockbridge, Lynn, and Kingston, composed his district. But, although his name stands thus on the minutes of conference, for the year 1791, yet from his journal, we do not find that any particular superintendance of the circuits was attended to by him. The presumption is, that he merely had the superintendance entrusted to him, so far as to give direction to the preachers, while he himself confined his labours more particularly to Lynn, and the adja-

16 *

cent towns, as the following extracts from his journal
will show.

"Saturday, July 30th. I rode to Lynn, and met
the children at 5 o'clock.

"Sunday, 31st. At 11 o'clock, I preached on Jer.
xxii. 29. *O earth! earth! earth! hear ye the word of
the Lord.* The people appeared to be very solemn,
and I believe they were happy under the word, though
I did not feel so much comfort myself as I have often
done.

"Then at 2 o'clock, I preached again ; I had a
very refreshing season in speaking, and there appeared
to be some move among the people. Then I rode to
Marblehead, and at 6 o'clock, I preached on Luke
xvi 31, *If they hear not Moses and the prophets, neither
will they be persuaded, though one rose from the dead.*
I found much satisfaction in my own mind while I
was teaching the people, and there was some appearance of religion in the looks and behaviour of the
people. There is a considerable stir in this town,
respecting the sentiments of the Methodists, and a
great many wish us to depart out of their coasts ; but
the more the Lion roars, the more I am encouraged.
I found a few that were almost persuaded to be
Methodists, as well as Christians.

"Monday, 1st of August, I returned to Lynn, and
met a class at 5 o'clock, and another at night. Several
persons appeared to be under deep conviction, and
the professors of faith seemed to be moving forward.

"Wednesday, 3d. I went to Salem, and at night I
preached on Prov. xxviii. 13. I felt a good deal of
life and liberty, and spoke pretty close to my hearers.
I had some of the Hopkinsians to hear me, but they
do not like my way of preaching, because I advise

sinners to pray that their sins may be forgiven, and
they think that no one ought to pray till their sins
are forgiven.

"Wednesday, 10th. I rode to Manchester, and at 5
o'clock I preached on 1 Sam. ii. 30. *For them that
honour me I will honour, and they that despise me, shall
be lightly esteemed.* After I had gone through my
text, I spoke half an hour on the possibility of falling
from grace. I spoke freely, and endeavoured to bring
forward every argument I could to establish the point.
Many of the people seemed to stare very much.
After I had done the people came out, collected
together in companies to talk about the sermon, and
some said my arguments could not be answered, or
that the scripture was on my side; but others complained heavily. I committed the cause to the Lord,
and could not doubt but what good was done.

"Friday, 12th. I rode to Appleton, in the old parish
of Ipswich. When I got there, the woman of the
house met me at the door and began to weep, and said
she had found the Lord precious to her soul; that
she was deeply affected by my preaching when I was
round two weeks before; and when she heard me the
last evening, she was so distressed that she could not
rest, and returned home crying to the Lord to have
mercy upon her, till about 2 o'clock in the morning,
at which time the Lord set her soul at liberty. She
was well satisfied that her sins were forgiven. She
then added, 'let others say what they will against
you, I bless the Lord that I ever heard your voice!'

"Saturday, 13th. I rode to Lynn, and met the
children; we had nearly forty of them together.

"Sunday, 14th. At Lynn at 10 o'clock I preached
on Gen. xvi. 24. *See that ye fall not out by the way.*

I felt the power and presence of God with me ; my
soul was both humble and happy ; many tears dropped
from the eyes of the people. God, even our God,
was amongst us. Then I baptized three women who
professed to have been born again. We then administered the Lord's Supper, and we had a most precious season at the table. We had about forty-seven
communicants, all of whom seemed to be of one
heart.

"Monday, 15th. We met the women's class at
Wood-End, at 5 o'clock : several were under deep
conviction, and wept bitterly while I spoke to them.
One had lately been converted, and seemed lost in
wonder, love, and praise. We met the men's class
at night, and had several persons amongst us that did
not belong to our class ; some of them were deeply
distressed, and seemed to be determined never to rest
till their souls were converted.

"Friday, 26th. I rode to Greenland, in New-Hampshire state, and dined at Doctor March's ; then rode
to Portsmouth, and put up at Mr. Walton's, who is a
Separate minister. We had a meeting in a private
house. At his request, I preached on Psa. i. 6. I
found it to be a time of much life and love, and some
of the people appeared to be much affected. When
meeting was ended, some of the people blessed God
for our meeting ; and when the minister asked some
of the people what they thought of shutting such
preaching as that out of the meeting-house, some of
them said, if they shut that man out, they did not
know who they would let in. All seemed very
friendly.

"Friday, September 2d. I rode to Newburyport,
and at night, at the court-house I preached, The

house was greatly crowded in every part, and the hearers were very attentive, and I spoke with more than common liberty ; I felt a love for precious souls, and maintained that Christ had died for all ; and that the Lord was willing to save them all. I bore a public testimony against particular election, and showed the cruelty of absolute reprobation. The Lord seemed to open the hearts of the people to receive the truths that were delivered. I do not know when I saw a congregation that was better pleased. Several persons came to my lodgings and plead very hard for me to preach again in the morning, at any hour that would suit me. I was very loath to deny, but being unwell, I was afraid to engage.

" Friday, 23d. I rode to Windham, and at Josiah Sweet's at night, I preached on Phil. i. 22. *For me to live is Christ, and to die is gain.* This is the first time that a Methodist ever preached in this town. I had a good congregation, and some of them were much affected by the word. I think the time is near, when the work of the Lord will begin to revive in this part of the world, and if the Lord work by us, our good mistaken brethren will be brought to say ' send, Lord by whom thou wilt send.'

" Sunday, November 6th. I set out early in the morning and rode to Needham, and preached with some comfort in my soul. Then at 2 o'clock I preached again. I had many hearers, and felt help from the Lord. The looks of the people showed that many of them felt the weight of what was spoken. I had several invitations to preach in other places, and was greatly desired to preach again that night, but being quite unwell, I could not consent.

"Monday, 7th. I set out early and rode to Providence in Rhode-Island state. I was kindly received, by my old friends and lodged at Mr. Jacob's.

"Tuesday, 8th. I remained in town all day, and at night I preached on 1 John v. 21. Part of the time in which I was speaking I found freedom, but the rest of the time I felt but little comfort.

"Wednesday, 9th. I rode to General Lippet's in Cronston about 10 miles from Providence, and was very kindly received.

"Friday, 11th. In the General's house, I preached on 2 Cor. v. 17. *Therefore if any man be in Christ, he is a new creature.* I felt more than usual comfort in speaking. My heart was drawn out in love and pity towards my hearers. In this place the people know but little of the life and power of religion, and it is very seldom that they can get to any place of public worship. Seeing how destitute they are of the preaching of the gospel, I was brought again to pray earnestly that the Lord would send forth more labours into his vineyard.

"Saturday, 28th of January 1792. I rode to Lynn and was greatly pleased at the sight of Brother Robert Bonsall, who had just came from New-York to preach the gospel in this part of the world, with brother Smith and myself. I hope the Lord will make him a blessing to this people and to myself. At night I met a class at Brother Hallowell's."

After receiving the timely assistance of R. Bonsall, he set out on a tour through the different circuits which had been formed, and supplied with preaching in the state of Connecticut. He felt some reluctance at parting with the people in Lynn, in as much as he had a peculiar interest in their welfare. Christian affection is strong; but the affection subsisting between a minister and those converted under his ministry is stronger still : this makes the pain of parting so severe.

From Lynn he proceeded to Boston, from thence to Needham, where he preached with some satisfaction. He also took Sterling and Wilbreham on his way, and found the hearts of the people open to receive him. He then rode to Enfield in Connecticut, and was well pleased to find that religion had prospered in that place, and that a good class had been formed. From Enfield he went to East-Windsor, Middlefield, Derby, Oxford, New-Town, Reading, Dan-Town, Middlesex, Wilton, Stratford, Hartford, Tolland and Ellengton, besides many other places : during this excursion, it was with great pleasure that he observed, the change which had been effected within the space of a few months. ' I see visibly (says he,) ' that the Lord has prospered his work amongst the Methodists since I visited this part of the vineyard.'

After returning to Lynn, which was the 4th of May, he has these remarks :—" When I look back on my late journey, I am constrained to acknowledge that the Lord has been with me. I have rode about 517 miles in 33 days, and preached 40 sermons. I have reason to hope that the Lord has given me fresh strength and courage, to go forward in his ways. "

From the time he attended the conference at New-York, until the last of July, in the present year, he had preached three-hundred and twenty-one sermons, and gave twenty-four public exhortations ; and in order to show the exact manner in which he noted the improvement of his time and of his mind, we will for once, give a list of the authors, with the number of pages in each, which he had read during the same time.

BOOKS.	*No. of Pages.*
The Saints' Everlasting Rest, - - -	399
The New Testament, - - - - -	
The 1st Vol. of Fletcher's Works, - -	330
Preachers' Experience, - - - - -	370
Robert Barkley's Apology, - - - -	574
Sellon's Answer to Elisha Coles, - - -	347
The 2d Vol. of Fletcher's Works, - -	320
Mr. John Wesley's Funeral Sermon, by John	
Whitehead, - - - - - -	69
The Christian's Pattern, - - - -	306
Mrs. Elizabeth Rowe's Devout Exercises, -	214
A View of Religion by Hannah Adams, -	410
The New Testament, - - - - -	
Freeborn Garretson's Experience, - -	252
Sweeting's Narrative, - - - - -	64
Marks of a work of God, extracted from Mr.	
Edwards, - - - - - - -	45
William Hammet's Appeal, - - - -	24
The 1st Vol. of Wesley's Notes, - -	416
2d do. do. do. - - -	349
3d do. do. do. - -	342
Aristotle's Works, - - - - -	568
David Tappan's Election Sermon, - -	36

Total, besides the Testament,   5434

In addition to the number of sermons which he had delivered, he had heard seventy-four preached by other ministers; all of which are duly noticed in his journal.

On the 1st of August, 1792, conference was held in Lynn, from which he was appointed Elder over Lynn, Needham, Boston, and Providence.

In a few days he set out on a missionary tour, to the state of Rhode-Island, for the purpose of forming a new circuit. He visited Providence, Pawtuxet, Warren, and Bristol. Then leaving the state of Rhode-Island, rode to Taunton, then to Easton.

Saturday, 18th of August, he thus writes :—"I rode to brother Stokes', in Easton, and met the class at 5 o'clock. When I consider the goodness of God to me in this journey, I am constrained to call upon my soul to bless his holy name for his goodness to me. I know I have found delight in the service of God, and comfort among the people. I have had an opportunity of preaching to many who never heard a Methodist before. I have generally found satisfaction in labouring among such people as know but little about us.

"Monday, 20th. I set off early and rode to Boston, and at night I met the class, which has been but lately formed.

"Wednesday, 29th. Brother J. Corsden came to Lynn for me to go to Boston, to view a piece of ground that he was inclined to purchase to set a meeting-house on. I went, but did not approve of the spot.

"Thursday, 30th. I rode to Concord, and at night I preached in Mr. Samuel Lewis' house. I had a clever little congregation, and I felt much of the Divine presence while I was preaching. The people appeared to be all attention; for most of them never heard a Methodist before. I hope some of them heard to profit.

"Tuesday, 10th of September. I met the class at Wood-End at 3 o'clock; the Lord was with us of a truth; one woman said that the Lord had converted her soul a few nights before, and she spoke of it with

17

much confidence and tenderness, so that many were melted into tears. O God! let all the people praise thee.

" Monday, 1st of October. I visited several friends in Lynn, and at night, I preached my farewell sermon, on Phil. i. 27. *Only let your conversation be as becometh the gospel of Christ : that, whether I come to see you, or else be absent, I may hear of your affairs, and that ye stand fast in one spirit, with one mind.* The Lord was with us of a truth ; there was great weeping among the people, both men and women. I felt very sorry to leave them, and they seemed to be as sorry to part with me, as I expected to go home, and to be absent from them for the space of four months. But the will of the Lord be done.

" Tuesday, 2d. I left Lynn, with a good deal of sorrow, and set out on my journey.

" Thursday, 1st of November. The general conference commenced in Baltimore.

" Monday, 5th. We spent the whole day in debating one point (viz.) 'Whether or not a preacher that thinks himself injured in his appointment to a circuit, shall have an appeal to the district conference.' We had close and long debates, and at 5 o'clock we went to the Dutch church, and about 8 o'clock we broke up, and a majority was for no appeal. Some of the preachers were much dissatisfied about it, after it was decided.

" Tuesday, 6th. James O'Kelly wrote a letter to the conference, that he should leave the travelling connexion, on account of the vote that was taken the night before. When the letter was read many of the preachers wept heartily. It was a sorrowful day to me, yet I could say the will of the Lord be done.

"Thursday, 15th. Our conference ended in the evening in much love and friendship. At night Doctor Coke preached his farewell sermon; he gave us a good discourse.

"Friday, 16th. The most of the preachers left town in the forenoon. I waited till the afternoon, and then brother Cooper and myself set out, and rode to the widow Dorsey's, about twelve miles, and stayed all night.

"Saturday, 17th. We rode to Alexandria, Virginia, and got there a little after dark, and put up at brother Hickman's.

"Monday. 19th. The Alexandria conference commenced its business.

"Tuesday, 20th. The conference broke up early in the morning, and we set out on our journey, and rode to a friend's house a little beyond Dumfries, and tarried all night.

"Sunday, 25th. We rode to Richmond, and at 3 o'clock in the Capitol, I preached on 1 Peter ii. 9. I suppose I had more than half of the members of the general assembly to hear me, and many of them appeared to be very attentive : I felt great freedom in speaking. I am sure the Lord was in the midst of us. My own heart was much melted within me. I felt a hope that some good was done in the name of the Lord Jesus.

"Monday, 26th. I rode over to Manchester : the conference began about 9 o'clock.

"Wednesday, 28th. I left the conference, a few hours before it broke up, and rode with a few friends to Petersburgh, about 25 miles. At night we attended meeting at brother Harding's. I lodged at my brother Nathaniel's ; I felt very glad to be with my old friends and relations.

" Saturday, 1st of December. I rode out to my father's, and was much pleased at meeting with my father and friends. At 12 o'clock at my father's, I preached on Rom. xiii. 12. *The night is far spent, the day is at hand : let us therefore cast of the works of darkness, and let us put on the armour of light.* I found a good deal of satisfaction in speaking to the people, and they appeared to be attentive; but it is not with these people, as it was when I was here before, which was about four years and eight months ago. At that time they were much alive to God, but religion is very low now.*

" Monday, 31. I took my leave of my friends, and set out on my journey to Boston. Brother P. Hoffman set off with me We rode to Manchester, and put up at brother Cook's.

" Saturday, 5th of January, 1793. We rode to Baltimore, and got there by dinner time. I felt quite weary with my journey, and thankful to the Lord for bringing me amongst my old friends again.

" Tuesday, 8th. Brother A. Fonarden, who seemed much concerned for Boston, went with me to see many of the friends, and to ask their assistance in building a meeting-house in Boston ; we were pretty successful in our undertaking.

" Thursday, 17th. The weather cleared up about 10 o'clock, and I set out on my journey; the roads were amazingly muddy ; however I got to Cokesbury College by dusk : the bell was rung and the people collected, and I preached on 1 John ii. 17. *And the*

* He spent about one month in visiting his friends and relatives ; during which time he preached not less than seventeen times, besides attending many other meetings.

world passeth away, and the lusts thereof: but he that doth the will of God abideth for ever.

"Saturday, 26th. I rode early, and found it to be the coldest day that I have felt during the winter, for the winter has been uncommonly warm. I got to New-York a little after dark; myself and horse were both quite weary.

"Sunday, 27th. At 3 o'clock in the stone church, I preached on Jude 21. *Keep yourselves in the love of God.* I had a very large congregation, and found help from the Lord in speaking. A solemn awe seemed to rest upon the hearers. I may well say, 'one day in the service of God is better than a thousand.'

"Wednesday, February 20th. I rode to Boston, and got there a little after dark, much fatigued, and my feet somewhat wet, by reason of the roads being very sloppy. I found some comfort with the Boston class, that met soon after I got to Mr Burrill's.

"Thursday, 21st. I arrived in Lynn amongst my old friends: I had been absent almost five months: I felt thankful to God for bringing me back again: I was very glad to find that religion had revived amongst the people in my absence.

"Sunday, 24th. At half past ten, I preached on 2 Sam. xx. 9. *Art thou in health, my brother?* I pointed out some of the disorders of the soul, the means and manner of being cured, and then made a close inquiry. 'Art thou in health at the present time?' I had preached a farewell sermon before I left them, and I thought it necessary now to inquire how they were, and how they had been. It was a good time to the people, and profitable to myself. We then administered the sacrament, and three grown

17

persons were baptized, and several added to the church.

"Monday, 18th of March. I set off on my tour to Rhode-Island and Connecticut states. I rode to Boston, and at night, I preached on Gal. iii. 11. *But that no man is justified by the law in the sight of God, it is evident; for, the just shall live by faith.* I found satisfaction in preaching, and the people were quite attentive. Then brother E. Cooper exhorted, and his words seemed to have much weight with the hearers."

During this tour, he visited Easton, Pawtuxet, Warwick, Greenwich, Weckford, Charlestown, New-London; from thence to Gen. Lippet's, in the state of Rhode-Island, and from thence to Providence, and Needham, in the state of Massachusetts, and on to Boston; after which he returned to Lynn.

"Thursday, 30th of April. I went to Marblehead, and at night, I preached on Lam. iii. 26. *It is good that a man should both hope and quietly wait for the salvation of the Lord.* The people had been at the trouble to hire an upper room of Mr. Bowler, for 15 dollars per year, and to fix a number of seats in it for the use of the Methodists, which is more respect than they ever showed us before. To night we met in it for the first time, and the Lord owned our meeting, and his presence was felt amongst us. I found great liberty in teaching them the way to heaven; and felt more encouraged about the place and people than I used to be."

From this time until the first of August he was employed in travelling, and preaching in the towns of Marblehead, Manchester, Salem, and Boston; but spent more time in Lynn than in any other place, being more attached to the latter than to any other within the bounds of his district.

Though he made occasional excursions through the different towns in New-England, it does not appear that he travelled so constantly about this time as in former years. Having gone over the ground and formed societies, in order to build them up in faith and holiness, he was obliged to restrict his ministerial labours, and leave it to others to extend themselves. in more remote places. This, however, originated from no want of zeal in the cause of Christ; for wherever we find him, we perceive the same active fidelity in his Master's work, the same ardour of devotion, and the same attention to the spiritual wants of the people. And, although he was not instrumental in awakening as many sinners, and forming as many new societies, yet we may presume he was equally useful in establishing believers in the grace of God, and in giving a permanency and consistency to the societies; a work this, as essential to the success and prosperity of the cause of God, as the alarming the consciences of sinners, and bringing them to Christ.

CHAPTER XIII.

No conference prior to the year 1792, had been
held farther north than New-York or Albany, and
until the year 1789, Connecticut river was the nor'
thern boundary of Methodism in the United States.
Since the period last mentioned, several circuits had
been laid out in the New-England states and many
societies formed. Amongst the rest that in Lynn had
continued to flourish, and bid fair to outstrip in numbers and zeal, any other in that section of the work.
It was in fact the strong hold of Methodism in the
north. It was now deemed advisable to hold a conference in Lynn, to give the preachers an opportunity
of attending, who were so situated as to render it
inconvenient to travel to the conference in New-York.
The expediency of forming a conference in the New-
England states, was obvious to those who were acquainted with the extent of country between the borders of Connecticut and the lines of Canada.

Agreeably to a previous arrangement, Conference
met in Lynn, on the first of August, 1793. Only
eight preachers attended. Though they were few in
numbers, they were not deficient in those qualities so
essentially requisite for missionaries to possess; bold

in the cause of God, and zealous for his name, breathing the spirit of love to God and the souls of their
fellow men, they were willing to encounter dangers,
and endure toil, for the sake of spreading the flame of
religion, and of furthering the increase of the Saviour's
kingdom.

From this conference Mr. Lee was appointed to the
Province of Maine, a place far removed from the
grounds heretofore occupied by the Methodists ; not
being less than two hundred miles from any circuit
which had been previously formed.

The greater part of the country which he intended
to explore was but newly inhabited, and little improved
in point of husbandry or morality.   Few ministers
of any order had thought fit to brave the difficulties
which the climate and state of society presented at
that period.

The most of them preferred waiting a season, until
the enterprising settlers had availed themselves of the
advantages to be derived from the soil, and had accu-
mulated a portion of wealth sufficient to ensure comfort
and independence.   But those who recollected the
declaration of Christ, that " the poor have the Gospel
preached to them," were not willing to lose so much
time, lest evils of a more serious nature should obtrude themselves, and prevent the spread of divine
truth.

It is generally found in newly settled countries that
the inhabitants have minds more teachable and less
under the influence of preconceived notions, and what
is called " religious prejudices," than in the more improved and wealthy parts of the community.   That
this is a fact, many can testify who have taken the pains
to make the experiment.

We may reasonably suppose that in taking this appointment, Mr. Lee felt some solicitude of mind respecting his friends whom he was about to leave behind. He could not but feel interested in the welfare of those who had been raised up under his ministry, and to part with them, though but for a season, was to him a source of some regret ; but his state of mind will best appear from his own words.

" Wednesday, 4th September. I was busy most of the day in fixing my clothes, &c. for my journey. I took a little time to visit some of my friends. I felt a degree of sorrow at leaving my acquaintances, and going down to the Province of Maine, where I should be an entire stranger. Lord prepare me for the difficulties which lie before me.

" Thursday, 5th. I went to see a good many of my friends, and took my leave of them; some I talked to, and some I prayed with. But it was almost too much for me to bid them farewell. About 12 o'clock I left home and set out on my journey. I rode to Captain Patch's, in Hamilton, and stayed all night.

"Friday, 6th. I rode to Newburyport. Some of my friends went to see if they could not get the court-house for me to preach in, but it was refused So I did not preach ; I lodged at Mr. Belchi's.

" Saturday, 7th. · I rode to Dr. Marsh's, in Greenland, and took dinner, and rode to Portsmouth, and went to see Mr. Walton, a minister, but he did not appear to be so friendly as he did when I was there before ; so I went and put up my horse at a tavern, and then went to a boarding house, and lodged.

"Sunday, 8th. I went to hear Mr. Walton in the forenoon, and in the afternoon. After he was done, I went with some friends to the court-house, but the *great men* would not consent for us to go into the house to preach ; so I got on the step of the door of the court-house and began. When I commenced, I had about a dozen people, but they soon began to flock together, and I had some hundreds of them to hear me before I was done. They stood in different parts of the streets. I found much freedom in speaking ; and the word reached· many of the hearts of the hearers, who were as solemn and attentive as though they had been in a meeting-house. I lodged at Mr. Samuel Tappan's.

"Monday, 9th. I set off early, and crossed the river into the Province of Maine.

" Tuesday, 10th. I rode to Saco, and put up at Doctor Fairfield's, and at night in another house, I preached on Acts xiii. 41. I had the house much crowded with attentive hearers, and I felt the assistance of the Holy Ghost in preaching to them. Lord make it profitable to many."

From Saco he went to Portland, where, by the kind interference of some persons, Mr. Kellogg's meeting-house was opened for him to preach in. From Portland he travelled over a rough and hilly road to Free-port, and preached to as many as were willing to hear. From thence he went to Bath, where he preached three times. He then crossed Kennebeck river and rode to Newcastle, and from thence to Thomastown, to Union, and crossed the Penobscot river, and lodged at Abraham Stover's, in the town of Penobscot. He then went to a little village called Baggadoore Neck ; but finding it would be difficult to travel much further on horseback, and the settlements on the road being very thin, he resolved to return to the town of Penobscot, where he sent out an

appointment, and preached on the sabbath-day.—
He then rode to Major Buck's, in Bucktown.—
After this he took a route up the river within a few
miles of the Indian Settlement, and returned down
the river to Frankford; here the people received
him gladly, and strove hard to retain him amongst
them; but, although they offered to hire him to come
and settle amongst them the ensuing spring, "it had"
(says he) "no weight with me, for I am no hireling."

The inhabitants upon Penobscot at that time, were
principally new settlers, consequently destitute of any
regular preaching, and therefore the more thankful for
the visit they received from Mr. Lee.

He continued in these settlements, travelling to and
fro and preaching, with good hopes that his labour
would be blessed of the Lord, until the latter part of
October, at which time he returned to Lynn.

In January 1794, he repeated his visit to the settlements on the Kennebeck and Penobscot rivers, and
enlarged his borders by preaching in many new places.
His difficulties were many, but God gave him strength
to bear up through them all, with becoming patience
and resolution. He succeeded in forming a circuit in
the Province of Maine, which by the way, is all that
can be said of it, for we are not assured that there was
a single society of Methodists within its whole bounds.

In July Mr. Lee left his circuit and returned to
Lynn, where conference was held the 25th of the same
month, and he received his appointment to the district
of New-Hampshire.

The following extracts from his journal, we hope
will be acceptable to the reader.

"Thursday, 7th of August. I parted with all the
preachers, and set out to a new circuit, which had been

lately formed. I rode to old Mr. Lee's, in Concord, and got dinner, and then rode to Wm. Haskill's, in Harvard, and stayed with him all night.

"Friday, 8th. I rode to Fitchburgh and put up at David M'Intire's. I felt very much fatigued. The family was very kind, but I felt very doubtful whether I should be useful amongst these people. My mind was variously exercised, and I was in a mournful condition. Lord help me.

"Saturday, 9th. We went to a meeting in the afternoon, to Mr. S. Shattuck's ; but when we arrived they said they had not heard of our appointing meeting there. But after a while a few people came together, and I preached on Gal. ii. 20. We had a good little meeting, and we were thanked for coming to preach at the place.

"Sunday, 10th. At the new meeting-house in Fitchburgh, I preached in the morning, and also at two o'clock in the afternoon. The Lord seemed very near me at times, but I did not have that faith for the people that I have generally had in other places.

"Monday, 11th. I rode to Mr. Jones', in Ashburnham ; they sent word to their neighbours ; at 4 o'clock preached to them on Matthew iii. 2. I was a little pleased with those people, and have reason to believe that they were engaged in religion. I had little to say to any of them in private conversation, about their souls, for I was so heavy and sleepy, that I felt much inclined to be on the bed or alone, partly owing to bodily infirmities.

"Tuesday, 12th. I rode to Mr. Newhall's, in Peckerfields, in New-Hampshire, upwards of 20 miles from where I started in the morning, and the road was very bad, both stony and hilly, so that I was quite weary when I got there ; however they sent word to their neighbours, and they met at night, and I preached. I found but little liberty.

" Thursday 14th. I was very unwell in the morning, the St. Anthony's fire broke out in my face, which was much swelled and inflamed, and was very painful. I rode to Esq. Roots', in the south part of the town, (Marlborough,) and was forced to keep my bed most part of the day. Upon strict examination, I felt a confidence in God, and a pleasing hope of heaven.

" The next day I preached at Mr. Roots'. I felt better pleased with these people than with any company I have met with in these parts ; but I felt so unwell, that I could hardly make out to stand and preach.

" Saturday, 16th. I rode to Orange, in Massachu- setts. The day was very warm, and I was quite sick with my complaint. The next day being sabbath, I preached at Orange meeting-house, both in the morn- ing and afternoon.—Was quite sick at night.

" Friday, 5th of September. We set off early in the morning, and rode to Wilbraham conference. But when I got there, I found that the conference had began the day before. I went and sat with them. At night, attended preaching.

" Saturday 6th. Conference sat in the morning; then at 11 o'clock, I preached on 2 Cor. xii. 9. *My grace is sufficient for thee.* I found a great deal of liberty in speaking, and the power of the Lord was amongst us. I was much affected; and many of the people wept in every part of the house. I felt the grace of God sufficient for me at the time ; and I was willing to trust him all the days of my life. O ! what a precious sense of the love of Jesus my soul enjoyed at that time! Let the worldling boast of pleasure, I will not envy his happiness; give me the love of Jesus, and I desire no more.

"Sunday, 7th. We met in the meeting-house at 8 o'clock in the morning, and after spending near an hour in singing and prayer, brother F. Asbury preached on Mal. iii. 1—4. Then we had the ordinations. Three young men were ordained elders, and one a deacon. Then the Lord's Supper was administered, and we had a very solemn time. I found my soul much quickened and refreshed. The people withdrew a few moments, and then came together again, and I exhorted. First, I addressed my *remarks* to sinners. 2d, to mourners in Zion. 3d, to Christians. 4th, to backsliders. 5th, to young people. 6th, to the aged. And, lastly, to ministers. It was a time of God's power. The people wept, and some cried out so as to be heard all over the house. Then brother Amos G. Thompson exhorted with a good deal of life and liberty. Then Joel Ketchum exhorted; he is a promising young man, and if he keeps humble, is likely to be a useful speaker. The meeting finally closed, after having held seven hours and a half. It was a blessed day to my soul. The conference broke up, and most of the preachers left town. About 10 or 12 preachers of us rode to Enfield, in Connecticut, and arrived a little after dusk. I eat a little, for I had neither got dinner or tea that day, and then went to the meeting-house, where the people were waiting for us. I preached on Rom. vi. 11. I found some freedom in preaching, and the power of the Lord was measurably felt by myself, if no more. Then brother G. Roberts exhorted. We had a good company of attentive hearers; and it was a profitable time to my soul. I went to old sister Knight's, and stayed all night. I was a good deal weary and fatigued.

"Wednesday, 10th. We rode to brother Perkins', in Coventry. At 4 o'clock, I preached on 2 Cor. iv. 7. I found my soul refreshed with the presence of the Lord, and my hope in the mercy of God was confirmed. Some of the people were much affected, and melted into tears. The Lord has dealt kindly with this people, and a great many have been awakened and converted.

"Thursday, 11th. We rode to Tolland, and preached in our meeting-house. At night, I preached on Acts xvii. 6. I found a good degree of liberty in speaking. The next day I rode to Windham, and at night, preached in the court-house.

"Saturday, 13th. We rode to Norwich and dined, and then rode to New-London, and put up with brother Richard Douglass; I found my mind a good deal engaged with God, and felt a longing desire to be more than ever given up to him.

"Sunday, 14th. I preached twice in New-London. In the evening we drank tea with a friendly widow; and Mr. Darrough, a Baptist minister, came to tea with us; he was very friendly. I told him if he did not take care, the Methodists would out do him. He said, 'I don't know how they will go about it.' Why, said I, they will out preach you, and out live you, and out love you. 'Well, says he, they may, but if they do, they shall have hard work for it, for I intend to love God with all my soul; and then, if they out love me, their vessel must be *bigger* than mine' I felt much pleased with his friendly conversation, and loving demeanour. The Lord has dealt very kindly with the people in this city; and there has been a gracious

18 *

revival of religion amongst them last spring, and the first of the summer ; and above fifty have joined the Methodists.

"Monday, 15th. We rode to Norwich Landing, and met with brother Jesse Stoneman, one of our preachers. At night, in a private house, I preached on Matt. vi. 10. I had quite a large congregation to hear me. The Lord was with us of a truth, and the word seemed to reach the hearts of the people. Glory be to God for ever. My soul was lost in wonder, love, and praise. Then brother Mudge exhorted, with a good degree of life and freedom ; and the people seemed, by their looks, as if they were willing to receive the truth, and turn to God.

"Tuesday, 16th. I took breakfast near where I lodged ; one of the neighbours came in to see me, who had been converted a little time before, and had never been baptized, she desired me to baptize her : her children as well as herself, pressed me hard to do it ; although I was in a great hurry I consented. Some of the neighbours were called in, and we had a comfortable hour in waiting upon God, and performing the ordinance. I then rode to Coventry, in Rhode-Island, and being directed to call upon Colonel B., I rode up to his door about sunset, and spoke with him, and asked him if he had not entertained the Methodist preachers sometimes. To which he replied, I have sometimes. Would you, said I, be willing to entertain another ? he said, I would *full as leave*, if it would suit them as well, if they would go along. Well then, I told him I would *go along*. So I rode on and got into a blind path by dark, and then for the greater part of the way I could not see the path at all, and very often I could not see my horse's head ; however,

I arrived at Colonel Lippet's, in Cranston, a little after they had got to bed, which was about 10 o'clock. I missed my way a little once. I had to depend upon God for protection, and to put a little trust in my horse, for he had been once that way before. Thank the Lord for all favours. The next day I tarried at friend Lippet's, and spent my time chiefly in the house, reading and writing. The Colonel's wife and daughter professed to have been awakened by a sermon which I preached at their house. I felt my soul much humbled while I was talking to them on the subject. The next day I rode to Greenwich, and was assisted in preaching to a good company of hearers, on 1 John iii. 38. The Methodists have been labouring here sometime, but have very few in society. I lodged at the Widow Munford's.

" Saturday, 20th. Came to Warren in the afternoon, the weather was extremely warm, and I rode late, and made it a little in the night before I arrived ; I put up at Mr. Martin Luther's.

" Sunday, 21st. In a barn in Warren, at 10 o'clock I preached on Jer. xxiii. 29. I found freedom in speaking, and was much comforted. At 2 o'clock I preached again on Ephes. iv. 27. I found much of the divine presence, and could bless God for the favourable opportunity of teaching the people. The Lord has dealt kindly with the inhabitants of this place since I was here last, and we have a considerable society formed, a preaching-house raised, and the top of it covered. I have no doubt, but what God is among these people. Then I rode to Bristol, and preached at night in the court-house. My subject was on Heb. iii. 12. It was a good time to my soul, and a solemn time among the hearers. The day was very cold and the change being so sudden, I took cold. However, I felt willing to spend my life, and my all, for God, and for the good of precious souls.

" Monday, 22d. I crossed the ferry to Portsmouth, on the Island, and preached at Mr. Cook's. I had a most precious season in delivering my message to the people. There appeared to be a pleasing prospect of doing good amongst them ; I was pleased with the little class when I met them at night.

" Wednesday, 24th. Rode back to Portsmouth, dined at brother Cooks : and then crossed the ferry and rode to Bristol, and spent a little time with the friends, and then rode to Warren, and at four o'clock in the new meeting-house, I preached a dedication sermon on Haggai ii. 9. I had liberty in preaching. It is the first Methodist meeting-house which has been built in the state of Rhode-Island, and this the first sermon preached in it. I hope God will own the Methodists in this town. I met the class at night, and the power of the Lord was amongst us, and many souls were happy in his love.

" Wednesday, 1st of October, I came to Lynn, and got there a little before night.

" Monday, 13th. I left Lynn and journeyed to Waltham Plains, and preached in the school-house at night. My text was Isa. xxvii. 11. I found life, liberty, and comfort in preaching ; the house was much crowded and the people very attentive. Brother Cooper exhorted. We rested at Beamu's tavern.

" Tuesday, 14th. We rode to Westown, to the quarterly meeting. At 11 o'clock I preached on Phil. iii. 10. We had a precious season, and a melting time. Then we administered the Lord's Supper, and many of the communicants were bathed in tears ; at

2 o'clock brother Cooper preached, and A. G. Thompson exhorted. I rested at brother Fisk's that night.

"Thursday, 23d. We had our quarterly meeting at Lynn. It was a very good meeting to my soul, and the souls of many of the people.

"Saturday, 25th. I intended to have left town, but we had a northeast storm which lasted all day, and the rain increased towards night, so that I remained most of the day at home.

"Sunday, 26th. Meeting in Lynn, brother Ketchum and myself preached : the former in the forenoon and myself in the afternoon.

"Monday, 27th. The rain continued part of the day, and then the weather cleared off. I went to see a few people. O how much I am wanting in faithfulness, and watchfulness, in all my religious visits ; but I do desire to be wholly the Lord's, without reserve.

"Tuesday, 28th. We proceeded to Marblehead, to quarterly meeting : we held a love feast in brother Prentice's house. A few people spoke with life and freedom. The company was melted into tears. I was pleased to find them so much engaged in religion. At night, we held a watch night ; I preached ; brother Ketchum exhorted, and the people were attentive.

"Wednesday, 29th. Returned to Lynn, met a class at Gravesend, and found the Lord present amongst the people.

"Monday, 3d of November, I set out on my eastern tour for two months, and came to Newburyport a little after dusk.

"Tuesday, 4th. I rode to Portsmouth, New-Hampshire state ; heard a dry discourse at night, in a private house, preached by I. Walton ; his text was, Rom. v. 1, 2.

"Friday, 7th. I rode to Portland, and stopped at Major Ilsley's, but he was that day moving out of town with his family; however, he went to some of the men, and engaged the court-house for me to preach in at night. I visited several of the friends, and at night, preached in the court house ; my subject was 1 Tim. v. 22.—A very full house, and attentive hearers. I cannot doubt but what the Lord will yet favour this people. I lodged with friend Cob, a Quaker ; he was quite reconciled to prayers, night and morning.

"Sunday, 9th. At Mr. Randall's in Gray, I preached on Lam. iii. 22. I had life and liberty in preaching, and the people paid great attention. At 1 o'clock in the afternoon, I preached again, on Luke xi. 9. The words seemed to pierce the hearts of some of the hearers. They are seldom favoured with preaching. Then I rode to New-Gloucester, and preached at 4 o'clock. The people were not much moved by the sermon.

"Wednesday, 12. At Mr. Spague's, in Green, I preached at 2 o'clock ; my text was, Phil. ii. 15. I had a small congregation, and but little life in speaking. I believe the text did not suit the state of the people, being mostly unacquainted with the power of religion. I then rode to Esq. Dearborn's, in Monmouth, and stayed all night.—Was greatly delighted in hearing of many precious souls that had been awakened, and several that had been converted in the town, within a short time past. Surely, the Lord is saying to the north, give up. Amen, even so: come Lord Jesus.

"Thursday, 13th. Brother P. Wager came to me from his preaching place. I was greatly pleased with the account he gave me of the prospect of a work

of God in several places on his circuit. At 2 o'clock
I preached at Captain Hopkin's tavern, and the Lord
moved upon the hearts of many of the people. Brother Wager exhorted with freedom. I met the class
and was happy to hear from the people's own mouth,
what the Lord had done for their souls. There were
about fifteen in class, and most of them profess to be
happy in God. This class has been formed but a few
weeks, and is the first ever formed in the Province of
Maine. May they be as the little cloud, which at first
was like a man's hand, but soon covered the heavens.

"Saturday, 15th. I rode to Nathaniel Whiteir's
in Readfield, and was much pleased with my old
acquaintances. Sabbath I preaced twice at Mr.
Hutchen's, and the people were much melted under
the word. I felt my soul much taken up with the
things of God, and could truly say it was my meat and
drink to do his blessed will. Then I went to N. Whi-
teirs' and met the class. The Lord was very precious
to our souls and the people were much melted. This
was the second class formed in this province, and has
in it about seventeen members ; several of them have
lately been converted ; some are old professors, and
some under deep convictions, and a very great concern seems to be on the minds of many of the neighbours. There is a prospect of having a great inga-
thering of souls to the Lord. Then at dark I held forth
again on 1 Thes. i. 5. Many were present ; a good time
in preaching. Surely the Lord is about to do great
things for this people. Even so : amen and amen.

"Monday, 17th. I tarried in town all day ; and
went to look at our meeting-house. It is almost
covered in. Through my influence, the people began
this house last summer, and it is now nearly ready

to preach in. It is the first Methodist meeting-house ever built in the Province of Maine. I expect we shall see Methodism greatly spreading in these parts before long. Here Antinomianism has much prevailed for a few years amongst the Baptists. Their minister, Isaac Case, a good old man, often says of his followers, that they are *case* hardened. They are greatly afraid the Methodists will do much harm.

"Wednesday, 26th. I set out early in the morning, the day was remarkably cold, and I had to travel a lonesome road to Sandy river. One place, I had to go seven or eight miles, without seeing a house, and it appeared as if my feet would freeze; but I drew one of my mittens over the toe of my shoe, and made out to keep it from freezing. When I got to Farmington, I found no appointment had been made for me to preach. Here I took dinner, and spent a little time with the people, then rode up to Reed's, in Middletown. It was dark, and I felt so chilled that I shook as though I had an ague. My cheeks, and under my chin, were so pinched by the cold, that they felt quite sore for a week; and what made the matter still worse, was the exceeding roughness of the road, which made the journey unpleasant; however, I met with a kind reception at night, and was greatly delighted at hearing of the work of God upon the river, and of souls being brought to know God since I was here before.

"Thursday, 27th. They collected the neighbours together, and at 11 o'clock I gave them a sermon, on Col. iii. 14. It was a delightful season; my heart was humbled within me before God, and the people were melted into tears. I could not repent coming to this place, though I came through great tribulation. I dined, and went on towards Farmington. On my

way, I overlook a company of women who had been
at meeting; one among them was praising God for his
goodness, and those in company were weeping. When
I came up, the one who was praising God, took me by
the hand, and told me how good the Lord had been to
her. My soul was transported with the pleasing
sound; but how unfashionable it is to hear people
praise God along the road! I came to Mr. Bradford's,
in Farmington, and at 3 o'clock, I preached on John
iv. 14. Here the Lord was pleased to visit us again
with his blessed presence. Tears flowed from many
eyes, and it seemed to be a time of love. Several
persons in this neighbourhood have been lately
brought to the knowledge of God. The righteous are
becoming as bold as lions.

"Monday, 1st of December. It snowed all day.
A man went with me on a new tour, where the Methodists had never been before, excepting one place.
We rode through the snow to the Vineyard, and
stopped at deacon Norton's; but his wife being sick,
we could not stay there, as they had a large family, and
but one room that was fit to lodge in. However, we
obtained something to eat, and prayed with them;
and a little after dark, went to Daniel Luce's, and
stayed all night; the next day preached at Luce's.
The people heard the word with attention, and with
tears in their eyes. It is very seldom they have an
opportunity of hearing a sermon. After meeting we
travelled a very bad road to Capt. Dagget's, in the
east part of the town. I was kindly entertained, and
slept comfortably.

"Wednesday, 3d. We rode through the woods to
the mouth of Sandy river, where it enters the Kennebeck. Some part of the way we had no path at all,

19

but had to follow the chops in the trees ; the snow
was ten inches deep ; the travelling was disagreeable
enough. About noon, we saw a house, which was the
first we had seen on the way; so we rode up to it,
and went in. I talked to the man and his wife on the
subject of religion. The woman told me she had not
heard a sermon in two years. The man said he had
heard one or two in that time, by going a long way.
They were quite solemn while I spoke to them about
their souls. After this, they had an opportunity of
hearing me. We came to Mr. B. Hilton's, a little
before night, and after letting them know who I was,
and what my business, they gave word to their neighbours, who came together, and I preached to them. My
subject was John iii. 20. I found comfort in delivering to this people a message from the Lord ; and they
received it with great attention, and appeared very
thankful for this opportunity. They never heard a
Methodist before.

" Thursday, 4th. We rode up Kennebeck river to
Mr. James Burn's, to Zitcombtown, a little below
Seven Mile Brook ; and at night, I preached on 1 John
iv. 9. I had a clever company to preach to ; they
were all attention, and some of them much wrought
upon, so that they could not forbear weeping. I felt
a hope that the word was profitable to the souls of the
people. They importuned me to come amongst them
again, or try and send one to preach to them, for they
seldom hear a sermon of any kind. My heart was
moved with compassion for the people. There never
was a Methodist preacher in these parts before.
Lord send forth more labourers into thy vineyard,
and into this part of the world. I had not time to go
any higher up the river, but the people are settled

about thirty miles higher. The next day I came back to the mouth of Sandy river, in full view of old Norridgewock Point, where, in former years, the Indians had a meeting-house for public worship, and a priest; but in time of war, while at their devotion, the English soldiers rushed upon them, and killed their priest, and most of their men.

"I preached at Mr. Wilson's, crossed Sandy river upon the ice, and rode up to Mr. Arnold's, and tarried all night.

"Monday, 8th. I rode to Mr. J. Cochran's, in Goshen, and at 2 o'clock, I preached on Ephes. ii. 20. I found a good deal of freedom in preaching, some of them were much wrought upon, and could not refrain from tears. I baptized three children, and the parents appeared to be very solemn while I was speaking. There is great attention paid to religion in this place at present. I hope several persons are determined to seek and serve the Lord.

"Friday, 12th. Readfield. This day was appointed as a day of fasting for the society, as we intended to commune on the following Sabbath. At 11 o'clock I preached; my subject was '*We then as workers together with him,*' &c. I found much of the presence of God with us while we were together. There was a considerable move amongst the people. I then met the class, and consulted about administering the Lord's Supper. One of our friends gave us an agreeable account of a gracious work of God amongst the people at Sandy river. Lord increase it abundantly. Tarried all night at the widow Johnson's. Several persons were present who wished to know what they should do to be saved.

" Sunday, 14th. I preached in Readfield and administered the Lord's Supper to about eight persons.
This was the first time that this ordinance had ever
been administered in this town by the Methodists, or
in any part of this province ; we had a happy time
together.

"Tuesday, 16th. Setting out with Samuel Dudley,
we rode to the Hook, and crossed Kennebeck river on
the ice, though it appeared to be very dangerous, for
the ice would often bend under the horses, when on
the other side it broke in ten or fifteen feet from the
shore, but they came out safe, and we went to another
place, and walked to the shore. We then rode to
Pittson meeting-house, and called at Major C.'s. but
he was not at home. I told his lady who I was, and
that I should return that way in two days, and if her
husband would give notice, I would preach as I came
back. Then we rode to Eastern river, and dined. I
then went on to John Plummer's, in New Milford,
and was kindly entertained.

" The day following I preached at Plummer's, in
New-Milford ; some wept freely. After meeting I
had some pressing invitations to come again.

" Thursday, 18th. I set off alone and came to
Major C.'s. but they had made no appointment for me
to preach there. This text of scripture came to my
mind, *Shake off the dust of your feet for a testimony
against them.*

" Tuesday, 23d. I rode to Mr. Laine's, in Little-
borough, and at 2 o'clock, I preached on John xi. 3.
I had a crowded congregation, and the melting presence of God was amongst us. Many of the people
could hardly refrain from weeping aloud. After I
had dismissed the people, and went into another room

a man came in to speak to me, and burst into tears. Another came in with tears in his eyes, and begged that I would preach again at night. I could not refuse. Some of the people then went home, but soon returned. One man being in deep distress, began to cry aloud to God to have mercy upon his poor soul ; and thus he continued to cry with all his might, until some of the people were much frightened. I talked, prayed, and sung, and while I was singing a visible alteration took place in his countenance, and I was inclined to think his soul was set at liberty. He afterward spoke as though he believed it was so. About this time another man was seized with a trembling, and he began to pray to the Lord to have mercy upon his poor soul, and cried aloud for some time. I then took my text, and preached on 1 Peter v. 7. It was not long before another man was taken with a violent trembling, and crying, so that my voice was almost drowned. I was forced to stop. I then prayed for him, and he became more quiet. I then went on with my sermon. There was a great weeping in every part of the house. It appeared as if the whole neighbourhood was about to turn to God. I hope the fruit of this meeting will be seen after many days, and that the work of the Lord will revive from this time.

" Thursday, 25th. At Captain Hopkins', in Monmouth, being Christmas-day, I preached on Isa. ix. 6. We had a remarkably large congregation, and a very remarkable season. The people seemed to swallow every word. Toward the end of the meeting, the power of God was mightily displayed ; there were but few dry eyes in the house. I wept over my congregation, and had to stop for a season. I begged the poor sinners to be reconciled to God, till I was per-

19 *

suaded that some of them would obey the truth. P. Wager exhorted, with a good deal of life. We then administered the Lord's Supper to several persons. This is the first time the Methodists ever communed in this town. Then I gave the friends some advice about building a meeting-house in this place. I hope they will pay attention to it.

" Tuesday, 30th. I set out on my journey to the westward. The travelling was exceedingly rough, and the day very cold, but I came to Saco by night, and put up at Hooper's tavern. After praying with the family, I went to a neighbouring house to see a Baptist woman of my acquaintance, but she was gone to a dance, and had not returned! John the Baptist lost his head by reason of dancing, and I thought the Baptists had never been fond of dancing from that day to this.

" Thursday, January 1st, 1795. I made an early start, and rode to Portsmouth, in the state of New-Hampshire, and put up at Mr. Hutchins'. They collected a few of their neighbours together, to whom I preached with liberty and satisfaction, but religion is at a low ebb in this town at present. I felt thankful to God for bringing me in safety to see the beginning of another year.

" Sunday, 25th. Bristol court-house, at half after 10 o'clock, I preached on Isa. liii. 1. I had but a small congregation, but I found some freedom in speaking. At 2 o'clock I preached again to a crowded house, and had a solemn meeting. I spoke with faith and delight ; and the people were all attention. I felt a pleasing hope that good was done in the name of the Lord Jesus. I then crossed the ferry to Portsmouth. At night at Mr. Earl's I preached on Matt. xi. 30. I had a crowded house; and I was much assisted in speaking. The people were attentive, and some of them deeply affected. I was ready to conclude that the Lord was about to revive his work in this place. The people are teachable, and glad to hear the way to heaven.

" Monday, 26th. We determined in the morning to purchase a house that had never been finished, and to make a meeting-house of it. I drew up a subscription paper, and doubt not but they will soon have the house fit to preach in. It stands about a mile to the north of the Quaker meeting-house.

" Wednesday, 28th. I rode to the north end of the Island and crossed the ferry to Tiverton, and preached at Mr. Benjamin Howling's. I had a large congregation. It was a place where the Methodists never preached before. I found my soul at liberty, and spoke to the people with a great deal of freedom; some of my hearers were cut to the heart, and wept much.

" Friday, 30th. I rode to New-Bedford, and put up at Mr. George East's. I gave them a sermon at night, on Rom. xiii. 10. The people were quite solemn. It may be remarked that this was the first Methodist sermon ever preached in this town.

" Tuesday, 3d of February. I sailed in the packet for Nantucket Island, but having a rough, disagreeable passage, and very sick withal, I prevailed with them to land me on the Vineyard. I shook as though I had an ague, being cold and sick. I then walked to Mr. J. Dagget's tavern, at the head of the harbour at Holme's-Hole. I was kindly received, and gladly entertained. The next day I gave them a sermon in the meeting-house; we had a small congregation, and not much life. At night I preached again with more

freedom and faith than in the morning, and tho word
seemed to make some impression on the minds of the
hearers ; perhaps I am the first Methodist preacher
who has visited this place for the express purpose of
preaching, and even now I have visited this place
sooner than I intended, for I expected to have called
here on my way from Nantucket.

" Friday, 6th. I preached at Shubal Davies' in
Edgarton. I had a refreshing season, and spoke with
faith. I walked about two miles to the widow Norton's, and stayed all night; she is almost eighty years
old, and appears to be acquainted with the power of
religion.

" The next day I borrowed a horse, and went to
see old Mr. Zacheus Mayhew, who is a missionary to
the Indians on the Island. I met him on the road.
He went back with me to Mr. Morse's, the minister
of Tisbury, who lives in a place called Newtown. We
tarried till after dinner ; and then rode to the widow
Norton's. Mr. Mayhew went with me. We concluded to go down and spend the Sabbath with his
congregation of Indians. The old missionary is about
seventy-seven years of age, and seems to be acquainted
with the love of God. I asked him particularly about
his conversion, and was pleased with the relation he
gave. The other minister which we visited, Mr. M.
said he believed that when a person died, that the soul
slept with the body, and was not sensible of pain or
joy till the resurrection. Good Lord deliver me
from evil! The Island, called the Vineyard, contains
three townships and one county. It has several little
villages, but the land is generally poor, and not cultivated. They have but few horses on the Island, and
cut very little hay. They have no sleighing in the

winter. A great many of the men follow the seas, and
are engaged in piloting and fishing, beside many that go
to foreign ports. I fear there is little religion here,
though a few are to be found who adorn their profession.*

"Thursday, 12th. A small schooner being ready
to sail, I embarked, with three sailors as passengers,
beside the two men who belonged to the vessel. At
9 o'clock we sailed for New-Bedford; but having to
beat out of the harbour, and the wind dying away,
we were not able to get through Wood's-Hole; so
we put into the wharf just by Wood's-Hole, and
went up to Mr. Parker's tavern, in the town of Falmouth, and county of Barnstable. I concluded it was
all for the best, and feeling quite resigned to my lot, I
determined to try and do something for God. I spoke
to the tavernkeeper about a meeting; he was quite
willing to have a meeting at his house, so the people
were requested to meet at night. My text was Rom.
x. 4. I found liberty in speaking. Here I am detained,
but I hope it may be for the good of some poor soul.
I was kindly entertained *gratis.* The Lord reward the
family according to their good works.

"Friday, 13th, was quite stormy in the morning,
and some of the company seemed unwilling to go. I
thought it best to try it; so we set sail about 9 o'clock,
with the wind ahead, blowing very hard, and the
snow falling very fast. We beat through Wood's-Hole,
a very dangerous place for vessels to pass through;
and after tacking backwards and forwards for about
two hours, I was *dreadfully* sick; however, after

* He remained on the Island seven days, during which time he
preached twelve sermons. Some of the meetings were profitable.

much difficulty, we landed at New-Bedford a little after
dark. I felt thankful for a safe arrival at the long
wished for place. I lodged with Mr. East.

"Monday, 16th. I preached at Stoke's, at 1 o'clock,
on 1 Pet. iii. 9. Though we had a small company, i
was a melting season. Brother N. Chapin closed the
meeting by prayer. We then consulted about building a meeting-house, and determined to begin to build
it in the lower part of Easton, near Bridgewater, as
soon as possible. The people seemed to be in good
spirits about it, though they are but poor. At night, I
preached at old Mr. Churchill's, in Bridgewater. I
believe our meeting was not in vain. Brother N.
Chapin told me this evening that by hearing me
preach, which was the first Methodist he ever heard,
he was reclaimed from a backslidden state ; and so
brought to preach the gospel. While he was relating
this to me, I felt both humble and happy ; and was
brought to say, O, that it was with me as in days
past, when the Lord owned my labours in the conversion of many. But if there were not another soul
brought to know God, by my ministry, I should still
have cause to bless God that ever I preached the
gospel.

"Thursday, March 12th. My birth-day.—Was
thirty-seven years old. I have made a profession of
religion about twenty-two years. But when I look
back upon my life, I have great cause to mourn before
God, that I am not more given up to his service. I
have been generally healthy ; and for many years, I
have been, for the most part, a happy person. Some
things in my life I would gladly recall, if it were in
my power. Lord forgive my follies past. I wish to
give myself more to God than ever. I have reason to

hope that I have gained some strength in religion the
past year. We rode to doctor Hind's, and took dinner,
and then went to meeting. Mr. M. Cazier, the minister of the place, gave a lecture for the singers, on
Psa. lxvi. 2. *Sing forth the honour of his name : make
his praise glorious.* He preached without notes ; and I
think was as barefaced an Antinomian as I ever heard.
He said that no man ever yet sang forth the praises of
God aright, but what was brought to be as willing for
God to *damn him* as to *save him.* Speaking of the
Psalmist's saying he would sing of mercy and judgment, he said, he would praise God as much for sending men to hell, as for taking them to heaven : that is,
I will bless God for saving one man, and damning another. He further declared, that every action of man
was just as God would have it to be ; and whether it
appeared in our view, to be a good or a bad action, it
was intended of God, for the general good ; and the
moral system would be broken, if the action were not
to take place, &c. &c.

"At night, I preached at doctor Hind's, on Rom. ix.
22. Here I endeavoured to show the unreasonable-
ness of predestination ; and how the people had fitted
themselves for destruction ; and yet, God had much
long-suffering towards them. I further told them, a
minister ought to pray the people, in Christ's stead, to
be reconciled to God, warn them of their danger, and
weep over them, and let them know that the Lord was
not willing that they should be damned ; but that they
should come to the knowledge of the truth and be
saved. I also endeavoured to show how unreasonable
it was for a minister to say that God was willing to send
his hearers to hell ; and that they should bless God
for sending them there. I had a comfortable meet-

ing, and freedom in speaking. Just as I was going to
leave the house, the minister came in, and abundance
of people flocked into the room, expecting to hear us
dispute, but after asking him a few questions *civilly*, we
parted."

Would the limits we have prescribed to ourselves
permit, we should gladly continue the extracts from
his diary ; but the notices he has made for this year
only, would make a considerable volume, much of
which, therefore, must be passed over. From these
simple records of his travels and exercises, it evidently
appears that he exemplified the same uniform zeal in
the cause of God, and the same persevering industry
for the salvation of souls, which had heretofore
marked his conduct.

From Greenwich, he went through the deep snow
to Hardwick, from thence to Braintree ; the travelling
was so *intolerable*, that he concluded to stop a day or
two, and preach to small and careless congregations.
He, with much difficulty, reached Worcester, the snow
being deep and the way untrodden ; from thence to
Milford, Mansfield, and to Norton. At the latter place,
he met the preahers of the circuit, and held a quarterly meeting. Easton was the next stand, where
good prospects of a revival of religion cheered him
exceedingly ; then he hasted to Boston, where religious affairs remained unimproved ; but the quarterly
meeting at that place, was held in peace. He then
proceeded to Lynn, as the next place in course. He
found an evident declension of religious fervour in
Lynn. At Marblehead his next quarterly meeting was
held. He then returned to Lynn, and set things in
order, and prepared himself for an eastern journey.
He was detained a few days by inclement weather,

but on the 30th of March he commenced his journey.
He passed through Salisbury, Portsmouth, in New-
Hampshire, then crossed Piscataway into the Province
of Maine, and then on through Kennebeck to
major Ilsley's, at Back Cove, in Falmouth; from
thence to Portland, Monmouth, Readfield, the Twenty-five mile Pond; this, with most of the forementioned places, he had visited about eighteen months
previously; during which time there had been a gracious revival of religion; but some *religious quarrels*
had damped the rising flame. Leaving the Twenty-
five mile Pond, he had very bad roads to Hampden;
twice in one day his horse fell into the deep mud, and
he but narrowly escaped with whole bones. From
thence he came to Bangor, where he found it necessary to cross the Penobscot; there was no ferry-boat
at hand, but two small boats were procured, and made
fast together. and his horse was made to stand with his
fore feet in one, and his hind feet in the other boat,
and all were enabled to get over without accident. He
went on, taking Orrington, Buckstown, Goldsborough,
Eppin, the Falls of Pleasant river, and Mechias, in
his way. Swimming rivers, passing dangerous fords,
encountering with hills, rocks, and mire, were the
occurrences of every day's travel. Coming to colonel
Stillman's, within two miles of Mechias, he formed a
resolution of crossing the Passamaquoddy, and of
visiting the British provinces. He accordingly visited
Moose, and Dudley islands; and then passed into St.
Andrew's, in the Province of New-Brunswick. In
all these places, he found the people destitute of
preaching. He then proceeded to St. John's, and in
crossing a part of the Bay of Fundy, the vessel was
driven against the rocks by the rapid tide, which

20

created some alarm on board; but fortunately, they
came off without injury. The next day, the captain
put into a place called Dipper Harbour, within eight
leagues of St. John's. Here he continued two days,
and preached at a Mr. French's, who, although the
proprietor of three thousand acres of land, could not
afford a chair for his guests to sit upon. Having a
favourable wind, they set sail, and soon landed at the
town of St. John's. Here he met with an old friend,
William Jessop, a preacher, with whom he had often
been comforted in other parts of the world. He had
an opportunity of viewing the *fearful* falls of St. John's
river; a place which is, at certain times, calculated
to strike the spectator with fear, and in the roaring
rapids of which, many a bold adventurer has found
a watery grave; but none can attempt this dangerous pass, only at a certain time of the tide, when the
water is nearly on a stand, either going out or coming
in, and then it will not serve more than about fifteen
minutes at a time.

In this town, he spent seven or eight days very
agreeably, preaching, meeting classes, holding prayer
meetings, and visiting the sick, and others who
needed his company and advice.

Saturday, the 16th of May, he took his leave of
William Jessop, and St. John's, and sailed for St.
Andrew's, at which place he arrived the same day,
quite sick from his voyage, but was able to preach at
night. The next day, he embarked for St. Stephen's,
in Schoodic river, but being becalmed, they were
forced to come to anchor, a little below a large hill on
the American shore, called Devil's Head; here
he went on shore. visited a family, and conversed on
the subject of religion. In the afternoon they weighed

anchor again, passed Devil's Head, and proceeded up the river a little, and were again becalmed. There was no other alternative but that of casting anchor; he, however, hailed a row boat that was passing, was taken on board, and carried up the river to Duncan M'Call's. It was now past 11 o'clock at night, but the family arose at his call, and received him with open hearts. He found a hearty friend in Duncan M'Call, one with whom he had corresponded for several years. He had long felt a desire of seeing him, and now his desire was realized, and their kindred spirits were more closely united. For several days he tarried with his friend M'Call; and as he was now at the dividing line between the United States and the British provinces, he had an opportunity of giving his labours to each for several days. Here he was particularly pleased with an instance of the power of religion, which I give to the reader in his own words.

"Thursday, 21st of May. We had prayer meeting in the chapel, and had a good time, though there were but few people. I was much pleased at hearing two of our sisters pray: I have not heard a woman pray for many weeks before. Sister G—, drank tea with us. I understood that she was the first who experienced conversion in this place, (St. David's Parish,) and her husband was so much opposed to it, that at last, he determined to leave her, on account of her religion, and one day he was actually on the point of starting. 'Stop a little, (says she,) let us pray together before we part;' so he consented to join her in prayer, and God touched his heart, so that he gave up the notion of leaving her, and has since become a religious man."

On the 15th of July, conference for the New-England states, was to be held in New-London; his friend Mr. M'Call had come to a determination to accompany him thither; so, embarking in a canoe on the 25th of May, they went down the river, and over to the American shores, to Mr. Brewster's, and after spending a little time with the family in prayer, they hastened on to Mr. Voris', in Bobin's town, where he preached to a thin congregation. They then went to Moose Island, where Mr. Lee preached. Leaving Moose Island, they proceeded up Crobscook river in the canoe, and passed through the falls, though not without danger of being swallowed in the whirling eddies of this dangerous pass. They, however, arrived safe at colonel Crew's, at the head of the river. Here they left the canoe, and hired a guide for one dollar, to take them through the woods to the stage road. Lakes, ponds, and dreary swamps, opposed their march; sometimes wading, then floundering through mud, crossing the intervening waters in frail bark canoes, presented no small impediment in their way. At length they took shelter for the night, with colonel Stillman, after a journey of fifteen miles by water, and eighteen by land. Here he met with his horse, and pursued his numerous appointments until the setting of conference.

On Tuesday, the 21st of June, he preached a dedication sermon, in a new meeting-house, built by the Methodists in Readfield, which was the first ever built by the Methodists in the Province of Maine.

CHAPTER XIV.

—◦✦◦—

Conference in New-London—Goes to Boston, and assists in laying the corner stone of the first Methodist Meeting-House in that place—Singular conduct of some ill disposed persons in Provincetown—Visits Mount Desert—Receives a letter from Bishop Asbury—Attends Conference at Wilbraham—Meets with Mr. Asbury, and goes to Charleston—Pleasing change in that place—Travels through Georgia—The manner in which Mrs. Vannest was awakened—Conference in Readfield—Goes to the South.

CONFERENCE for the year 1795, was held in New-London, and commenced its sitting on the 15th of July. Much peace and harmony prevailed during its session. His station this year, was the same as in the preceding, only, that within the bounds of his district, he had seventeen circuits and stations, in the visiting which once a quarter, was sufficient to keep him actively employed. After the adjournment of conference, he accompanied Mr. Asbury on a tour through Providence, Norton, in Massachusetts, then to Boston, from thence to Lynn. Mr. Asbury then turned his course towards the south. Mr. Lee still bore him company to Waltham, Farmingham, and Milford; here they parted. The bishop pursued his journey to the south, and Mr. Lee went to Boston.

Five years had elapsed since the Methodists had been making exertions in Boston, in order to raise a society, and to build a house of worship. Mr. Lee had, during that time, used every effort within his power to promote the interests of the church, in that place. Considering the difficulties with which he had to contend, it is a wonder he had not given it up in despair : but now there was some prospect of witnessing, in part, what he and others had long wished to see. On the 8th of August, he arrived in Boston, for the purpose of making arrangements for the commencement of the meeting-house, which had been so long meditated. On the 28th of the same month, he had the pleasure of assisting, with all due solemnities, in laying the corner stone of the building. During a stay of about three weeks in the town, he again set an example worthy the imitation of all who are placed in a similar situation ; namely, preaching on the commons. .

The hired room in Boston, where the Methodists assembled, could not, probably, contain more than one hundred persons ; hence Mr. Lee very justly concluded that few, in that large and populous town, would be able to hear the gospel preached by the Methodists, so long as they continued to meet only in the old room. He, therefore, contrary to the wishes of some of his brethren, boldly resolved to go to the commons. He went ; and thousands flocked to hear him for three successive sabbaths. It was his calculation, that by preaching on the commons, it was likely to do twenty times as much good as by meeting at the usual place.

Having so far arranged matters in Boston, he then set out in order to superintend his charge, and to find some new places where he might preach the gospel. At Marshfield, he preached, perhaps the first sermon ever preached by the Methodists in that place. At

Sandwich, it was the same. In Provincetown, he preached twice ; and was encouraged to hope that some lasting impressions were made on the minds of many present. Here the Methodists had met with some opposition. The little society which had been formed, came to the resolution of building a house of worship.· To prevent which, a town meeting was called, which voted that the Methodists should have no house of worship there. Nothwithstanding this arbitrary *decree*, the society resolved to go on ; the timber was collected, and nearly in readiness for framing ; but it was　matter of great importance to those opposed to this measure, to prevent what they considered so great an evil ; and what they could not effect by vote, they were resolved to carry by force and cunning: accordingly, a company of choice spirits sallied forth under cover of the night, and repaired to the spot where the timbers were collected, hauled them over a hill, down into the valley, and set themselves to work, making sad desolation amongst the timbers, reared up a pile, and set up the effigy of the Methodists on the top, tarred and feathered. It would be hardly worth while to record this daring act, marked with extravagance and folly, did we not believe that those guilty of it, were the tools of the men who formed the town meeting.

We are far from taking delight in recounting the reprehensible conduct of our fellow men ; but such chivalrous deeds of darkness ought to be exposed to merited disgrace and condemnation, that others may fear ; and we are happy to have it in our power to record that the subsequent improvement of society in that part of the country, where formerly a bigoted attachment to particular forms and creeds, hurried many into unjustifiable measures, has justly reprobated all such violent proceedings. May the tolerant spirit of the gospel of Christ, universally prevail.

"I went to see it, (says Mr. Lee,) and felt astonished at the conduct of the *people*, considering we live in a free country, and no such conduct can be justified ; however, I expect this will be for the good of the little society, and that they shall find the truth of these words, 'the wrath of man shall praise thee.'

"Monday, 23d of November, I rode to Bristol, and at 2 o'clock, I preached on 2 Pet. iii. 14. This was the first Methodist sermon ever preached in Bristol. I could truly say the meeting was profitable to my soul. I then rode to Mr. Rust's, in Nobleborough, and at night, I preached on Prov. i. 22, 23. We had a solemn time. The people pressed me hard to send them a preacher, but I know not how I can do it, unless the Lord will send forth more labourers into his vineyard.

"Tuesday, 24th, I rode to New-Milford, and held forth in the new meeting-house, on Rom. ii. 6. I had but few to hear ; I suppose the head men were somewhat afraid, and therefore, did not have proper notice given. The young candidate rode with me a few miles after meeting, and was not satisfied with my inviting all to Christ, and persuading them to choose religion and turn to God. I asked him if he did not believe that God had decreed that some men should not be saved ? He said he did. I then asked him if he did not believe that Christ opened a way, by his death, whereby all might possibly be saved ? he said he did. Then I told him, according to what he said, Christ had opened the way whereby God's decrees might be

broken, and wished him to try and clear up the con-
tradiction : he did try, and tried it often, till he was
quite confused—and so we parted.

"Saturday, 7th of May, 1796. I returned to Trenton, to Mr. James Smith's, at a place called Kilkenny,
where, at 2 o'clock, I preached on Ezek. xviii. 11. This
was a thinly settled neighbourhood ; but I had quite a
good company of hearers, and the Lord was present
with us. I found great freedom in speaking, and was
melted into tears myself, and the people wept very
freely. I felt so much for their poor souls, that I was
willing to spend my life for their welfare. This was
the first Methodist sermon ever preached in Trenton,
and the people heard as though they were never to
hear another. After meeting I rode to Union river,
and left my horse, and went to Benjamin Joy's, and
stayed all night.

"Sunday, 8th. At Mr. Joy's, on Union river, at 11
o'clock, I discoursed on *the one thing needful*. The
day was wet, but thank God, we had a good meeting.
In the afternoon, my text was Dan. vi. 16. The
place seemed awful on account of the presence of the
Lord. O, what a pity that so many people in this
place, should be destitute of regular preaching : many
of them seem willing to hear the word. I felt thankful
to God for bringing me amongst them once more.

"Monday, 9th. It was very wet, and rained hard
till the middle of the day. After dinner, I travelled
to Mr. Foster's, on Jordan river, about six miles. I
had to walk a good deal of the way, for I could not
ride. I do not remember that I ever travelled a
worse road than this in all my life.

"Tuesday, 10th. A young doctor went with me
down the river, and got into a canoe with some

other people, and went over to Mount Desert, and
found many collected for training. Just after our
arrival the captain dismissed his company. Many
women had also collected to see the men muster, and
afterward to have a dance. But when they found
out that I intended to preach, they were at a loss to
know what to do ; some said they would have a dance,
others said nay, but we will have a sermon. The
woman of the house said, if they would not hear the
gospel, they should not dance. The man of the house
spoke out aloud, saying, 'if the Lord has sent the
man, let us hear him, but if the devil has sent him, let
the devil take him away again.' So I told them I
would preach at another house, at 4 o'clock. I then
set off, and one Mr. T. a Baptist by profession, went
with me ; he was *brim full* of religious talk, but I
soon discovered that he was a strong fatalist, and
when he found out that I believed that Christ died for
all men, and that the Lord called all men, he got into
a violent passion, and with abundance of fury, called
it a *damnable doctrine*, and appeared to be ready to
swear outright. Poor man! how small a thing is it
for a man to call himself a Christian, while he is
governed by wrath, and an evil spirit. At Esq.
Paine's, I preached at 4 o'clock ; my text was 1 Pet.
ii. 9. I had a *tolerable* company, and a very good
meeting. The Lord was very precious to my sou ,
and many of the hearers were melted into tears, and
heard the word as though it had been for their lives.
But while I was preaching, the forementioned Baptist,
and another of his party, kept shaking their heads at
each other, as much as to say, 'that's not true ;' at last
I stopped, and said to one them 'I should be glad if you
will try and keep your head still ;' he behaved better

afterward. Mount Desert, is now divided into two
towns ; the one I preached in, is called Eden.   This
was the first Methodist sermon ever preached in the
town ; and I feel a pleasing hope that a lasting blessing will attend it. I lodged with Mr. Paine that
night.

" Friday, 17th of June. We left the two brother
Hulls'; and brother Mudge came with me to brother
Baker's, in Falmouth, where I preached at 2 o'clock.
I found much of the presence of God with me while
preaching, and the word was attended with some
power : many tears were shed.

" There has been a good stir of religion in this
place, of late. An aged man upwards of seventy
years old. was asked something respecting his will,
he answered, ' I have no will.' They said, ' what have
you done with your will?' he said, ' I lost it upon the
ledge the other day,' meaning, he got converted the
other day upon a rocky hill, and there . his will was
swallowed up in the will of God.

So voluminous are the manuscipt journals of Mr.
Lee, that we can give only a small portion of them,
without swelling this memoir beyond all reasonable
limits.   And though it might be very desirable to
let him speak in his own language ; yet for the sake
of brevity, we are under the necessity of abridging
his remarks, and of presenting a more condensed
view of his travels and ministerial labours.

He continued in the faithful discharge of the duties
on the district until the conference for New-England,
which was held in the town of Thompson, in the state
of Connecticut, and commenced the 20th of September 1706. He was re-appointed to the same charge
as in the year preceding. From the annual confer-

ence he attended the general conference held in Baltimore. It commenced the 20th of October. Here he
opposed the motion " to strengthen the Episcopacy, in a
way which should be agreeable to Mr. Asbury," believing that it would be most proper to leave it to the
vote of the general conference to make their own
selection. The majority, however, voted for the
motion. Doctor Coke who was present as one of
the superintending Bishops, requested that the question might rest for a few hours ; at the expiration
of which time, he made known to the conference
his determination of giving his services to the Methodist Episcopal Church. This proposition was
acceded to by a large majority, and so the matter
rested. We take the liberty of saying, that Mr. Lee
was no less remarkable for his independency of mind,
than for his firmness in maintaining any point which
he had espoused. Though he, on some occasions,
might manifest more tenacity than needful, yet he
always had his reason, for his conduct. And from the
penetration of his mind in viewing the bearings of
every question of moment which was presented, he
was not very liable to be misled in his decisions. He
was disposed on all occasions, scrupulously to adhere
to the discipline of the church of which he was a member : he was ready to sacrifice his own feelings in
order to preserve it inviolate. The interests of the
church were too sacred to be compromised, to the particular caprice of any individual. If we are not very
much deceived, he has done much in his day to deserve
the gratitude of his brethren, in preserving the order
and economy of Methodism in America.

From the general conference in Baltimore, Mr.
Lee went to visit his relations in Virginia. He was

happy once more in seeing his aged father in good health, after an absence of four years. He also had an opportunity of being present at the Virginia conference, held at Mabry's chapel. After spending a few weeks amongst his friends and relations, he set out once more for the north, and was favoured in his journey, with meeting many of his brethren in the Lord, amongst whom he had once laboured, and enjoyed seasons of delight.

In January, 1797, he returned to his district, and was happy in finding that the cause of religion was progressing in the several circuits which were under his superintendance.

In August, he received a communication from Mr. Asbury, requesting him to get himself in readiness to leave the district, and to go with him from the ensuing conference to Charleston, and to visit other parts of the work. Mr. Asbury's health, at this time, was such as to incapacitate him for the arduous labours which he had to sustain. Mr. Asbury needed assistance, and the interests of the church required it ; he, therefore, looked to Mr. Lee as a man whose experience, talents, and integrity, entitled him to his confidence.

On the September following, Mr. Lee attended the conference at Wilbraham, (Mass.) Through extreme indisposition, bishop Asbury could not attend. He sent a communication to Mr. Lee, of which the following is a copy.

"*Byram River, Sept.* 12, 1797.

"My very dear brother,

"I am now convinced that I ought not to attempt to come to the conference at Wilbraham. Riding thirteen miles yesterday, threw me into more fever than I

21

have had for a week past. It will be with difficulty I
shall get back to the widow Sherwood's, my house at
present. I have sent brother Wells, who, next to
Jonathan Bird, has seen much of my continued labours,
and afflictions, for many days and miles—the burden
lieth on thee ; act with a wise and tender hand ; especially on the stations. I hope it will force the connexion to do something, and turn their attention for one to
assist, or substitute me. I cannot express the distress
I have had in all my afflictions, for the state of the connexion. We say the Lord will provide. True ; but
we must look out for men and means. The Lord could
have provided without such a poor, worthless creature
as I am, crossing the Atlantic. You and every man
that thinks properly, will find it will never do to divide
the north from the south. Methodism is union all
over ; union in exchange of preachers ; union and
exchange of sentiments ; union and exchange of interest : we must draw resources from the centre to the
circumference. Your brethren in Virginia wish you
to come forth. I think the most general and impartial
election, may take place in the yearly conferences ;
every one may vote ; and in general conference, perhaps, one fifth or one sixth part would be absent. I
wish you to come, and keep as close to me and my
directions as you can. I wish you to go, after the
conference, to Georgia, Holston, and to Kentucky : and,
perhaps, come to Baltimore in June, if the ordination*
should take place, and so come on to the eastern confe-

* This has reference to a communication which Mr. Asbury made
to the conference at Wilbraham, which proposed the election of
Richard Whatcoat, Francis Poythress, and Jesse Lee, as assistant
bishops in the United States. It was rejected, being thought con-
rary to the form of discipline.

rence. You will have need to follow my advice for your health, steel as you are.

"I now conclude with my best wishes, and earnest prayers for the conference and you.

"As ever thine in Jesus.

F. ASBURY."

Upon the receipt of this letter, Mr. Lee endeavoured to act in conformity to the instructions which it contained. He, therefore, presided in the conference at Wilbraham, and then went on to meet with the afflicted bishop, whom he found at Mrs. Sherwood's, in New-Rochelle, somewhat amended; though still labouring under considerable affliction.

Friday, the 27th of September, found them in New-York, where they were eye witnesses to the gracious displays of God's power in the conversion of souls.

Monday, October 9th, they reached the Duck creek Cross-roads, where conference was held, which commenced the day following. Here the Lord owned the labours of his servants, and made his word the instrument of effecting the work of conviction, conversion, and sanctification. At this conference, it was unanimously agreed that Mr. Lee should travel with bishop Asbury. The state of the work, and the ill health of the superintendant, were a sufficient justification for this measure. From Duck creek, they hastened to Baltimore, where conference opened the 21st. From Baltimore they moved on to the south, passing through Alexandria, King George county, crossed Rapahanock river at Port-Royal, thence through Essex, King, and Queen, and Gloucester. Here a good work was progressing. On the 17th of November, a few miles from Gloucester town, who should they meet but Doctor Coke, riding on a small horse, with a boy behind

him ; the meeting was agreeable ; they then went on,
leaving the doctor to follow them, and crossed York
river, at Little York, then on to Williamsburg, crossed
James' river at old James town, and then to Lane's
chapel, in Sussex, where conference commenced the
25th. Here the conference voted that Mr. Asbury
should preach no more until the April following; but
that he should go the most direct way to Charleston ;
and in the mean time, Mr. Lee should fill his appointments. Doctor Coke wished to return to England ;
the conference consented that he might do so. No
time was to be lost by Mr. Lee in getting to the conference in Charleston, considering he had the distance
of nearly five hundred miles to travel, in the space of
a little more than four weeks, and to attend twenty-
five appointments on the way.

On arriving in Charleston, which was on the 1st of
January, 1798, he surveyed with pleasure, the change
which had been effected in that city within the space
of thirteen years. Methodism had not commenced in
Charleston in the year 1785 ; but since that period, it
had taken root, and flourished, and many had found
shelter under its branches : two churches had been built,
many societies formed, and friends willing to receive
the ministers of Christ into their houses. From the
conference in Charleston, which began, continued, and
ended in great peace, he went on to Georgia, visited
Augusta, and on south as far as the Oconee river, the
then dividing line between the United States and the
Indian lands. It was no small gratification to him to
meet with many of his old Virginia friends, who, for
the purpose of settling upon a richer soil, had removed
to Georgia. The following extracts from his journal,
will close this chapter.

" Thursday, February 8th. We crossed Savannah river at Barsdall's ferry and left the state of Georgia ; it was a damp day, and rained a little. We then crossed Little river, and being overtaken by night, put up at a public house. I will here observe that I have been greatly comforted with my visit in Georgia ; where I spent twenty-seven days, and preached twenty-one sermons. The country is much better than I expected to have found it ; the land is good, and in the parts where I travelled is inhabited principally by emigrants from Virginia. At present they live well ; but the people in general appear to be of an ungovernable turn, both in church and state. I have seldom seen a new country that I like as well as Georgia. I travelled through seven counties. I expect there will be a revival of religion amongst them shortly. Georgia is a good country for corn, tobacco and cotton, and also for oats, wheat, peas and potatoes : it is very good for peaches, but apples do not thrive so well. In the low lands of the state, in the *pine* woods. there are found a great many Salamanders. *so called* ; they are not found perhaps in any other state of the union. They live under ground. and they tell me are made much like a mole, though larger; and throw up hills of loose dust, much like hills made by ants.

" Monday, 12th of March, was my birthday ; I am now forty years old. I have enjoyed religion twenty-five years, have been in the Methodist society twenty-four years and four days, and a travelling preacher about 15 years. I feel as much as ever, determined to spend my days for the Lord. My soul is still panting after God. I wish to be more than ever devoted to his service ; and if I live to the Lord, I expect to be in heaven before I see forty years more; however strange it may appear, so it is that I have often thought that I should live till I was about fifty-six years old.

I do not pretend to say that the Lord has revealed this to me. It may be from an evil spirit, or it may be vain thoughts. *Time will show ;** but if I were called to die to-morrow, I do not know that I should have any objections. I do feel a pleasing hope of leaving all my troubles, when I leave the world; but if my life is prolonged, I hope to be the instrument of bringing a few more souls to God, before I rest from my labours.

"Monday, 9th of April. Conference began at Salem ; the session opened at 9 o'clock, and we set till 12. Then I preached on Rom. ii. 7. *To them who by patient continuance in well-doing, seek for glory, and honour, and immortality, eternal life.* I had a most powerful, weeping, shouting time ; the house seemed to be filled with the presence of God ; and I could truly say, it was a time of love to my poor soul.— Bishop Asbury exhorted for some time, and the people were much melted under the word : it was a blessed day to me, and I believe to many

"Wednesday, 11th. We set close to business in conference all day, and settled our matters with much peace and harmony, and the conference broke up at night. It was a profitable time. Four of our preachers located. None had died ; none expelled. Several new preachers engaged in the work, and we had a very good supply of preachers for the circuits. Lord send forth more labourers into thy vineyard.

"Friday, 13th. Enoch George rode with me to the widow Smith's in Dinwiddie county ; then I rode to my father's, where I was glad to find the family in health.

* The event proved that he did not fall very far short of his calculations. He was spared a little longer, for usefulness, and for sufferings.

"Saturday, 14th. I spent part of the day in walking about the plantation with my father, to see how he had fixed matters ; and withal to talk with him about many temporal matters. I wished him to make his will, for the peace of those who might live after him, and for the sake of his negroes, who are yet in slavery ; but he was not determined about it. I went in the evening to James Perkin's, who married my sister, where I met with brother Edward and his family, and my brother John, where we stayed all night.

" Friday, 20th. I left my relations once more and set out for New-England, and my brother John being in bad health, set out with me, to see if riding would not be an advantage to his health. We rode to Richmond, and at night, in the court-house, I preached on 2 Cor. vi. 17, 18. *Wherefore come out from among them, and be ye separate, &c.* I felt weary and fatigued, and had but little liberty . speaking.

" Tuesday 1st of May. We rode to Baltimore, where we met with many of the preachers from different parts of the country, who had collected for the conference. At night in the Dunkard's meeting-house I preached on Heb. x. 24. *And let us consider one another, to provoke unto love and good works.* We had a good little stir amongst the people. It was a time of love and of weeping. I hope the Lord will prosper his work in Baltimore.

"Saturday, 5th. At 12 o'clock conference broke up, and several of the preachers left town. We had a great deal of peace and union for the four days and a half that we set together. No one was expelled, and none located. One preacher was received on trial.— There has been but little stir of religion in the bounds of the conference, except in a few circuits.

" Tuesday, 29th. I rode to the Vansant's, at the head of Chester, and preached at 12 o'clock on Gal. vi. 7. *Be not deceived.* I had a very crowded house. I felt great liberty in preaching. The power and presence of the Lord was with us, and most of the people were in tears. Our hearts were closely united together, and I was much blessed amongst my old friends. After meeting, Mrs. Vansant gave me an account of her being brought to seek religion. She said, after her husband was converted, he used to talk to her about her soul's welfare; and others, preachers and private members, would talk to her, and persuade her to serve the Lord; but she did not like to be spoken to on the subject, unless it was by wise and sensible persons; for she was too proud to be advised by every body. However, the Lord took a strange method with her. About ten or twelve years ago, she and her husband were standing at the door, and she said to her husband, ' I do wish we had money enough to buy another goose, for we have but one.' Her husband said, ' never mind, only trust in the Lord and he will provide you a goose.' In a few moments they heard the noise of a goose, and looked, and saw one flying in the air, which soon came and lighted down in the yard, with their goose and gander. ' There,' says her husband, ' I told you if you would trust in the Lord, he would provide a goose for you, and now he has done it.' She said she was so struck with the circumstance, that she began to believe that there was something in religion, and so began from that time to seek the Lord. She is now a steady Methodist, and says she is happy in the enjoyment of religion. She further told me, that they had inquired all about the neighbourhood, to know if any one had lost a goose, but could never find where the goose came from, from that day till now ; and the goose is still with them. How strange is this! that a woman who was too proud to be advised by common men, should be humbled and brought to seek the Lord by a strange goose.

"Wednesday, June 4th. We rode out of the state of Delaware, into Pennsylvania, and on to Philadelphia, and at night I preached on Ephes. iv. 3. I found freedom in speaking to the people, and the word seemed to find its way to their hearts. I felt thankful and happy. Most of our preachers had collected in the city, from the different parts of the yearly conference bounds.

"Thursday 7th, conference began.

"Saturday 9th, conference met at 8 o'clock, and sat till 2 o'clock in the afternoon, and then broke up. Just before the business was concluded, I had such a pain in my head, that I withdrew and went to my lodging. We had a comfortable time at conference, though there were some disagreeable things amongst us. We had but few preachers admitted on trial ; and a few located : one had died. Most of the preachers present appeared to be much devoted to God.

"Monday, July 9th. I took leave of my brother* John, perhaps for life. I felt very sorry to part with him, but duty called, and I felt willing to part with all my friends rather than neglect the work of God. My brother expected to sail in the afternoon or next morning, for Virginia. I left him as well as he had been for a few days. I left New-York at 10 o'clock, and rode out to Nicholas Berrien's, near King's bridge : and at 3

* His brother John, who accompanied him to the north, was in a low state of health. The symptoms of his complaint became more alarming as he progressed northward. He embarked in a vessel at New-York, and returned to Virginia.

o'clock I held forth on Rom. viii. 6. A few of the
hearers were solemn. Mr. Asbury and Joshua Wells
came to the house some time after meeting was over.
They had stopped on the road, and took their dinners.
The next day we rode to the widow Sherwood's ; I
preached and J. Wells exhorted. Mr. Asbury was
quite unwell all day.

Friday, 20th. We rode pretty early, and crossed
Connecticut river at the lower ferry, and travelled a
dismal road for a carriage, to New-London, better
than thirty miles from the place we started from in the
morning : night overtook us before we got into the
city. We put up at brother Gale's. He informed
us that they had just been raising the frame of a Methodist meeting-house, that afternoon, in New-London. I
hope this will be profitable to the souls of the people,
in some future day, and that the society here will
prosper more than ever.

"Wednesday, 25th. We rode out of Connecticut
into the state of Rhode-Island, and a very bad road
part of the way : but we arrived at General Lippet's
just before dark. I was rather uncomfortable both in
body and mind, but was much pleased to meet with my
old friends again.

Friday, August 17th. We rode early in the morning, and the day being uncomfortably warm, travelling was rendered very unpleasant : however, we had
a heavy shower of rain in the afternoon, which made
it more pleasant. Night found us at major Ilsley's, at
Back Cove, in Falmouth, where we rested comfortably. The next day I rode over the bridge to Portland, and spent the forenoon amongst our friends. I
had the society together, and talked and prayed with
them, and had reason to believe that the Lord was

with them ; but they had suffered by the loss of brother T. Boynton, a faithful leader, who had died a few months before.

"Tuesday, 21st. We rode to the widow Rowe's, and at 3 o'clock Mr. Asbury preached on Acts ii. 21. He gave us a good discourse ; then I exhorted. We had a heavy shower of rain, accompanied with awful thunder, in the evening. The thunder struck in several places, not far off. I went to the door to look out, and thinking it very probable we should have another clap of thunder, I thought I would put the chain of my watch in my pocket, that it might not attract the lightning : at the instant I took hold of the chain of my watch, we had a flash of lightning that struck an ox, and killed him dead in the field, just before the door, about three hundred yards from the house. Our horses were about one hundred yards from the ox, at that time. I saw that the horses were not hurt, but did not know that the ox was killed till next morning ; the people told me that the hair of the ox was singed from the rump to the head.

" Wednesday, 29th, conference began in Readfield ; we were closely engaged all day ; the next day we set in conference very early, and broke up at 8 o'clock. At 9, we held lovefeast, and had a large number of Methodists together, and none else. They spoke freely, and feelingly. It was a good time. At 11 o'clock Mr. Asbury preached a good sermon; and, though before meeting he appeared to be weak, yet while he was preaching, he was quite strong and courageous. Then we ordained Timothy Merritt, Robert Yellaley, and Aaron Humphrey, deacons, and Roger Searle, an elder. It was a very solemn time at the ordination ; but the people were so crowded in the

gallerys that were not finished, that some of the joists
gave way, and frightened the people very much for a
few minutes, and some were slightly hurt.   Then I
preached on Rom. xvi. 20.   My soul was much animated with the presence of the Lord.   The people
were melted into tears.   It was a precious time to many.
Then we administered the Lord's Supper.   I suppose
there were above two hundred communicants ; it was a
most solemn time at the table.   I stood astonished at
the sight! to see so many people at the Lord's table,
when it is not quite five years since we first came into
this part of the world.   After meeting, Mr. Asbury
borrowed my horse and set out on his journey, and left
me to settle the remainder of the conference business.
I was quite busy till bed time.   I felt thankful to God
for the privilege of being at the first conference that
was ever held in the Province of Maine.

"Wednesday, September 19th.   Our conference
began in Granville, at 8 o'clock ; most of the preachers
were present.   It was a very agreeable day.

"Friday, 21st.   We had a blessed time in preaching;
preachers and people, were melted into tears ; twelve
persons were ordained.   Mr. Asbury then gave the
preachers their stations, and our conference broke up.
We had some good accounts of the work of God in different circuits ; above two hundred had joined in the
state of Vermont, and in the bounds of the conference,
we had added about one thousand members ; we
received ten new preachers.   Praise God, O my soul!

"Saturday, 22d.   We left Granville, but I have
forgotten the name of the man at whose house we
lodged, although I stayed there four nights.   The
man of the house was not at home ; but I understood
he was a deacon of the Congregational church.   We

were kindly entertained at his house. We had a rough road to travel, but we left the state of Massachusetts before night, and came into the state of Connecticut, through Canaan, to Mr. Church's, in Salisbury, where we tarried all night.

"Friday, 28th. We made an early start, crossed the North river, seven miles above New York city; we rode quite fast, and soon left the state of New-York, and came into New-Jersey, passed through Newark, and night overtook us before we got to Elizabeth-town. Tired and weary, we rested with brother Morrell. The people informed us that the deaths in New-York, with the yellow fever, were as many as had ever been.

"Wednesday, October 3d. We rode to Burlington in the morning; and there we heard of the death of brother John Dickins, and his daughter; they both died the week before. I have not felt so much distressed at hearing of the death of any person for a long time. In the death of brother Dickins, we have lost one of the best of Christians; a good preacher; a worthy and much respected man; and an uncommonly faithful superintendant of the book concern. He died of the yellow fever in Philadelphia, which is stated to be much worse at this time, than at any former period. The accounts published in the newspapers, state that from sixty to eighty die of a day; and one day, upwards of one hundred died. This ought to be considered as an awful, and sore judgment upon the people. After spending a little time in Burlington, we rode on, and left the state of New-Jersey; crossed the Delaware river into the state of Pennsylvania, and on to Germantown, and put up at doctor Lusby's. The town was very full of people from

22

Philadelphia. It was generally supposed that four
fifths of the inhabitants of Philadelphia had moved
out of the city; and yet there died, in general, about
sixty a day. The news about the fever engrossed
most part of the conversation, and filled most of the
public prints.

"Saturday, 6th. We rode early, and left the state
of Pennsylvania, and got into the state of Maryland,
and so on to William Howell's, at North-East, and put
up with him. I was greatly pained at hearing of the
apostacy of R—— C——, an old minister, dismally
fallen.

"Sunday, 7th. We stayed at North-East, and at
11 o'clock, Mr. Asbury preached on Heb. xii. 15, 16,
17. He gave us a good discourse, and I think, was
profitable; I exhorted: there was some little stir
amongst the hearers. Two men were called to an
account in class-meeting, for their conduct at a late
election. Parties were strong in their opposition;
and the Methodists were too busy about politics; and
these men both drank too much. One fought, and
the other pulled off his coat. When called upon to
speak for themselves, they confessed their faults, and
wept aloud, and begged both God and man to forgive
them. All present sympathized with, and forgave
them.

"Tuesday, 9th. We rode to Baltimore; the
weather was warm, and remarkably dry; there had
been very little rain for many weeks. At night, I
attended a prayer meeting in the new church, and the
presence of the Lord was there, and the people were
much quickened.—My soul was happy.

"Monday, 15th. Brother John Harper set out
with me about sunrise; we rode to Georgetown, and

put up at colonel Bell's. It was a hard day's ride, about forty-four miles The next day we made an early start, took breakfast in Alexandria, and there met with Mr. Asbury. We then set out, rode through Colchester, and Dumfries, to brother Ward's, where we stayed all night.

"Saturday, 20th. I left my company and rode to Petersburg, where I met with some of my brothers.

" Tuesday, 30th. We rode to George Trotter's, where we met with Mr. Asbury and several preachers. It was a day appointed for Mr. Asbury to meet the local preachers, but we had but three or four of them present. We talked and prayed together, and were much united in love and friendship.

" Wednesday, 31st. At Paup's meeting-house, Mr. Asbury preached on Eph. v. 25, 26, 27. He gave us a good discourse. Then I exhorted, and the power of the Lord was amongst us ; many wept, and some cried aloud with deep distress. Then Miles Harper exhorted, and dismissed the assembly. The class was desired to remain. Brother Mead, who was present, began to sing, and in a little while many were affected, and a general weeping began. John Easter proclaimed aloud, ' I have not a doubt in my soul but what my God will convert a soul to day !' The preachers then requested all that were under conviction to come together. Several men and women came, and fell upon their knees ; and the preachers, for some time, kept singing, and exhorting the mourners to expect a blessing from the Lord ; till the cries of the mourners became truly awful Then prayer was made in behalf of the mourners, and two or three found peace. My soul did magnify the Lord, and rejoice in God my Saviour. Here I end the

month, in which I have travelled about five hundred
miles ; I have felt much peace and comfort in my
soul.   I hope the next month will be more devoted to
God than what this has been.   Even so : amen, and
amen !

"Thursday, November 8th.   We rode to Daniel
Shine's, who married Gabriel Long's widow.   I
inquired where brother Long was buried, and went to
his grave, and stood by it a few minutes with a grateful remembrance of his past kindness to me.   When I
lived with him nineteen years ago, I do not remember
ever to have seen a man, who was a private Christian,
that equalled him for piety and a depth of religion.
His surviving consort told me he died very happy.
He left no will.—The reason why he left no will, was
owing, probably, to his being opposed to slavery, and
the laws of the state would not allow him to free them,
and he was not disposed to will them to any particular
person."

He continued his tour, principally in company with
bishop Asbury, through the Carolinas, then crossed
the Savannah river at the Cherokee ford into Georgia ;
and the last day of the year found him in Charleston,
ready for the conference, which was to commence the
next day.

CHAPTER XV.

—◆—

Reflections at the commencement of the year.—Conference at Charleston.—Commencement of a revival at Lockwood's Folly, related by Mr. Belvieu.—Conference in Baltimore.—Conference in Philadelphia.—Do. in New-York.—An earthquake.—An account of Martin Boehm's conversion, and call to the ministry.—Goes to the south.—Forms Oconee circuit, in Georgia.—Views the ruins of Mr. Whitefield's Orphan Asylum.—Returns to Virginia.—Conference at Blunt's in Isle of Wight.—Goes to Maryland.—Conference at Stone Chapel.

TUESDAY, January 1, 1799. I have now entered upon a new year. O my soul! enter thou into greater depths of the joy of the Lord. I felt fresh desires to spend the year, if spared, more to the glory of God, than what I have done in my former years. Our conference met in Charleston, at 9 o'clock. We had thirty-three preachers present, which belonged to the travelling connexion, including those who were just received to travel the ensuing year. Several young men were received, and some of them were highly recommended.

"Friday, 4th. Conference met at half past 8 o'clock. At half after 10, Mr. Asbury preached on Heb. xiii. 17, 18. After sermon we ordained seven deacons, and three elders. We met in conference again at 3 o'clock, and finished our business. We had much love and union amongst us during the time we were together. We parted in much love. Thomas Humphries, Mark Moore, Henry M. Gaines, and

22 *

Richard Posey, located. John N. Jones had died the summer before. We sent George Clark to form a circuit about St. Mary's, in Georgia. O that we may ever love and serve the Lord, and continue united in love, all our days!

" Wednesday, 30th. Mr. Asbury and myself left Charleston, and crossed Cooper river at Clemon's ferry, and rode to brother Jackson's, at Cainehoy, and stayed all night. Here I would observe, that I stayed four weeks and almost two days in Charleston ; in which I preached seventeen times, besides attending many other meetings, both in public and in private, and I often had such faith in the promises of God, and such a sense of his presence, that I could not doubt but what the Lord would revive his work amongst the people ; I frequently spoke of my feelings concerning this matter. Mr. Asbury seemed to think differently, and frequently expressed his awful fears, that the people were growing worse and worse. Well, let the matter turn out as it may, I know that God was amongst the people, and that my expectation of a revival of religion afforded comfort to my soul.

" Friday, February 1st. We rode about fifty miles, and made it till after 10 o'clock, before we got to Mr. Boon's. Mr. Asbury ran his carriage against a stump, and turned it over, and hurt his arm a little by falling out.

" Thursday, 7th. At Little river meeting-house, Mr. Asbury preached, and I followed, on 1 Cor. xv. 33. Several people were much wrought upon. Lord, make our labours a lasting blessing to many souls. We then left South Carolina, and rode into the state of North Carolina.—Came to Mr. Gause', and stayed all night.

" Sunday, 10th. At Charlotte meeting-house, Mr. Asbury preached. and after an intermission of fifteen minutes, I preached. God was in the midst of us. Several young converts were present ; and they, with others, were deeply melted into tears ; some of them could hardly refrain from roaring aloud. Glory be to God in the highest, for this meeting. We then rode to friend Belvieu's. There I received some account of the beginning of the late revival of religion, which began at this house.

" On the 24th of December last, one of our friends was at Mr. Belvieu's house, and prayed in the family. The next night, Mr. Belvieu said to a young man, ' what shall we do about prayer to nigh: ?' The young man said he did not know, he would read, and sing a hymn, if the other would pray. The other said he could not pray. However, after supper the young man came out of the other room, and said to Mr. Belvieu, ' I feel a desire to pray in the family, and I wish you would call the black people together.' Mr. Belvieu told me he felt struck with astonishment, and did not know whether he was in earnest or not ; however, he went to the door to call the black people, but before he had time to call them, one of the women in the house began to pray earnestly, and he ran back into the house, and they were soon in a flood of tears. All the people now flocked into the house, and the young man began to pray ; and they continued praying till Mr. Belvieu's wife got converted ; and the young man who prayed, also became a subject of converting grace, and others were deeply distressed on the account of their sins. And thus they continued praying and rejoicing, till late in the night ; this was the beginning of a revival of religion on Lockwood's Folly ;

and it has prospered since; many having been born again, and brought into the liberty of the children of God. There is still a blessed prospect of religion in the neighbourhood. Lord increase it.

"Sunday, March 17th. We rode to William's meeting-house, Mr. Asbury preached; he finished his discourse, dismissed the assembly, and went to his lodgings. After a few minutes, I preached on 2 Peter iii. 17. I spoke very plainly and pointedly to the people, and the power of the Lord attended the word to many hearts. A little more than sixteen years ago, I came with brother E. Drumgoole, into these parts, before any Methodists came to form a circuit. At that time I felt much concerned for the souls of the people; but have never had it in my power to come amongst them from that time until now. The Lord has wrought wonders since that time; and the work of grace has not stopped: Lord carry it on more abundantly! We lodged that night at Edward Burrell's."

After visiting Norfolk, Portsmouth, and Princess-Ann, where a good and gracious work of religion was progressing, they came on to Sussex, where conference was to be held.

"Tuesday, April 9th. I rode to Stith Parham's, and put up. At 9 o'clock conference met in Jones' Chapel, in Sussex county, Virginia, and upwards of fifty preachers had assembled. Conference broke up the 11th. At this conference we received nine preachers on trial, and admitted seven into full connexion. Thirteen located, and one had died. We had lost some in the number of our members.

"Wednesday, May 1st. Our conference began in Baltimore. Many preachers were present. We set three hours in the forenoon, and about three hours in the afternoon.

"Saturday, 4th. At sunrise, Seely Bunn preached on Heb. xi. 24—26. He gave us a good discourse, and it had some weight on the minds of the people.— We set in conference again both in the forenoon and in the afternoon, and then finishing the business, we dismissed the conference. We had a good peaceable time amongst the preachers. They were affectionate, but had no great stir of religon, or any very lively meetings.

"After we had finished our business in conference, four of the largest preachers amongst us went to a friend's store, and were weighed. My weight was 259*lbs.* Seely Bunn's 252, Thomas Lucas' 245, and Thomas F. Sergent weighed 220 ; in all 976*lbs.* A *wonderful* weight for four Methodist preachers, and all of us travel on horse back.

"Wednesday, 8th. We went down to the ferry to cross the bay, and the wind appeared quite too high for us to venture over, so we turned back to the house, and Mr. Asbury concluded to go round the head of the bay. and leave me to cross alone, and to attend to the appointments till he could come to me. I waited about two hours, and then took boat, and crossed the Chesapeake Bay, in an hour, where it was about seven miles wide. I went to Doctor Anderson's, where I spent the afternoon and night. I felt thankful to the Lord for his preserving goodness towards me that day.

"Tuesday, 14th. We rode down to Doctor Allen's, and spent a little time with him, and then went to Easton, where I preached. My subject was Jude 3. I had a blessed time in speaking to the people, and my soul was much quickened ; there was a good.

move in the congregation. Mr. Asbury and C. Spry exhorted with power. I was quite astonished to see what a number of people had collected at our meeting. The house was filled from end to end, gallerys and all, and abundance of people, out of doors, that could not get in. Glory be to God, for that precious meeting! We then pursued our journey, crossed Choptank river at Dover ferry, and went home with William Frazier, and stayed all night. This place was once a home for me, when I rode this circuit, almost fourteen years ago. I was truly thankful to the Lord for bringing me there once more.

"Friday, 31st. We rode early, and reached Milford a little after the middle of the day. At 4 o'clock I preached on Eccle. xii. 13. I had a good degree of liberty and power in preaching. It was a solemn time and a melting season with many of them. Surely God was there! Mr. Asbury then ordained three deacons, and then exhorted; we had a crowded congregation, and a very profitable meeting. It has been about twelve years since I was in this town. Since then, the place has considerably improved, and religion has gained some ground. I here had the pleasure of seeing many of my old acquaintances, and one who was formerly a very pious man, is now a poor backslider. He wept greatly while I was speaking; and afterward when I talked to him, I could scarcely refrain from tears.

"Saturday, June 1st. I preached at sunrise in Milford; and then rode to Barrett's Chapel in Fredirica, and preached at 11 o'clock. The Lord owned his word and made it profitable to some souls. We then rode to Dover, and put up at Abraham Ridgely's, who is secretary of the state of Delaware, took dinner with

him, and then went over to Richard Bassett's, who is
the governor of the state, and took tea with him. He
and the secretary and their wives are all Methodists.
At night the secretary of state went to the state-house
and rung the bell for meeting. We met, and Ezekiel
Cooper preached, and Ephraim Chambers exhorted.

"Thursday, 6th. Our yearly conference began,
in Philadelphia. We met at 9 o'clock in the forenoon,
and at 3 o'clock in the afternoon, we had a large number of preachers together; at night I preached on
Matt. iii. 2. *Repent for the kingdom of Heaven is
at hand.* I had great freedom in speaking, and was
led out far beyond my expectation in explaining the
text, and the word took hold of many hearts; some
roared aloud, and some shouted: glory be to God!
it was a good time to my poor soul. I felt as if I
could have met my Lord with pleasure, and have gone
from the pulpit to glory.

"Friday, 7th. We met in conference again. We
had a pretty good day, and the hearts of the brethren
were much united. Business at night, prevented me
from going to meeting.

"Wednesday, 12th. At 5 o'clock, in the morning,
Anning Owen preached. He gave us a lively discourse, and several of the people were melted into
tears. We set in conference again, and after spending a little time together, we finished our business,
and conference broke up, and the preachers dispersed.
The next day we made an early start, and just before
night we left the state of Pennsylvania, crossed the
Delaware river into the state of New-Jersey, and
rode to brother Cobb's, in Trenton. At night I
preached to a little congregation, and with some
liberty. The day following we met with Mr. Asbury

at Brunswick, and after dinner rode to Mr. Harnet's, and stayed all night with him.

"Saturday, 15th.   We rode early, stopped a while in Elizabeth-town.   Then rode to Newark, and crossed the North river into the state of New-York, a little before night.   I put up in the city at brother Philip I. Arcularius'.

"Wednesday, 19th.   Our conference began at 9 o'clock, in New-York. We had several candidates brought forward to travel, and they were mostly received.   We had a large number of preachers at conference ; and they brought pleasing accounts, from their respective circuits, of a gracious work of God amongst the people.

"Thursday, 20th.   We set in conference again, and examined the characters of the preachers, and I was thankful to find that they had generally adorned the gospel in their lives and conversation.

"Saturday, 22d.   We met in conference again, and in the forenoon we finished our business, and the preachers left the city : we had a good conference, and we had an increase of members in society, especially in the New-England states.   The Lord has been very good and gracious to the preachers in the bounds of this conference.   On sabbath, in our different congregations, we collected three hundred dollars for our travelling preachers.

"Wednesday, 26th.   Crossed Croton river, and stopped at Gen. Courtlandt's, where we took dinner. At Croton church, 2 o'clock, I preached on 1 Cor. ix. 27.   I had a happy time in public ; my soul was much quickened and refreshed with the presence of God. Then Mr. Asbury exhorted.   We then rode on, but had to stop a while to get out of a shower of rain, and then rode again, when there came on a very heavy thunder gust, and we had to stop an hour or upwards. We then put on again. When we got to Peekskill, I rode up to a house, where lived a *Methodist*, and wished to stay all night, the good woman made many excuses. I told her Mr. Asbury was sick ; it was then dusk, and raining : but she said it would be best for him to lodge at the next house, and we went there, but the man said they were not prepared to entertain strangers. So we went on, and got to old governor Courtlandt's, some time after they were all in bed ; however, they arose and received us gladly. I was truly thankful that we did not stop till we got here. We were well entertained, and comfortably accommodated in the governor's house.

"Tuesday, July 30th. About 5 o'clock, in the morning, having just arose out of bed, I heard a very strange noise, but could not tell whether it was thunder, cannons, or a roaring in the chimney. I went to the window, but saw nothing. I then concluded it must be an earthquake, which was confirmed that day by others who heard it in other places. Just before night we rode to old friend Martin Boehm's ; he was formerly a minister amongst the Menonists, chosen by them to preach before he was converted, or had any intention of preaching. The custom of the Menonists in making choice of a preacher is this : When they want a minister, they assemble together, and choose one by ballot, and then they take two, three, or more of those that have the largest number of votes, and take as many tickets, and put them in a book, and write on one, ' This is to be the minister', and each of these men draw out a ticket. and he that draws the one with the writing on it, is to be their minister. Old

23

friend Boehm told me he was thus chosen. He inquired of the people what he must preach. They told him, ' Repentance and faith.' He began preaching, and soon after got awakened, and converted, and then preached so much of repentance and faith, that he was afterward disowned for it. He is now united with us, and has children and grand children in our society. The old man wears his beard at its full growth. He preaches altogether in the German language ; after I prayed in the family at night, he prayed in German.

" Wednesday, 31st. At friend Boehm's meeting-house I preached on Isai. xxx. 21. I had a very precious season in preaching, and the power of the Lord was with us : and there were many tears shed by the hearers ; thank God for another happy meeting. Then Mr. Asbury preached on Heb. vi. 12. He gave us a good discourse. I then went and took a view of the grave of William Jessop, who was buried at the meeting-house between three and four years ago. He was a favoured friend of mine, and a travelling preacher for many years. I felt very solemn when I thought of his departure. I understood that he departed this life in the full triumph of faith. His last words were ' my work is done, Glory ! Glory ! Glory !' and so died away. O Lord, let me die the death of the righteous !

" Saturday, August 17th. It rained considerably in the forenoon, which was greatly needed, for there had been a remarkable drought for many weeks ; we set off about 11 o'clock, and rode to Winchester. I preached in the meeting-house to a small congregation, and most of them were from the country, it being quarterly meeting. After meeting I went and visited the prisoners, and there I found E. J—— confined in irons, waiting to be tried for his life. He was the same man I visited in Washington, in the state of Georgia, last December, on the day he was to have been executed, being condemned for stealing a negro ; but the day of his execution was put off for a few weeks, and he says he was afterwards pardoned. When I talked to him in Georgia, a few hours before he expected to be hanged, he said he had made his peace with God, and believed he should be saved. His life is no better, for all his pretended religion. I fear most part of the penitents in a dungeon are but little better. Yet I believe some have sought and found favour with God."

From Winchester, he proceeded in company with Bishop Asbury, attending numerous appointments in Virginia, then through North and South Carolina into the state of Georgia. Having yet some time to spare, before the commencement of the southern conference, Mr. Lee endeavoured to employ this time actively : and formed a new circuit in Georgia, between the Oconee, and Appalachy rivers. This circuit was called Oconee, after the river of that name. This new settlement, which was then formed into a two weeks circuit, has since widened into a district, and many have been brought into the fold through the instrumentality of the Methodists. After forming the Oconee circuit, he spent a few weeks in travelling through other parts of the state of Georgia, and then went to Charleston, to attend the conference, which commenced in that place the 1st of January, 1800. The conference continued four days, and every thing was conducted with peace and propriety. Seven young men were received into the travelling ministry, as probationers ; none had died during the year, and not one location was called for ; accounts from all circuits were favourable.

Leaving Charleston on the 7th, he set his face again towards Georgia. In his journey he had to encounter with weather unusually severe for that climate. On the 10th he found the snow two feet and a half deep on a level. " Such a snow (says he) I suppose was never seen in these parts before by the oldest person living ; the family, black and white people, were frightened half out of their wits. I don't remember that I ever saw more snow fall in one day and night in New-England, than what fell in South Carolina and Georgia. It was very cold withal." This snow made great destruction amongst the trees and undergrowth, so as to render travelling extremely difficult. However he continued to push on, and on the 12th reached Savannah in Georgia, where the depth of the snow continued almost undiminished ; and he was induced to tarry in Savannah one day, which gave him an opportunity of preaching for the first time in his life in that place. The next day he went on, crossed the Ogeechee, and on the 13th aimed to get into Barrington, but was bewildered amongst the ponds, and at night was glad to get shelter in a log cabin without any doors, and thirty or forty hogs sleeping under it : these were some of his *consolations* in that newly inhabited country. On the 16th he crossed the Altamaha with much difficulty, and not without danger, as the flat in which they were ferried over, was so old and rotten that it would hardly hold together. On the 17th he rode fifty computed miles, which brought him to the Sattilla river, and from thence the next day he reached the town of St. Mary's. " Here (says he) I was brought to think of the great goodness of God towards me in my extensive travels, through the United States. I have been twice through them to the north, into the British government, and am now at the dividing line, between the States and Florida in the south. Surely I ought always to rejoice and praise the Lord, for his kindness both to my soul and body."

On Sunday, 19th, he preached in the court-house, in St. Mary's, to a large congregation of attentive hearers, and felt a hope that good was done, both in the forenoon and afternoon. And even in this remote place he met with friends and an old acquaintance from Virginia. From St. Mary's he hurried on, through mud, water and swamps, making long rides, and preaching every day. On the 25th he rode fifty miles, and preached on the way; arrived at night at Mr. John Linder's, where he makes the following remarks. "I have been absent from this place six nights and seven days. I have rode in this time about one hundred and sixty-five miles. I have remarked that the country is very level, and the land very poor, except near the water courses, being mostly low pine, barren, and almost covered with what is called *saw pimento*, but on the river Sattilla and a few other places, the land is good. The country is no doubt very sickly, except on the Sattilla, which is a tide river, and the town of St. Mary's, which is open to the sea, and situated on a dry sandy bluff. The country is very good for cattle, but at present it is a poor place for piety or morality, few people making any profession of religion, and many who are addicted to very bad habits, find a dwelling in these parts. Drunkenness is very common amongst the people. Persons who violate the

23 *

laws of their country find it convenient to flee from justice, either to the Indians on the west or the Spaniards on the south, and thus get out of the laws of the United States. I heard of some people in those two counties, Glenn and Camden, that were grown up, and some that had families, who had never heard a sermon or a prayer in all their lives, until last summer, when brother George Clark first came amongst them. Surely these people will receive the gospel, and press into the kingdom of God."

"Friday, 24th. We rested at brother Linder's. I found a rest day to be very profitable to me. The day past away very agreeably, but after we had been in bed a few hours, we were waked out of our sleep by a drunken man, who beset the house with a heavy club in different places, and called to the family to get up, and swore that he would be the death of the preachers. I was fearful he would do mischief, so I arose and fastened the room door. At last he went to another house hard by, and they gave him a torch in his hand, and he went off."

Here he rested again the day following; made out the plan of the new circuit which he had formed in his late tour, which was called St. Mary's. From thence he went on toward Savannah, at which place he arrived the 29th.

"Friday, 31st," he has these remarks in his journal. "Mr. Miller, and Mr. Holcomb, a Baptist, and myself, rode down about twelve miles to Bethesda, to see Whitefield's orphan house. I felt very solemn in viewing the ruins of that institution. There were two wings of the building standing; they were of brick, one story high, and about one hundred and thirty feet long, with four chimneys in each. These

buildings are going to decay very fast, one of the
chimneys has fallen down. In one of these wings lives
a small family ; some negroes live in a part of the other
wing ; and a part is used for a horse stable. There
was an old dwelling house also, that was likely soon
to fall down. The brick walls which formerly enclosed
the yard, were levelled with the earth, and in places,
ploughed up to the foundation. The place, taking in
land and buildings, rented for thirty dollars a year.
There was no school of any kind kept on the pre-
mises. I understood that the general assembly of
Georgia had taken possession of the place, and also,
another plantation, and the slaves which belonged to
it ; the whole is rented out, and the profits arising
therefrom are applied in maintaining a small school of
orphan children, who are educated not far from that
place. I viewed these ruins with great sorrow ; and
called to mind the great collections of money for the
use of the institution, and the many prayers offered
up to God for his blessing upon it ; and the pains
which had been taken to carry it into successful ope-
ration ; and then to see the gloomy appearance which
it made, I felt a secret wish that the Lord would open
the way for some good to be done by it yet.

"Monday, February 3d. I left Savannah, and
preached at a meeting-house called Goshen. The
next day I rode, pretty early, up to the Sister's ferry,
crossed the Savannah river into the state of South
Carolina, and so went to William Manius', about five
miles from the ferry, and stayed all night. In these
parts, the snow that fell when I was there before, had
lain in some places two weeks. Here I will observe,
that I had been in the state of Georgia twenty-four
days ; in which time I preached eleven times ; rode

four hundred miles ; and most of the time, the
weather had been disagreeable either for travelling or
preaching."

Friday, 7th. He reached Charleston, and at night,
preached to a congregation, who received the word
with much apparent delight. On the 11th, he left
Charleston, went on by Cainehoy, crossed Santee
river, and with much difficulty, reached Mr. Boon's.
The roads were exceedingly bad. On the 13th, he
reached Georgetown, and preached. He left Georgetown on the 15th, crossed Black river, and Peedee,
went on by Kingston, and then into the state of North
Carolina; took Charlotte, and Lockwood's Folly, in
his way ; and from thence to Wilmington. At this
place, he had an opportunity of paying a tribute of
respect to the memory of General George Washington. America was in mourning at that time, in consequence of his death. Mr. Lee partook of the common sentiment and feeling of a nation, on this mournful occasion. Though it is needless to award the
meed of praise to a man who so richly deserved, and
so unanimously received the applause of mankind, yet
we cannot pass over the notice of this event, without
paying our tribute of respect to the man whom a
nation delighteth to honour. By Americans the name
of WASHINGTON will always be pronounced with
respect and gratitude, while foreign nations will unite
in eulogizing his political and domestic virtues, and in
perpetuating his fame as the father of his country.
" Honour to whom honour is due, and tribute to whom
tribute is due."

From Wilmington he proceeded on through North
Carolina, chiefly in company with bishop Asbury,
whom he assisted in his travels, and in his labours,

For three years had he been engaged in travelling
extensively through the several conferences, as a
helper to Mr. Asbury. It has been stated before, that
Mr. Asbury's health was such as to make it absolutely
necessary that some person should be with him, and
assist him. Mr. Lee was the man who rendered him
every assistance in his power ; and the conferences
confided in his integrity, while he manifested an
unshaken determination to promote the interests of
the church ; and this he continued to do as long as
his services were required.

In April, the Virginia conference was to have met
in Norfolk ; but in consequence of the small pox,
which prevailed in Norfolk, at that time, it was thought
most expedient to remove the setting of conference to
Blunt's meeting-house, in Isle of Wight county. This
point being determined, the preachers met at Blunt's
accordingly, and conference opened on the 9th of
April. "Here a certain person (says Mr. Lee)
laboured hard to keep the preachers from going to
the ensuing general conference, and endeavoured to
make them promise him to go immediately to their
circuits." Of the propriety or impropriety of this,
we shall not undertake to determine.

From the conference at Blunt's, he went on
toward the north, crossed James' river, at old James'
town, where the first inhabitants of Virginia settled.
"I went (says he) to the site of the old town on
the island, and spent some time amongst the tombs,
in viewing the stones, some of which had been
engraven more than a hundred years ; but the church
is quite demolished, except the brick walls of the
steeple." He then proceeded on through Williamsburg, and Yorktown, crossed York river, into Glouces-

ter, and went to Joseph Bellamy's ; from thence through King, and Queen, on by Port Royal, Dumfries, and Alexandria, and then into Maryland, to the conference, which was held at the Stone chapel, about ten miles from Baltimore, and commenced the 1st of May. Here he was a little surprised that a certain person did not insist on any of the preachers going immediately to their circuits, but appeared entirely willing for them all to attend the general conference. But the reason appears to have been, that they were all now within ten miles of the place where the general conference was to be held, a few days after.

The conference at Stone chapel, finished its business on Saturday, the 3d, and spent the sabbath in peaceful worship ; and on the 5th, rode to Baltimore, ready for general conference, which commenced the day following.

CHAPTER XVI.

—◦◦◦—

Retrospection.—Attends the General Conference in Baltimore.
—Very near being elected Bishop.—False reports cleared
up.—Goes to the north, as far as Lower Canada.—Returns
to New-York.—Remarks at the close of the year.

THE traveller in pursuing his journey through a
country, variegated with lofty hills, pleasant dales,
and flowing streams, takes a pleasure, sometimes in
stopping upon some eminence, and turning his eyes
towards the place from whence he set off ; and thence
of ruminating upon the path which his feet have trod,
and the incidents of his journey, until his thoughts are
arrested in the contemplation of the pleasing land-
scape spread before him ; or follows the turbulent
stream bounding over the rocks and seeking its way
to more peaceful waters afar off. Thus the writer of
this memoir, feels an inclination to pause a moment,
and take a short retrospect of " *days gone by;*" days
indeed, in which the subject of our remarks was inti-
mately connected.

  At the close of the eighteenth century Methodism
had existed in America only about thirty years. The
spirit which animated a Wesley, and prompted him to
attempt a reformation in religion throughout the kingdom of Great Britain, inspired also the mind of a Capt.
Webb, who, in a military costume, preached the gospel in its purity, in the city of New-York. He was a
loyal subject of George III. and a faithful servant of
the King of kings.

The faithful exertions of Capt. Webb, and of Mr.
Embury, in New-York and Pennsylvania, and of
Robert Strawbridge, in Maryland, afforded substantial
proof to Mr. Wesley, that there were materials
in America, of which Methodism might be formed.
The British Conference was called to offer its assistance in furnishing men and means, to spread the gospel on the shores of America. Two volunteers,
Messrs. Boardman and Pilmore, nobly stepped forward, and tendered their services, which were accepted; and they came with a present of fifty pounds in
their hands, as a testimony of affection from the British Conference, to their brethren on this side of the
water. When they landed, which was on the 24th of
October, 1769, they found a great and effectual door
opened for the preaching of the gospel. They often
preached in the open fields, and thousands flocked to
hear. The reception which these men met with,
enabled them to send a favourable report *home* to Mr.
Wesley, and within two years after their arrival, they
received the aid of two others; viz. Francis Asbury
and Richard Wright. The Methodists in Europe and
America, were governed by the same rules, and all
aimed at the same thing; namely, the spread of vital
religion. The rules and discipline which had been
adopted by the brethren in the old world governed
those in the new. Mr. Wesley, being well apprised
that in all associations there must be some one to take
the lead, selected Mr. Asbury as a fit person to have
the superintending charge of the preachers and societies in America. Providence seems evidently to have
directed him in his choice. Though the labourers
were but few, and the fields large, they endeavoured
to surmount difficulties, and apply their strength to

the best advantage. In 1773, Mr. Wesley sent to
the assistance of those preachers already in America,
Messrs. Rankin and Shadford. As Mr. Rankin had
been engaged in travelling and preaching longer than
any who were in America, Mr. Wesley therefore
transferred the superintendency to him. Soon after
his arrival, a conference of preachers was called,
which was convened in Philadelphia; and it was
ascertained that the strength of the Methodists con-
sisted in ten travelling preachers, and eleven hundred
and sixty members. The work extended from New-
York to Virginia; but there were many intermediate
places where they were not known.

The revolutionary war, which commenced in a few
years after, greatly checked the missionary enterprize
amongst the Methodists; many of the societies were
dispersed, and the preachers were much disquieted by
the confusion which prevailed amidst the collision of
political parties.

After a long and arduous struggle, the sanguinary
conflict came to an end, and the independence of the
United States was acknowledged by the European powers. This event was no less favourable to the church
than to the nation. Through the labours of God's
servants his cause began to prosper, and Methodism
felt the fostering hand of the benevolent Father of our
spirits. In the year 1784, the societies in America,
were organized into a church. In 1800, the time of
which we are now speaking, and about 30 years from
the commencement of Methodism in this country, the
Methodist preachers were spread all over the United
States, and had penetrated into the wilds of Upper
Canada, and the province of Nova Scotia. They enumerated one hundred and fifty-six travelling preachers,

24

and between sixty and seventy thousand church members.

From the year 1784, the time in which the church
was regularly organized, and Messrs. Asbury and
Coke were appointed bishops, or general superintendents, there was a regular and annual increase of labour.
Doctor Coke, however, could not be prevailed upon
to confine himself to America; but from the multipli-
city of plans which engaged his attention, he was
obliged to spend the greater part of his time either in
the island of Great Britain, or the West Indies.
Bishop Asbury was, therefore, left with the whole
burden of the superintendency, which, through affliction of body, he was not able to sustain. He had made
application to the preceding general conference for
an assistant; but upon Doctor Coke's giving some
assurance to the conference that he would give his
services entirely to the Methodists in America, Mr.
Asbury did not insist upon the appointment of any
other at that time. Doctor Coke soon discovered that
he had promised more than he was able to perform;
for we do not learn that he was present at more than
one or two conferences, from the year 1796, until the
year 1800. During this period, Mr. Asbury, through
extreme weakness and debility, found it necessary to
call to his assistance Mr. Lee; who, by the voice of
the annual conference, held at Wilbraham, in 1797,
was appointed to travel with, and to assist Mr. Asbury
in his labours; but whilst Doctor Coke was absent,
there could be no ordination unless Mr. Asbury was
present. Weak as he was, he found it necessary to
exert all his remaining strength in attending to the
frequent calls for ordination, at the several annual
conferences, and elsewhere. Worn down under these

toils, he came to the conclusion, that unless the Episcopacy was strengthened at the general conference of
1800, he would be under the necessity of resigning,
and it is said, had even prepared his valedictory
address. The conference, therefore, took his case
under consideration, and resolved that another bishop
should be appointed.

At that time there were two men, among many
others, who deservedly stood high in the estimation of
the members of the general conference—Mr. Whatcoat and Mr. Lee. The former came to this country
in 1784, in company with Doctor Coke and Mr. Vasey.
Mr. Whatcoat commenced his ministerial labours in
Great Britain, about the year 1769 ; and was, therefore, older than Mr. Lee, both in years and in the
ministry. His experience and deep piety, and tried
integrity, entitled him to great respect ; but his
strength of body had evidently much declined through
labour.

Mr. Lee was known amongst the preachers, as a
persevering and indefatigable man, of acknowledged
integrity, and of uniform piety ; who possessed zeal
which was not easily damped, and his experience
could not be called in question. He had followed the
fortunes of the Methodist church, almost from its first
rise in America ; and he knew how business should be
transacted ; he was plain and undisguised in his manners, and was greatly gifted as a speaker. To these
two men the attention of the general conference was
directed ; but when put to the test, a small majority
was in favour of Mr. Whatcoat, who was, therefore,
elected bishop. Although to be a bishop of the Methodist church, was an office which Mr. Lee was far from
coveting, yet it was a source of some regret to him

that the election was not conducted with that coolness
and impartiality which the solemnity of the occasion
required.

The following extract from his journal will fully
explain his views and feelings on this subject.

" Tuesday, 13th of May.   There was some uneasiness in the minds of some of the preachers respecting
a report which had been circulated by some person or
persons, in order to prevent my election to the
bishop's office.   The report was this :—' that Mr.
Asbury said that brother Lee had imposed himself on
him and on the connexion, for eighteen months past,
and he would have got rid of him long ago if he could.'
They came to me about it, and I told them I did not
believe that Mr. Asbury said it ; but if he had reported
it, I could prove to the reverse ; so I went to Mr.
Asbury about it, who denied it, and said he wished
me to consent to travel at large in future, and to attend
the conferences, and assist in the business thereof, for
he and brother Whatcoat could never do it ; and added
that if I would not consent to go, he thought he should
be forced to resign at the close of the conference.   I
told him I despised the idea of doing any thing out of
resentment, and that I had but two things in view,
respecting my manner of travelling : one was the peace
and happiness of my own mind ; and the other was,
the good of the church, and Methodism at large ; and
that I had but little expectation of complying with his
request, though I was not fully determined against it.
I then told him if he found freedom, I wished he would
speak in conference about the report above mentioned.
So we went into conference, and he spoke to the subject, and denied the charge, and said he was thankful
for my past services, and did wish for them in the con-

ferences in future. We traced the report until we fixed it on T——— L———, and he did not clear himself."

So true it is, "that envy always finds a mark to shoot at." These insinuations, thrown out at a time of general excitement, no doubt had a tendency to influence the minds of some against Mr. Lee, and in all probability, was the cause why he was not elected.

From this statement of facts, we may perceive that he had many warm friends, who esteemed him highly for his work's sake ; but though he doubtless had enemies, it is not necessary to suppose all were such who opposed his election to the office of a bishop. While they gave a preference to another for this high office, they might have had the fullest confidence in his integrity, and the warmest affection for his person. But we dismiss this subject by observing, that though much more might have been said, yet to have said less would have been an act of injustice to the dead. "He that desireth the office of a bishop, desireth a good thing."

After much business as well as faithful preaching, the conference closed its session in peace and harmony.

There was scarcely a sermon delivered but was attended with the displays of divine power. While the attention of the people was awakened, and the meeting-houses were thronged with hearers, Mr. Lee thought once more of the commons, and the market-house ; places at which he had formerly preached to thousands ; and he now concluded to make another trial in the market-house. The following extract will show that he had no cause to regret his labour.

"Sunday, 18th of May, at 5 o'clock in the market-house, on Howard's hill, I preached on John xvii. 3.

24 *

And this is life eternal, that they might know thee the only true God, and Jesus Christ whom thou hast sent. The power of the Lord came down amongst us while I was speaking, and the people wept and roared aloud, and prayed most earnestly. Joseph Totten exhorted with life. Afterward several prayed with those that were under conviction. I was afterward informed by letter, that seven souls were awakened by the sermon and brought to God. Thank the Lord for a few more seals to my ministry under the market-house."

Tuesday, 20th, conference finished its business. Mr. Lee's remarks are worthy of observation, and by the way, prove that his mind was not at all chagrined at the circumstance of his not being elected to the office of a bishop. We are inclined to think that he viewed it as a matter of minor importance that another was, in that respect, preferred before him. " I believe (says he) we never had so good a general conference before ; we had the greatest speaking, and the greatest union of affections that we had ever had on a like occasion."

Leaving Baltimore, he proceeded to conference at Duck creek, which commenced the 2d of June. Here extraordinary power was displayed under the preaching of the gospel, during the five days in which the conference was employed in transacting its business. One hundred and fifty souls professed to experience converting grace. Indeed we have no account of any conference that was ever blessed in the same degree before. Mr. Lee acted as secretary to the conference. His travels and labours for the remaining part of the year will be seen from the following extracts.

" Saturday, June 7th. I took my leave of Duck creek, and left several preachers there, who intended

to hold meeting the next day ; one of them had given
out word in public, that they intended to continue
their meeting day and night, as long as the Lord would
convert souls. We had a warm ride to Wilmington,
and some rain ; I got there just before night, and put
up at Allen M'Lane's. In all my serious hours,
whether I was riding or sitting, I would, at times, find
myself lost in meditation, and fancy that I could hear
abundance of people shouting glory! glory to God!
and for some time, if I fell asleep, when I awoke, it
appeared to me as if I could hear many voices shouting glory! honour, and salvation, &c. and being
pleased with the imaginary sound, I would start to
attend to it more particularly, and behold it was a
dream ; but, glory to God! my soul was on the wing,
and I mounted higher and higher by faith and love,
towards heaven.

"Sunday, 8th. I preached in Wilmington at 10
o'clock : my text was, Numb. xxxii. 23. *Ye have
sinned against the Lord : and be sure your sins will find
you out.* The Lord was amongst the people. At 3
o'clock Ezekiel Cooper preached ; and at 5, in the
market-house, Samuel Thomas preached to many
hearers. Then at night, in the meeting-house, I
preached on James i. 21. I had a crowded house,
and there was a great shaking amongst the dry bones ;
and at the close of the meeting the people made such
a noise, that many fled and ran out of the meeting-
house. They could not bear to stay where God was
powerfully present. Just so it was with *guilty Adam,*
when he heard God coming in the garden, he ran to
hide himself; but not to ask forgiveness for his
sins.

" Monday, 9th. We rode to Philadelphia, and at
night I found satisfaction in preaching to the people ;
there was a little move upon the minds of some.

" Tuesday, 10th. I visited several friends in the
city, and at night I preached on 2 Kings vi. 16. We
had another good meeting. A little before night, Mr.
Asbury took me up stairs, and told me, that a good
many of the friends wished me to stay in Philadelphia, and if I chose to stay I might. I told him I did
not wish to stay ; and had rather take a country circuit ; but if he appointed me there, then I must stay.

" Wednesday, 11th. We left Philadelphia, and rode
up the river ; crossed into Burlington, in the state of
New-Jersey. A Baptist minister had an appointment
made for himself at the Baptist meeting-house ; he
asked me to take his place. I accepted the invitation,
and preached on Acts x. 35.

" Saturday, 14th. I rode early ; dined at Elizabeth-
town, and then rode on through Newark, and crossed
the North river at Powles-Hook, into the city of
New-York.

" Sunday, 15th. I preached at the North church
in the afternoon, at 3 o'clock, and in the Bowery at
six ; at night went to hear Joseph Pilmore.

" Thursday, 19th. Our conference began in New-
York at 9 o'clock in the morning. At night in the
old church, I preached on Luke ix. 60. I spoke a
good deal to the ministers, and endeavoured to stir
them up, to continue in the work of the ministry. It
was a weeping time amongst the preachers, and there
was a solemn sense of the goodness of God resting
upon many. Glory to God for his goodness to me,
and for his presence in the congregation.

"Saturday, 21st. We sat in conference again, and the bishop put a few lines privately into my hand, which I here transcribe verbatim.

"Jesse Lee is appointed to act as an assistant to the bishops, at the yearly conferences, and to aid the book interest in every part of the continent where he goes.

" DEAR BROTHER,

We wish to close the minutes in York, if we can; you must have some place therein; will the above do? York will be a blank at present; if you choose to stay until you think it meet to go down south, you may; and more, you may make your own appointments south, and omit going eastward, or go if you choose to the east, or if you choose you may come to Kentucky.

FRANCIS ASBURY,
RICHARD WHATCOAT."
Saturday morning.

"I then wrote them a few lines, and informed them that I did not feel altogether at liberty to take the appointment, or to travel at large, but if I had any choice, it was, after making a visit to the east, to take a single circuit.

"Saturday, 28th. I left New-York state, and rode into Connecticut, to Joseph Hawkins', in Nodd. At 2 o'clock, I preached on Luke xi. 28. I had a small congregation, and they were very tender; and some of them wept heartily. I talked to several persons about their souls, after I was done preaching, and some of them were not so much engaged as they used to be when I was in these parts before; they promised me with tears in their eyes that they would try and be more engaged in future. I then rode to Samuel S. Smith's, and stayed all night with him; he is a lawyer, and a pr acher among the Methodists.

"Tuesday, July 15th. I rode to Boston, but had no opportunity of preaching. The workmen were engaged in finishing off our meeting-house, and were to have it done in a little time.

"Tuesday, 22d. I left Lynn after dinner, and set out on my eastern tour, having concluded, at Mr. Asbury's request, to visit the eastern states, and then turn up to Vermont state, to Canada, and so round to the city of New-York, and spend the winter in that city. I went on through Salem, and met R. Williston, in Beverly, and we rode to capt. Patche's, in Hamilton. The family were desirous of our preaching with them, but it was too late to get a congregation.

"Tuesday, 29th. I rode through Dover, and so out of New-Hampshire, into the province of Maine. I had a long day's ride to deacon Clark's tavern, in Wells, where I stayed all night. In that place it was remarkably dry, and the crops were greatly injured by the drought; every thing looked very gloomy.

"Tuesday, August 5th. At Mr. Blake's, in Monmouth, at 11 o'clock, I preached on Matt. vi. 10. I had a precious time in preaching to a loving happy people, who wept and rejoiced together: my soul was sweetly lost in love and praise. The Methodists there were all on fire of love. Then at our meeting-house in Monmouth, at 4 o'clock, I preached on 1 John ii. 28. I had a very large congregation, and a happy time. The people were deeply affected, and the power of the Lord was in the midst of us. I was greatly revived at seeing many of my old friends, and many of my own spiritual children, who were engaged in religion.

"Wednesday, 6th. I rode to Kent's hill, in Readfield, and preached in our new meeting-house, to a large congregation of attentive hearers ; they were much engaged with the Lord. I found my soul happy in God, and was much assisted in preaching. The friends stopped after meeting, and I spoke largely to the society by way of advice, and directed them how to conduct themselves as Christians. I also stopped the local preachers and exhorters, and drew a plan for them to hold meetings on the Sabbath, so as not to be idle, or in each others way. I was closely engaged in the business till dark. I had a happy time amongst my old friends ; and found them much more alive to God than they were when I left them. Our friends have built a good meeting-house in the place. I hope it will be a lasting blessing to the neighbourhood.

"Monday, 18th. I swam my horse across Penobscot river, and in Hampden meeting-house, at 3 o'clock, I preached on Luke vii. 50. I had a comfortable time in preaching to the people. As the meeting-house was not finished below stairs, I took the congregation into the gallery, and preached to them there. Then I took leave of my Penobscot friends, but not without painful sensations, as I thought it probable that I should never see them again. I then rode to brother Isaac Davis', on Jordan brook, and stayed all night with him.

"Tuesday, 19th. I rode through to the Twenty-five mile Pond, about twenty miles. When I first travelled this road, about seven years ago, there was no house on that road in all the distance, and now there are nearly twenty houses. I got to John Chaise's, at the Twenty-five mile Pond, about 3 o'clock, and at 4 o'clock I preached. We had a happy time together; saints and sinners felt the power of truth.

"Saturday, September 6th. We set out early in the morning, and rode out to Connecticut river, at Northumberland meeting-house; there I left my travelling companion, and rode down the river, through Lancaster, Dolton, and into Littleton, where I was hailed and stopped by Josiah Newhall, an old acquaintance of mine, who had moved up into the country; I consented to stay all night with him, and was thankful to find a house, though but a small log cabin, where I could lay my head in peace; myself and horses were weary. I was greatly pleased with that part of the country. It was generally level, and rich land near the river, though most of the settlements were new. The mountains on both sides of the river, and the rising grounds at a distance, made a beautiful appearance. The country promises to be very fruitful, and I doubt not but religion will flourish in this country before long. Our preachers have lately formed a circuit there, called Landaff. I rode one hundred and forty-five miles, and preached six times that week.

"Wednesday, 10th. I preached in Bradford. We had prayer meeting at night. There I saw old sister Pickett, who formerly lived in Mr. Wesley's family in London. She came to America, and settled where she now lives, in the state of Vermont. She was, for a great number of years, deprived of the privilege of hearing the Methodists preach, for we had no preacher in that part of the world; yet the Lord spared her to see an answer to her many prayers, and the gospel is now preached in her neighbourhood, by the Methodists, and the Lord has done wonders by their ministry already.

"Saturday, 20th. I rode very early in the morning, and went through Fairfax to St. Alban's, where I dined. Then through Swantown, and crossed Missisque river, and went through Highgate to St. Ormond's, or Dunn's Patent, in Lower Canada, and put up at Peter Miller's, who was very kind. There I met with Peter Vannest, one of the preachers of the circuit; this was the first time I ever visited Lower Canada. I was charmed with the country; it was very rich and level, and healthy withal. I was then at Missisque bay, on the north-east side of Lake Champlain. When I look back on my past travels, I am astonished at the goodness of God towards me, in preserving my health, and keeping me from departing from him.

"Sunday, 21st. At the widow Hogle's, at 8 o'clock in the morning we held a love-feast, and the young converts, as well as some old disciples, spoke very feelingly and freely of their experiences. I was truly happy in God, and wept much amongst my brethren. Then at 10 o'clock, I preached on Gen. xix. 17. There was a great move amongst the people, and they wept in every part of the house. Then we administered the Lord's Supper, and our good God was pleased to meet us at his table, and we did set in heavenly places in Christ Jesus. At 1 o'clock I preached again, on Psa. i. 1. Some of the people were so overcome with the power of God that they fainted, or sunk down into the arms of their friends, or upon the floor. I then took leave of Canada, and my Canada brethren, and rode back to the state of Vermont, and down to Church's, in St. Albans; and at night I preached on Titus ii. 12. I had a sweet

25

time in preaching to the strange people, and they were remarkably attentive, and heard as though it had been for their lives. Then brother Peter Vannest exhorted with some life. We had a crowded house. I have seen no town in Vermont that appears to be so good for farmers as St. Alban's. I was glad to get to bed as soon as the people were dispersed, having rode 18 miles, preached three times, held a lovefeast, and administered the Lord's Supper; and, withal, it was a wet day. Brother Peter Miller, after we left his house that day, came after us, fixed to travel with me for a week. I was thankful for his company.

"Saturday, 27th. We rode through Pawlet and Ruport, and then out of the state of Vermont into the state of New-York. I had been in Vermont eighteen days, including one day which I spent in Canada, and had preached twenty-three sermons. We then rode through Salem to Peter Swetezer's, where we stayed all night. On that plantation Philip Embury died, who was the first Methodist preacher who ever preached in New-York. He was an Irishman by birth, and a house joiner by trade. I heard that he died very happy in God."

He then proceeded on, preaching in Cambridge, Troy, New-Lebanon, and then into the state of Massachusetts, and Connecticut; and on the 14th of October, arrived in the city of New-York; on which day he has the following remarks :—"Here I will observ that it was twelve weeks to a day, from the time I left Lynn, near Boston, till I got to New-York; in which time I rode twelve hundred and sixty-three computed miles, and had preached eighty-nine ser mons. In that tedious journey, the Lord favoured me both in body and soul."

I will here add one more extract from his journals for this year, which will close the chapter.

"December, 31st.   Here let me take a view of the past year.   In the beginning of the year 1800, I was in Charleston, South Carolina ; and had a good time amongst my brethren in the ministry, during the sitting of conference.   Then I went through the lower parts of South Carolina, and Georgia, to the south of Georgia, on to St. Mary's river.   In that journey I had many difficulties, and much consolation in my own soul. In the beginning of February, I returned to Charleston, and after spending a few days there, I set out on the low lands by Georgetown, and so on to Wilmington, in North Carolina.   In the beginning of March, I visited Newbern, and Washington, and then on through Roanoke circuit, and got into Virginia in the close of that month.   I then visited my relations at Petersburg, and in the neighbourhood.   Then I attended conference in Virginia, where we had much union and brotherly love.   From thence I travelled through the lower parts of Virginia, by old Jamestown, Williamsburg, York town, Gloucester, Urbana, and then by Dumfries, Colchester, and Alexandria, and so into Maryland, and attended conference at the Stone chapel, on the first of May.   Then I attended the general conference in Baltimore.   After this, crossed the Chesapeake Bay by Chestertown, head of Chester and Duck creek cross roads, and was at the conference there in the beginning of June.   Then I went by Wilmington, Philadelphia, Burlington, Brunswick, Elizabethtown, Newark ; and crossed Hudson river to New-York, where we held our conference in the latter part of June.   From thence I went by New-Bedford into New-England, by Reading, Newtown,

Southburry, Middletown, Hartford, Pomfret, Milford
Watertown, Cambridge, Boston, to Lynn, where we
held our conference in July.   Then I went by Salem,
Ipswich, Newburyport, Salisbury, Kingston, Poplin,
Epping, Lee, Dover, Berwick, Portland, New-
Gloucester, Poland, Readfield, Hallowell, New-Mil-
ford, Bristol, Union, Belfast, up Penobscot to Orring-
ton, back to the Twenty-five mile Pond, Fort Halifax,
Norriguoor, Seven mile Brook, up Sandy river,
Readstown, Farmington, Jay; up Androscoggin river,
by Bethel, north of the White hills to Upper Coos, on
Kennebeck river, down to Landaff, Haverhill, into
Vermont, by Newbury, Vershire, Onion river, into
Canada; then by St. Alban's, Onion river, Otter
creek, Rutland, Salem, Troy, Albany, New-Lebanon,
Stockbridge, Canaan, Rhinebeck, Poughkeepsie, and
so on to New-York, which finished the year."

It ought to be observed that in all these places, he
preached the gospel of the Son of God to all who
were willing to hear.   So that we may presume that
much spiritual good must have resulted to the souls of
the people ; and long will Jesse Lee be remembered
by those who were profited by his ministry in these
parts of the country.

CHAPTER XVII,

—◦◦◦—

Progress of Methodism in New-York.—Leaves New-York to return to Virginia.—Remarks on Fredericksburg.—Attends Conference at Drumgoole's.—Appointed to the southern district.—1802, Conference at Salem.—1803, Drumgoole's.—Remarks upon Camp Meetings.

THE commencement of the year 1801, found him in New-York; on which station he continued until the beginning of the following March. It will be but just here to remark, that his labours in New-York, were blessed in a considerable degree. With regard to the progress of Methodism in that city, he has given the following concise history. " I will here set down an account of the beginning of Methodism in the city of New-York, which was the first society formed in the United States. This society was formed by Philip Embury, from Ireland, in the beginning of the year 1766, when a few of his own countrymen were joined together with him. He then exhorted and prayed with them, and spoke to them about the state of their · souls. After a short time some of the inhabitants of New-York joined with them. They then hired a sail loft, in which they met, and Mr. Embury used to preach, exhort, &c. Captain Webb, an officer in the British army, came amongst them, and was much engaged in religion, and preached frequently. After some time they purchased a lot of ground, in John-street, on which they built a church, in the year

1768; and on the 30th day of October, in the same
year, the church was opened for divine worship; and
Mr. Embury preached the dedication sermon. It is
now a little upwards of thirty-two years since our
society had a house of worship in this place, and they
have been increasing and multiplying ever since.
We have now five houses of public worship. The
first church is commonly called Old Church, the
second is called the *Bowery*, the third, North River;
the fourth is called the Two mile Stone, being two
miles from the centre of the city. The fifth is the
African Church, which was erected by the people of
colour, for themselves to worship in; yet they are to
be governed by the Methodists in all their spiritual
matters. But they themselves are to settle their temporal matters. This church was built in the latter
part of the past year. Besides these houses, we have
a charity school of thirty poor children supported by
the society, and several dwelling houses belonging to
the society. Three travelling preachers are stationed
in the city, and are assisted by several local preachers.
When we took the last account of the numbers in our
society, we had six hundred and forty-five whites, and
one hundred and thirty-one coloured persons.—
Hitherto the Lord has helped us."

On the 3d of March he left the city; and though
he was much united to his friends in this place, he
was extremely glad to be freed from the bustle and
confinement of the city. Accustomed as he always
had been to travelling, it was no small tax upon his
feelings to confine himself within the narrow bounds
of a city. In taking his departure, therefore, from
New-York, the scenery of the country seemed to
present him with new charms; and he felt himself

extremely happy to breathe the pure air and converse with the variegated scenery of the surrounding landscapes.

Thursday, March 5th. We find the following notice in his journal. "I got to old Joseph Hutchinson's before night. He gave an account of his mother's death, who had been dead a few weeks only ; she lived in three centuries, and was one hundred and one years, nine months and seven days old when she died ; and her friends had counted up her offspring as far as they could, and had made the number three hundred and seventy-five. The old lady had lived till she lost her sight, and afterward her sight was restored to her again ; and what was more extraordinary was this, she lived till her hair turned white and then came off, and her hair became dark again.

" Tuesday, 24th. I rode early in the morning, and crossed Rappahannock river at Falmouth, and stopped at Fredericksburg. At night, in our new meeting-house, I preached on Rom. iv. 7. *Blessed are they whose iniquities are forgiven, and whose sins are covered.* I had a good time in preaching, and the power of the Lord was amongst us, I was glad of an opportunity to preach in that town. It has often been said of George Whitefield, that when he passed through Fredericksburg that he shook off the dust of his feet as a witness against that wicked people : and I never heard of any persons being converted in the town from that time till lately ; and it is said, that there is not one person living in town now, that was living there when Whitefield shook off the dust of his feet as a testimony against them. Some time past the Lord began to revive his work in the town, and now they have a society formed ; and within a few months they have built a small meeting-house, though it is not quite finished. I hope the Lord will visit, and bless the people. The preacher that tarries with them is much encouraged, and labours with great satisfaction."

He then proceeded on to Petersburg, and was glad to find his friends all in health, except his brother, John Lee, who was still afflicted. He here received information of the death of the Rev. Devereaux Jarrat, a minister of the church of England, "who," says Mr. Lee, "was the greatest preacher, and the most pious person, that I was acquainted with, amongst that order of ministers."

Thursday, April 9th. Conference began at Drumgoole's meeting-house. Here he was appointed to travel what was then called the south district of Virginia. Though he was not exactly reconciled to the appointment at first, yet afterward he became resigned, and entered cheerfully upon his work. His only reason for objecting to a district was, that he could enjoy more peace of mind in travelling a circuit; but he was willing to sacrifice his own opinion for the public good. During this itinerant year he attended twenty-five quarterly meetings, was present at twenty-seven love-feasts, and preached two hundred and ninety-four sermons.*

It was during this year, in the month of November, that he received the sorrowful tidings of his brother's death. He died on the Yadkin river, in Surry county, North-Carolina, on the sixth day of October, 1801.

* I have since heard it remarked, much to his praise, by many who recollect his labours with pleasure in that district, that he made it a point to preach at every regular preaching place in the bounds of his district, at least once a year.

Should any wish to know the circumstances of his end, let him read the following :—

"He had been travelling, for the advantage of his health, for near six months, from the time he left home last, and had been over the mountains to the Sweet springs, and southerly to the Yadkin river, and from thence he expected to return home in a short time ; but while he was travelling the road, he spoke to the man who travelled with him, and observed, that he felt a difficulty in breathing, and believed he was near his end. His man tried to divert his mind a little, but he told him it was no trifling matter, for an ulcer was formed on his lungs, and he expected it would break on the outside of his lungs, and if it did, he should die in a few hours. After a little time, he said the ulcer was broke, and in the way he expected. He drove on to a house, and requested admission, which was granted. He then went out to his man, who was taking care of the horses, and told him, he should die in a few hours ; and gave him some of his papers, with directions concerning his burial. He then went into the house, and asked the woman if any of them could sing ? she replied, she made but a poor hand at singing. He asked, if any of them prayed in public ? but received no answer. He then said, "I must pray," and kneeling down he prayed, and repeated it again and again ; and continued on his knees as though he wished to die in that postu.e ; but his man went to him, took him up, and laid him on the bed. He told him to tell his friends not to weep for him, for he was sure of going to heaven. At last he died without either sigh or groan. He did not live four hours after he got out of his chair. All the wheels of life stood still at once!"

The last day of the year he makes the following
summary remarks, after preaching at Blunt's meeting-house, in Isle of Wight. "Here I finished the
year 1801. In the beginning of the year I was in
the city of New-York, where I continued until the
beginning of March. I then came to Virginia, with
a full intention not to travel a district as a presiding
elder, but to take a circuit; but at the conference I
was over persuaded to take charge of a district, and
at last consented. Thus far I have endeavoured to
fill my station faithfully, and have been greatly comforted amongst the preachers and people. However
I have seen but little stir of religion in a general way;
yet several souls have been converted to God ; yea,
several dozens of them in the district ; and there is a
little prospect in several places now. I think I have
had but one day's sickness in the whole year. I bless
God that I do love him, and I love his people ; and it
is the determination of my soul to serve my God all
the days of my life. Whether I live or die, I dedicate my soul and body to the Lord, to be wholly his
without reserve, for ever and for evermore. Even
so, amen, come Lord Jesus."

In the beginning of the year 1802, he was considerably afflicted in Portsmouth, and was confined for the
space of two weeks ; in which time he endured much
pain, which was occasioned by a severe attack of the
gravel. He observed that he lost, during his illness,
twenty pounds of his weight.

March 1st, he attended conference at Salem, and on
the 4th, they finished their business. "The prea   s
(says he) took their stations without murmuring, and
appeared to be well pleased generally. At the conference we took four men on trial, and four preachers

located. We had not a full supply of preachers, and
therefore, several of the circuits could have but one.
I continued in the same district by appointment. I
felt sorry at parting with the preachers." During
this conference there were some awful displays of
divine power, and nearly a score professed to obtain
pardon for their sins.

This year indeed, seemed more remarkable for the
progress of religion than the year preceding. At a
quarterly meeting in June, at Mabry's chapel, on
Sabbath there was a great outpouring of the Spirit.
" The place (observed Mr. Lee) was awful indeed.
After a while one proclaimed aloud that God had converted her soul. Another spoke out aloud and said,
God had reached a young man's heart. One of the
preachers called to one of the sisters saying, 'sister,
your daughter has promised that she would set out for
heaven.' Thus they continued for a considerable
time."

Also, at a quarterly meeting at Jones' chapel, in
Sussex, in the month of July, Sabbath was a high
day indeed, as the following extract will show. " The
meeting continued till sun sitting, in which time, it was
said, sixteen souls were converted, including one or
two who was converted the day before. The work
was also among the blacks. About the going down of
the sun, a young lad got converted, which was the
last, there being but few people left in the meeting-
house. One of the preachers shouted aloud, and
praised God that the Christians had taken the field,
and kept the ground, for there was not a sinner left.
Another preacher asked some of them to look out of
doors, and see if they could not find one more sinner,
for he thought if they could find another, that he

would get converted. But there was not another
unconverted sinner to be found at the meeting-house.
So they praised God together, and returned home.
Most of those who were converted, were children of
Methodist parents, though some of their parents had
been dead for many years. This was the best quarterly meeting I have had since I have been on the
district."

The following year, 1803, he attended the conference at Drumgoole's, which was held in March. His
appointment for this year continued as in the preceding. The year past had certainly been favourable to
the cause of pure religion, for it was ascertained that
one thousand members had been added within the
bounds of the Virginia conference.

This year was remarkable for the introduction of
camp meetings, as they have been not improperly
called. These meetings did not originate with the
Methodists, nor with any human design, but merely
from the circumstance of so many asse ıbling at some
sacramental occasions, among the Presbyterians, that
no house was sufficiently large to contain them. It
does not comport with the limits of this memoir to
enter into a detailed account of the origin and progress of these extraordinary meetings. That they
have been made a blessing to thousands, I have no
doubt. And though much has been said against them,
yet the opposition has generally proceeded from a
quarter which, instead of lessening our confidence in
their utility, only serves to increase our belief in their
being, in the order of Divine Providence, established
for the benefit of immortal souls. That they have a
natural tendency to inspire a spirit of devotion, especially in the minds of Christians, is evident to all who

have attended them with any degree of impartiality ; and the accidental evils which have accompanied them, ought not to be attributed to the meetings themselves, but to the native wickedness of the human heart, which, pervading many individuals now collected together, appears in a concentrated force : the disorder originates from the disorderly spectators, and not from the orderly worshippers who assemble for the sole purpose of spiritual benefit.

These remarks are made as introductory to Mr. Lee's account of the first camp-meeting which he attended, and which shall be given in his own words :—

" I will here observe that we had, in my judgment, about 2500 or 3000 hearers on Sabbath, and as many white people on Monday, but not so many blacks. We had many sermons preached at the camp-meeting, for, at different times, we had preaching at both stands, at the same time. I have only taken an account of what I saw and heard. We had twenty-nine Methodist preachers. According to the best account I could get, there were about thirty-five souls converted at the camp-meeting ; most of them were white people. Many had objections to the meeting before it came on ; but those who attended it, were generally pleased, and very desirous of having another. I have seen no meeting in this part of the world for years, that was so pleasing and profitable to me."

In August he attended another, held at Ellis' meeting-house, in Greensville, Virginia, which exceeded the former, both as it respected the number which attended, and the number converted. Every discourse, and every exhortation given during the meeting, was attended by the displays of divine power. Almost every hour and every minute, was employed in the worship of God. A little time was spent in eating, drinking, or sleeping, but each endeavoured to improve his time to the best advantage ; and seemed satisfied only with the hidden manna of God's love, and the living streams of his grace. More than a hundred living witnesses for Jesus, were raised up at this meeting.

But the work of reformation did not entirely depend upon the success of camp-meetings, for at various meetings, which he attended in the course of the year, the power of God was manifested in the awakening, conviction and conversion of many souls.

In the year 1804, he was, from the conference held at Salem, appointed to travel Williamsburg circuit. In the month of May, he attended the general conference held in Baltimore. Having returned to his circuit in June, he commenced his appointments at Williamsburg. " After preaching and meeting the class, (says he.) I went with a few friends to the hospital for lunatics ; at which place twenty-nine persons were confined. I saw most of them. Some were in the yard prepared for that purpose ; the men in one yard and the women in another. At the opposite end of the house, some were in their rooms, and some in close confinement in their cells. I was much pleased to find every thing so neat and cleanly in their apartments. None of those which I saw, were any way violent, or outrageous ; some walked about in pensive dejection, and others were cheerful and merry ; but at times, would show marks of insanity. I saw one woman who was sitting reading her Bible, in the German language, and when I spoke to her a few sentences in German, she appeared pleased, and began to converse freely, and sensibly. While I stayed I saw no mark of melancholy in her, yet I understood she had frequent fits of insanity."

He continued on his circuit until the latter part of July, at which time he visited his father; then attended a camp-meeting at White oak; and from thence he went to the Sweet springs, for the benefit of his health; and, as is probable, with a view to avoid the autumnal sickness which generally prevails at that season of the year, in the circuit on which he was appointed to travel. In October he returned, and as Daniel Hall was too unwell to attend his appointments on the district, Mr. Lee agreed to take his place for a few weeks. This year and part of the following, he was engaged in writing the memoirs of his brother, John Lee, who, as observed in a former part of this chapter, departed this life 1801. This, together with some other matters which engaged his attention prevented his travelling and labouring as regularly as he had done in former years.

In 1805 he attended the Virginia conference, at Edmund Taylor's, in Granville, N. C. At this conference it was ascertained, that Methodism had made considerable progress since the preceding conference. An acquisition of nineteen hundred had been made to the church, in the space of one year, within the bounds of the Virginia conference; and fourteen candidates for the ministry were received. Mr. Lee was appointed to travel Mecklenburg circuit. He however was not able to get to his circuit until the 9th of November following, in consequence of his having to make a visit to Baltimore and Philadelphia, for the purpose of publishing the *Life of his brother, John Lee.*

The following year, 1806, was an important year, both to the subject of this memoir, as well as to the

church to which he belonged. A few extracts from
his journal shall be given.

"Friday, February 14th. Our annual conference
began in Norfolk. At 9 o'clock we commenced
business, and sat till 11. Then Bishop Whatcoat
preached on Rev. xxii. 17. He gave us a good discourse, and with some animation. We met for business again at 3 o'clock.

"Saturday, 15th. At 11 o'clock P. Bruce preached
on 1 Cor. i. 18. He gave us a good discourse, and with
much animation. From that time the work of the
Lord began to spread, and seven or eight souls were
converted before the meeting broke up. Thank God
for his unspeakable blessings towards us. At night
J. C. preached on Acts xiv. 22. He gave us an excellent sermon, and with much power, and the word
had great weight with the people ; the heavenly fire
spread through the congregation, and there was a
great cry for mercy amongst poor sinners.

"Wednesday, 19th. At night I went over to
Portsmouth, and preached on Amos ii. 7. *By whom
shall Jacob arise? for he is small.* I had a crowded
house, and a solemn assembly. It was a time of
comfort in the assembly, and many were deeply
affected towards the close. The Lord has wrought
wonders in Portsmouth within a few days. I suppose not less than fifty souls have been converted in
this place.

"Thursday, 20th. We sat in conference again,
and continued until 1 o'clock, when we finished our
business, and received our stations, and concluded
our conference. The preachers were generally well
satisfied with their appointments. We had added to
the number of the society in the course of the year,

and in the boun's of the Virginia conference, two thousand four hundred and twenty-four members. No preacher had died, withdrawn, or been expelled, and so many young preachers came up to the help of the Lord amongst us, that the circuits were better supplied than they had been for many years before. I suppose, that in Norfolk and Portsmouth we had as many as eighty souls, or upwards, converted during the sitting of conference; but the greater number was in Portsmouth.

"Sunday, March 9th. I took Amelia circuit, where I was appointed by the bishop. I had a good meeting with the people, both in preaching and in class. I felt thankful for the comfort which I enjoyed in my own soul. I rode up to Jordan Reese's, and stayed all night.

Wednesday, 12th, was my birth day. I was then forty-eight years old. I have found in the course of the past year, that my head has turned gray, and that my sight begins to fail me, so that I cannot read small print without pretty good light. As I advance in years, I hope to advance in grace. I preached at Deep Creek, and the people were refreshed with the Divine presence. I lodged with John Morgan.

"Saturday, 21st. At Franklin's I preached on Psalm lxvi. 16. I had a happy little meeting. The man of the house is an object of pity, but is a happy Christian. He told me, that it had been twenty-one years since he was on his feet. He is perfectly stiff from his head to his feet. He can move his toes, has a tolerable good use of one arm, and can use the other a little, but cannot raise it to his head. He has the use of his tongue, mouth, eyes, and ears, but he cannot move his head upwards, or downwards, or side-

ways. He lies on his back continually; has no power
to change his posture, or to rest a weary limb. However he has a hickory withe supended over his bed,
and by taking hold of it with one of his hands, and
pulling, he can rest himself a little. He reads, sings,
talks, and shouts the praise of God with great solemnity. He supposes he was brought to that situation
by the rheumatism. I rode to brother H. Fether-
stone's, and stayed all night.

"Tuesday, April 1st. At May's meeting-house, I
preached on Job xv. 4. I had a sweet time in speaking to a tender people; and we were all pretty lively
in class-meeting; some of the friends praised God
aloud, and with many tears. Glory be to God for
the meeting! We had rain in the afternoon. I suppose the oldest men amongst us can scarcely remember ever to have known a winter so warm and dry,
as what the last has been. March has been very
dry, and very cold.

"Friday, May 9th. We began our camp-meeting
at a meeting-house called the Olive Branch, in Brunswick county. At 12 o'clock D. Hall preached in the
meeting-house. He gave us a lively discourse, and
the people felt the power of truth. Then Lewis
Taylor exhorted; and after a while a shout began,
and one person I understood was converted. We
had preaching at 4 o'clock, and at night.

"This meeting continued until the Monday following. The number of converts was considerable; but
one circumstance contributed not a little to interrupt
the harmony of the meeting, and retard the progress
of the work, which was the wild enthusiasm displayed
by a certain female, not a member of our church.
Her exercises were such as to attract the attention of

all present, and were of a character novel enough to
be sure; for she exhibited at some times the *jerking*
exercise, at other times the dancing exercise, and not
unfrequently the basking exercise; and taking them
all together, made as ridiculous a set of exercises as
ever attracted the gaze of the multitude." Mr. Lee
was opposed to all such extravagances, and therefore endeavoured to arrest the progress of the evil,
but by so doing he doubtless gave offence to some,
whose weak judgments caused them to justify every
kind of religious extravagance. While piety prompts
us to commiserate the case of those whose weakness
exposes them to the impositions of a distempered imagination, and charity leads us to draw a veil over the
infirmities of those who appear, in some of their religious exercises, to transcend the bounds of modesty
and decorum, we are not prepared to anathematize
every thing which may appear disorderly in the estimation of the cold philosophizing Christian. The
warmth of devotion can only be duly appreciated by
those who are under its sacred influence. Where
wisdom and sincerity predominate, they will keep
every disorderly passion in subordination to their con-
trol, and give a brilliancy and heavenly joy even to
its outward expression, which the hollow hearted
hypocrite cannot easily counterfeit.

The following account, taken from Mr. Lee's journal, for the same year, may be classed among those
extraordinary cases which baffle human calculations,
and indicate a supernatural influence. It took place
at a camp-meeting at Hobb's meeting-house in Brunswick circuit, which began October the 10th.

"The case of a young woman, N. W. being very
singular, I will here set down some account of it. At

this meeting on Sunday night, she fell down, and lay
helpless; they took her into a tent, and set up with
her all night; she continued helpless and speechless,
all the time. Next morning I had a tea spoon full
of water given her. About 9 o'clock in the forenoon she revived, and said, Love, love, love!
Glory, glory, glory! and then died away again, and
appeared like a person in a sweet sleep. In
the afternoon she was taken home in a wagon, but
remained as she had been before. Her parents,
fearing that there might be some bodily complaint
attending her, sent for a physician, who came, and
then sent for another. The physicians both agreed,
that they could not perceive that she had any bodily
complaint, believing it to be a supernatural power.
They did not attempt to do much for her, only took
a little blood, gave a few reviving drops, and put a
small blister on the back part of her neck, but took it
off in a little time. One of the physicians continued
with her until the following Sunday, but saw very
little alteration. She continued thus until Tuesday
night, at which time she revived, and spoke freely
and sensibly, though apparently in a weak and feeble
state. The next day she went about the house, and
out of doors, just as she pleased, and was quite well
and happy in God. She had been in that state from
Sunday night, until the next Tuesday night week,
which was nine days and nights. I understood that
during that time she ate nothing except such things
as were poured into her mouth, and she took but
very little of that. She was, for the most part of the
time, sensible of every thing that was said or done
to her in her presence. For some days before she
revived, she knew all her friends that came to see

her, and would answer any question by a nod or
shake of the head, and in some cases would hold out
her hand to a friend; when spoken to about the state
of her soul, and asked if she was happy, she would
move her head by way of assent, and raise her eyes,
and the tears would flow down her cheeks, which
satisfied her friends that she was converted. After she
regained her strength, she said, that the Lord blessed
and converted her soul, on the Monday after she was
struck down, at which time she spoke, and shouted, love! love! love! glory! glory! glory! I saw
her soon after she recovered from this ecstasy, and
took her into society, and had no doubt but she was
truly happy in God. Many people who visited her
in her helpless condition, were deeply affected, and
some of them were brought to think more seriously
about their souls. Such a strange circumstance I do
not remember to have known or read of before, and
yet there was nothing like a trance, or any particular
discovery of the other world professed by her."

He continued on his circuit until January, 1807,
and in February he attended the Virginia conference,
in Newbern, North-Carolina, from which he was permitted to make a visit to the south, as far as Georgia.
See the following extracts.

"Tuesday, February 10th. I took leave of my
friends and the preachers, and set out in company with
D. Hall, he for South-Carolina, and I for Georgia.
We rode that day to Thomas Lee's, a little south of
Trent river, and stayed all night at his house.

"Thursday, March 5th. We set off down Cooper
river, crossed one of its branches, at a small ferry,
and then crossed the main river at Clemon's ferry,
where it is about two miles wide; and from thence

we came to Charleston at dark, and lodged at the parsonage by the new church.

"Sunday, 8th, was a wet day; but I preached three times, in the forenoon in the new meeting-house, in the afternoon and night in the church in Cumberland-street.

"Tuesday, 11th. We left town, and travelled a most shocking road, on account of mud and mire, to Dorchester, and then put up at Abraham Riddle-sperger's; and at night in his house I preached on John v. 25. I found but little liberty in speaking to them. However I sowed in hope, and leave the event to God.

"Thursday, 19th. I took leave of brother Hall, after having been in company with him nearly three months. I felt some sorrow at parting with him; however, necessity required it. I crossed Congaree river, at Columbia ferry, and rode on to John Cargill's, where I tarried all night.

"Saturday, 21st. I rode early, and crossed Savannah river into Augusta, in Georgia, some time before night, and put up at Asaph Waterman's." The next day he preached three times in Augusta.

"Monday, April 13th. I rode down to Savannah, and put up at John Miller's; and there I met with Samuel Dunwody, one of our preachers, who has lately come to this place, having been lately appointed to labour here for the present year.

"Sunday, 19th. I rode out to the White Bluff meeting-house, about seven miles from Savannah, and at 11 o'clock I preached on Acts xvii. 27. I had a good degree of liberty in speaking to a strange people, and they heard with great attention. Some were moved upon and tendered by the word. I then re-

turned to town, and after dinner I went to hear the
Presbyterian minister, Mr. Henry Kollock. His text
was 1 John v, 4. He gave us a beautiful discourse,
and with much life. His sermon was written, but
it was well read, was sensible, and calculated to do
good.

"At night, at Mr. Myer's, I preached on 1 Pet. ii. 5.
I had a crowded house, and more attended than could
get in, many were forced to remain out of doors. I
preached to them with some freedom, and they fed
on the word with much apparent pleasure. All were
solemn, and some were affected. It was a good time
to many souls. After I dismissed the congregation I
desired that all that had been Methodists in other
places, and wished again to be in society with us, to
remain, and we would form a class. I took four of
them into a class. There were others present, but
I told them, that I did not desire any person to join
at that time but such as had been formerly in society
with us ; and if any others wished to join, they might
have an opportunity after a few meetings. This was
the first class that was ever formed in Savannah.
Who knows but the Lord will multiply his blessings
upon us, and make us a great people in this place, as
well as in other places ? At present there is a good
stir of religion in this town ; other churches have an
increase of members.

"Saturday, 25th. I rode in company with a couple
of men to Whitefield's orphan house, and was surprised to find how it was changed for the worse since
I was there seven years ago ; one wing has been
burned down, an old dwelling house entirely gone ;
there was only one wing left of all the buildings ; that
had been repaired and had several good rooms and a

piazza before it, into which a door opened from
every room in the house. At present there is no
school kept on, or sup ported by the property belonging
to this institution. I felt sorry to see how all the
improvements had been demolished ; and to think how
many thousands of dollars had been wasted on the
institution ; but what else could we have expected
when the property was left by Whitefield to Lady
Huntington, a woman who ought never to have had
the government of the institution. The lady's likeness at full length, was remaining in the house ; that
I believe was the only thing like furniture or orna-
ment which remained, and even that was in a shattered
con lition.

"Monday, 27th. I left Savannah and set out for
St. Mary's, not knowing what difficulties I had to pass
through. I crossed Ogechee river at the lower ferry,
about fifteen miles from the city, and then rode to
Joseph Clay's and stayed all night with him. He was
educated at college, and for some years he was a lawyer ; but when he obtained religion he joined the
Baptists, and is now a preacher ; and is much esteemed
by most of his religious acquaintances.

"Wednesday, 29th. I rode early in the morning,
and had a most desperate road to travel, for a chair ;
mud, mire, and water to go through, and logs, roots, and
stalks of the saw pimento to go over ; all which made
it *desperate* for most part of the way. I came to
Obey's ferry, on Altamahaw river, and there I had to
pay three dollars for ferriage. The ferry, including
the island we had to cross, was about two miles wide.
In going through the island, the men had to wade some
small lakes, which were more than waist deep,
and the water ran up in the foot of my carriage,

however, we got over safe a little before night. I stopped at Ezekiel Cockburn's, and stayed all night.

"Thursday, 30th. I had a lonesome, disagreeable road to travel for many miles, until I came into the old Barrington road, which was some better. I dined at Wm. Clemon's, and then rode about 16 miles to Mr. Nicks', just south of Little Satilla river, and put up there all night. I had rode near thirty miles that day, and then had to shut my horse up in a hen-house all night, without a mouthful of any thing to give him to eat. I was sorry for my poor brute, but could not help it.

"Friday, May 1st. I made an early start, and when I found a good place of grass, I stopped and let my horse graze a while ; this I did several times, until I found a house where I obtained a good feed for him. I came to brother Brown's, on Satilla river, about the middle of the day, and was greatly pleased to be at the house of a Methodist once more. In the evening, I was agreeably surprised by a visit from Abraham Bessent, of Jefferson town, with whom I was once acquainted in North Carolina ; he was then a local preacher, and continues in the same station amongst the Methodists.

"Saturday, 2d. I crossed Satilla to Jefferson, took breakfast, and then rode to the town of St. Mary's ; arrived there a little before night, and William Mickel entertained me. That night two men came to see me, and invited me to their houses, which invitation I considered a favour.

"Sunday, 3d. I preached three sermons in the town of St. Mary's. There appears to be a great alteration for the better amongst the people of this place. When I was here a little more than seven

27

years ago, they appeared to be more wild and careless about religion than they are at present; but many of the former inhabitants are either dead, or removed. The soldiers that were then stationed near this town, are gone, and many new settlers have come in; yet there are but few in this town that enjoy religion. Our preachers continue to preach here when they come around.

"Monday, 4th. I rode to Jefferson, twenty-three miles, and put up at brother A. Bessent's, where I was both pleased and comforted. The town of Jefferson contains about twelve or fifteen families. The court-house, for Campden is there.

"Wednesday, 6th. I preached in Jefferson court-house. I had a good congregation. It was a solemn, and a happy time; several persons were bathed in tears. Brother Anguis M'Donold exhorted with life and freedom.

"Thursday, 7th. At Richard Long's, at Colerain, I preached on John iii. 36. *He that believeth on the Son, &c.* I had but a small congregation, but there were as many as I expected, for that part of the country. Mr. Long lives in the old fort, formerly built to keep off the Indians. While we were there on the bank of the river, we got a man to take us over St. Mary's river into Florida,* which belongs to the king of Spain. When I got across the river, I went alone amongst the bushes, and fell on my knees before the Lord, and besought him in earnest prayer, to open the way whereby the gospel might be quickly preached in that part of the world. We returned to

* Since ceded to the United States, 1821. His prayers have been marvelously answered.

brother Crawford's that night, and tarried with him
again.

"Monday, 18th. I rode and crossed Ogechee
river, and came to Savannah about 3 o'clock, and was
very much fatigued with the journey, the day being
very warm. The next day I tarried in town, and at
night, in brother Dunwody's school room, I preached
on Luke xi. 4. I had more hearers than the room
could contain. It was a solemn and a quickening time.
The people were more affected than what they have
generally been, under my preaching in that place. I
felt uncommonly for souls; I did not know when to give
over speaking. Lord give success to thine own word.

"Wednesday, 20th. I was closely engaged in
writing in my journal most of the day, but at 5 o'clock
in the afternoon, I went to hear Mr. Kollock, the
Presbyterian minister. His text was Psa. xxx. 5.
In his favour is life. He gave us a good discourse,
with animation, and it was calculated to do good, with
the exception of a few sentences which savoured of
Calvinism.

"Monday, June 1st. I left the city of Savannah
and rode about fourteen miles to Robert Stafford's,
and preached with some freedom to a strange people.
I then crossed Ogechee river at Bird's bridge, and
went to William Rodes', and preached at night. It
was a profitable time.

"Monday, 29th. I crossed Oconee river at Mount
Pelier, and went to Salem, where I expected to have
held meeting, but the people had not been notified of
my coming; so that only three persons attended. I
prayed with them, and rode up to Sterling Bass', and
stayed all night. I spent about ten days in Baldwin
county, and I do sincerely think that it is the best

newly settled country I ever saw in any part of the
United States. The land is good; the water is good;
and the people are the most civil and religious that I
ever knew for such a newly settled place.

"Tuesday, 28th of July. Our camp-meeting began
in Hancock county, about three miles south of
Sparta. It began on Tuesday and ended on Saturday,
in which time I suppose we had as many as eighty
souls converted. We had thirty-seven Methodist
preachers. One hundred and seventy-six tents were
pitched on the ground. I suppose we had three
thousand people who lodged within the encampment.
I think our largest congregation amounted to about
four thousand five hundred hearers. We had fourteen sermons preached at the stage, and nine exhortations given at the close of the sermons. The ground
was laid out in a tolerably convenient place, containing four or five acres of land. The place was well
furnished with water.

"Thursday, October 29th. We rode to Wilkins
Jackson's, and I preached on Job xxi. 15. I had a
house crowded with attentive hearers, and I found
my soul much quickened by the meeting. Moses
Matthews exhorted with life and freedom. We had
more hearers than usual, in our new tour. We then
rode down to Lewis Saunders'. This day we finished
our new tour, which we had taken for ten days. We
were the first preachers that ever went into that new
country to preach the gospel. The people where
we went had settled there only the winter before,
and cleared land, and made a crop, without knowing
whose land they should be on. And since the land
is drawn for, they are mostly preparing to move elsewhere. The land for the most part is excellent in-

deed, and the country must become very wealthy; and
I doubt not but it will be famous for religion; though
it was in possession of the Indians but two or three
years ago. The wilderness shall blossom as the rose.

"Saturday, November 21st. I rode to Milledge-
ville, the metropolis of the state of Georgia. I put
up at brother Darrol's, and visited some of the sick
people; for it was unusually sickly in the town, and
several were at the point of death, and one of the
members of the general assembly died that afternoon.

"Sunday, 22d. I was to have preached in the
state-house at 12 o'clock, but the committee, appointed for Mr. Drane, who died the day before,
requested me to attend his funeral. I put off preaching until the afternoon. At 3 o'clock I preached in
the state-house. I had a good time in speaking. I
felt concerned for the salvation of my hearers. After
meeting I rode out of town to Robert Winn's.

"Monday, 23d. I was sent for to return to Mil-
ledgeville, to see William Stith, judge of the superior
court in the middle district of Georgia. I returned,
and found him worse than what he was the day before. I tarried with him until the middle of the day,
and then attended the funeral of a woman, whom I
visited the day before. I then returned to attend
the judge; I talked with him about his prospect of
heaven, and by his answers I had great hope of his
future happiness; he was a Methodist. He failed
fast just before night, and then revived a little. I
talked with him again, and encouraged him to venture
on the Lord, nothing doubting, and while holding him
by the hand, I sung

Happy soul, thy days are ended,
All thy mourning days below, &c.

27 *

He kept his senses perfectly to the last. Several members of the general assembly came in, just as he began to breathe hard and quick. I asked a friend to watch him while we prayed, and we all knelt down, and prayed earnestly, that the Lord would give him an easy death, and take him to heaven; when we rose up, one that sat by him said, 'he is gone.' He died very easy, and I believe in the favour of God. He left the world at five minutes after 8 o'clock, and left a mournful widow, but no children.

"Tuesday, 24th. At 2 o'clock, at Dr. T. Bird's, I preached the funeral sermon of Judge Stith, from Psa. xxxiv. 19. Most of the members of the general assembly attended. It was a very solemn time. I then left town, and crossed the Oconee river, and on to Peter Pryde's, and stayed all night.

"Monday, December 14th. I left Augusta, and the state of Georgia, early in the morning, and crossed Savannah river into South-Carolina, and rode to John Spunn's, about thirty-five miles. I felt some sorrow at leaving Georgia, for I was more pleased with the country and the people than I had ever been before.

"Wednesday, 16th. I rose early, and took breakfast by candle light, and started by the break of day, and had a tight ride of forty-four miles to Columbia. It was night before I arrived. I put up at brother Harrison's, and was weary and fatigued with my journey. The next day I rode out to Col. Hutchinson's, about four miles, and spent the day and night with him. The colonel has lately embraced religion, and joined the Methodists. I was agreeably entertained at his house.

"Friday, 18th. I returned to Columbia, and at night I preached on Isai. lv. 7. I hope the meeting

was not in vain. I lodged at Major Clifton's that
night. He is a lawyer, and has lately embraced religion, and joined the Methodists. The legislature
were sitting at that time in Columbia, and a little before night I went to hear them. I think of all the
general assemblies that I have seen in the different
states, this exceeded all for a grand appearance and
a showy dress. The speaker of each house had on a
grand robe of silk, adorned with ermine.

"Tuesday, 22d. I set out for Charleston in company with brother D. Hall, M. P. Sturdevant, and on
Friday, 25th, which was Christmas day, we reached
the city.

" Monday, 28th. Our conference began in Charleston."

In Charleston, S. C. he finished the year 1807.
His labours during the year were bestowed freely,
and freely did he receive his recompense from God.
No murmuring or repining at his sufferings was heard,
but often rejoicing on account of the presence of God,
which attended his ministry, and the love and peace
which he enjoyed in his own soul.

CHAPTER XVIII.

—◦◦◦—

His Journey from the South to Petersburg.—Attends the Conference in Lynchburg.—Is appointed to Cumberland.—Attends the General Conference.—Much ceremony at a Camp-Meeting.—Continues his Journey to the North.—Not pleased with some of the Methodist Churches, which had pews.—Enjoys the company of his old friends.—Set his face towards the South.—Returns to Virginia.

THE first day of the year 1808 found the subject of this memoir in Charleston. On the 4th of January he set out for Virginia. The second day's journey brought him to Georgetown, where he preached at night. The day after he rode forty miles to the widow Post's, in Pee Dee; the day was wet, cold, and damp. On the 7th he reached brother Ford's, on Little Pee Dee, drenched in a heavy shower of rain; but, according to his own account, the kindness of the family more than compensated him for his fatigue. On the 9th he reached Fayetteville, and the next day, being Sabbath, he tarried and preached in the forenoon and at night. On Monday the 18th he reached his father's, and found him and his family in health. He spent several days in visiting his friends and relations. The same laws which made this a duty made it also pleasant.

He left Petersburg on the 25th, and on Monday the 1st of February he was in Lynchburg, ready for conference, which commenced the day following. Conference finished its business on the 8th, and the

preachers dispersed. Some repaired immediately to
their circuits. Some, who had obtained locations,
hasted away to the cares and enjoyments of domestic
life ; whilst others were pleased with the opportunity
of once more visiting the paternal abode, and for a
short season participate in the endearments of the
society of their friends and relations.

Mr. Lee was appointed to Cumberland circuit,
Virginia. He returned to Petersburg, and visited
his father again, on some necessary business. On
Sunday the 25th, he acted as priest in his father's
house, and baptized a sister only a few months old,
while his father at that time was more than seventy-
seven years of age. It will be recollected that the
old gentleman had been married three times, and that
he had a child by the last wife. When the youngest
was baptized the eldest was more than fifty-five years
old. A great disparity in the ages of two daughters
of the same parent.

On Friday, the 25th of February, he took his
circuit, at Anthony Webster's, and continued on his
appointment until the 3d of April, at which time he
found it expedient for him to attend the general conference in Baltimore.

Some time previous to this he had contemplated
publishing a History of the Methodists in America,
and had actually commenced the collecting and ar-
ranging the materials for the publication of the work.
Perhaps we shall have occasion to mention this subject again toward the close of this volume.

It is scarcely necessary here to say any thing respecting the general conference, only that it commenced on Friday, the 6th of May, and closed on
Thursday, the 26th of the same month.

Mr. Lee had had it in contemplation for some time, to make one more visit to the New-England states; to see the many friends in that part of the world, to whom he was greatly endeared, he believed would afford him a peculiar felicity. He might also have in view something relative to the publication of his work. Be this as it may, his journals inform us, that he left Baltimore on the 31st of May for New-England, and that he pursued his journey, preaching every day, until he came to New-Jersey, and went to a camp-meeting in Penn's neck, which he was not able to reach until Sunday, the 5th of June. The order of this meeting, and particularly the concluding ceremony, deserves a notice.

He was not able to get to this meeting until the day before it was brought to a close. We shall only notice what may be called the concluding scene ; and in order to this, we have recourse to his journal. After observing, that as many as seventy-two persons were baptized, after he had preached at 10 o'clock in the morning, he goes on to say :—"At this meeting there were some things new to me. One was the form of their trumpets ; they had seven trumpets, which they blew all at once, for preaching on the stand. In the morning they went all round in front of the tents, blowing the seven trumpets as they went. Another thing, which was new to me, was their manner of taking leave of each other, which was as follows : the men with their trumpets went foremost, rank and file, blowing as they went; and then the preachers followed after; and then the men in general followed the preachers ; they then made a circular march, and when the preachers came round to the place from whence they started, they turned out of the ranks to the right-hand, and stopped and shook hands with all the men next to them till they all came round, and then the men who were marching in the circle, shifted sides, each with his companion, and went round again, and those who were on the opposite side from the preachers the first time, came next in turn to the preachers, and had an opportunity of shaking hands. Then the women marched around twice, in the same form, and all shook hands as the men had done before them. Most of them continued singing as they went. I was requested to march with them, and to stand and shake hands, but I excused myself; for, indeed, I did not like so much ceremony and form."

The disapprobation manifested by Mr. Lee at the pompous manner of this concluding scene, shows the correctness of his taste and of his views, respecting religious decorum, and gospel simplicity. Who, indeed, would approve of a practice which tended to convert the worship of a Christian assembly, professing plainness of speech and manners, into the gaudy appearance of military parade and pomp. We rejoice that such an unseemly practice was never generally introduced, and is now, we believe, universally condemned. Neither are these strictures to be construed into any dislike in the writer to camp-meetings.— Though, like all other good things, they may be abused, their practical utility will ever secure for them the hearty co-operation of all who have experienced a similar benefit from them, as that which the writer of these pages often has.

Monday, 13. He rode to Mount Holly, and preached, the next day at the New-Mills; from thence to Allentown, New-Brunswick, and Newark; at all of which places he preached.

Saturday, 19th. He reached New-York, at which place he continued until Monday the 27th, and preached nine sermons. He then attended a camp-meeting, held at Cow-Harbour; he was both pleased and profited by the meeting. From Cow-Harbour he embarked in a sloop, sailed over the sound, and landed in Norwalk, state of Connecticut. He was much gratified in saluting in the name of the Lord Jesus, some of his friends of former days. Almost twenty years had passed away since he first, as a stranger, entered this part of the world. On his first appearance, few were prepossessed in his favour; but his constancy and firmness conquered the prejudices of many. He encountered with floods of bigotry and persecution; but he was borne through them all, and lived to see "the crooked ways made straight, and the rough places made even," and living witnesses in abundance raised up, who could rejoice that ever they heard the gospel from the mouth of a Methodist minister.

A few extracts from his journal, while they show the feelings excited in his mind by this visit, will also give the reader an idea of the state of Methodism in New-England at that time.

"Saturday, July 2d. I rode to Stratfield, took dinner, and exhorted a few of the neighbours, and prayed with them; rode to Stratford, and stopped till a heavy rain was over, and then went on to New-Haven, and got there a little before 10 o'clock at night, and put up at old brother Jocelin's.

"Sunday 3d. In New-Haven, at 10 o'clock, I preached on Zechariah ix. 12. We had a comfortable time together; I preached also at 3 o'clock, and at night. I had great liberty in speaking, and the people were considerably affected under the word.—

28

Thank God for it. We have a new meeting-house now, though not finished, where we can quietly wait upon the Lord.

"Monday, 4th. Was independence day. I left New-Haven a little after sun-rise, and rode to Middletown, about twenty-five miles, and at night I preached in our unfinished house. The people appeared to feel the weight of the word spoken. I was glad to be there.

"Thursday, 7th. I rode to New-London, and at night I preached on Psa. xxx. 5. I had a large congregation to hear me, and it was a quickening time amongst the Christians, and while I was speaking, three women fell down on the floor, and lay helpless for some time. Many tears were shed under the word; we were truly glad to meet together once more in this world. The people thought that our meeting-house would not hold the congregation, and therefore appointed meeting in the Baptist meeting-house; but it was hardly large enough, for the house was greatly crowded, and my soul was happy there. I lodged at Richard Douglass'.

"Friday, 8th. In our meeting-house in New-London, at 5 o'clock in the morning, I preached, and had a precious time amongst the friends, and the Lord was with us of a truth. Many were affected. Thank God for it. There was then a good revival of religion in the city, and many had been converted within a few months, and some were still mourning for redemption in the blood of Jesus. I then rode to Norwich, and preached at night. I had a good congregation to hear me, but I did not feel as lively as I generally do. It was dull weather, and more rain at hand, which naturally tends to make me dull and heavy.

"Saturday, 9th. I left the state of Connecticut, and got into Rhode Island, before night; and about half after 9 o'clock, at night, I came safe to general Lippet's, in Cranston, where I met with a hearty welcome, and was pleased to be there once more. The next day being Sabbath, I preached at Lippet's meeting-house, in the morning, and administered the Lord's Supper; and in the afternoon I preached again. We had another precious time of the love and the presence of God.

"Tuesday, 12th. I rode to Providence, and put up at John Lippet's, and at night preached in the town-house. I believe some good was done at that time, and I hope the fruit thereof will be seen after many days. It has been many years since I preached in that town: but I felt something of the same union with the people, that I formerly felt.— There is now a small society in Providence. The next day I rode early, and stopped a little in Bristol, and travelled on to Newport, and put up with Samuel Merwin, who is our stationed preacher in town. I was pleased at hearing that the Lord was prospering his work in that town, and that some souls were seeking the Lord.

"Thursday, 14th. I went over to the fort to visit captain Loyal Beal, who commands the fort, and who is a steady Methodist. I returned, and just before dark the bell was rung for meeting. I went out to see, and hear it, for it was the first bell that I ever saw in a steeple to a Methodist meeting-house. The Methodists and others have united to build a Methodist meeting-house, which is not finished, but is fit to preach in. They have a steeple to it, with a pretty large bell; the house is fitted up with large square pews, so that a

part of the people set with their faces, and others with
their backs towards the preacher ; and these pews
are sold to purchasers. Male and female sit together.
Is not this a violation of Methodist rules ? At night I
preached, and we had a good time. The next day I
tarried in town, and visited many of my former acquaintances, and at night, in our new meeting-house I
preached on John xvi. 22. The house was much
crowded, and the people were all attention, and many
were bathed in tears. I warned them, and entreated
them, as though I was never more to see them. I hope
the blessing of the Lord will attend them.

  "Saturday, 16th. I preached in Portsmouth, in our
meeting-house. I had a precious weeping time amongst
my old friends. The word took hold upon their hearts,
and they wept freely. I was truly thankful to God
for the meeting. I spent the Sabbath in Bristol, in
which place there has been a revival of religion of
late. They have built a good meeting-house, but not
on the Methodist plan, for they have sold the seats, and
men and women sit together.

  "Thursday 21st. I rode to Boston, and put up with
the stationed preacher, Daniel Webb, and at night, in
the old meeting-house, I preached on 2 Cor. v. 18.
I found a sweet sense of the love of God in my soul,
and the people were quite attentive. The next day I
tarried in town, and at night, in the new meeting-house,
I preached on Rom. viii. 24. I did not feel as much
freedom in this house as I did in the old. This new
meeting-house is large and elegant, I think eighty-four
by sixty-four. It has an altar round the pulpit, in a
half circle, and the house is fixed with long pews, of a
circular form, to be in uniform with the altar. The
front of the gallery is of the same form. It looks very

handsome, and will contain an abundance of people, but is not on the Methodist plan, for the pews are sold to the highest bidder.

"Saturday, 23d. I left Boston after dinner, and rode to Lynn, and put up at brother John Broadhead's. I was glad to be there. Several of my old friends came to see me in the evening, and I was very glad to see and converse with them. The day following being Sabbath, I preached, at 10 o'clock, on Isai. xxxiii. 13. It was an affecting time. At 3 o'clock I preached, and the house was much thronged. The Lord was with us. And also at 6 o'clock, my soul was much comforted in speaking to the people, and many wept under the word. When I put the brethren in mind of my first coming amongst them, and the diffculties that I, as well as they, had to go through, they could not forbear weeping. I could but hope that a blessing would follow that meeting. I have not been so well pleased for a long time, at meeting my old friends, as I was at this place.

"Thursday, 29th. I rode to Portsmoth, in New-Hampshire state, and put up at Mr. Huchinson's, and at night preached in the old meeting-house belonging to the Universalists. I had a crowded house, owing to a previous notice being given that one of our preachers on that'night would preach on a particular subject : however, he gave place to me, and I found a good degree of freedom in speaking, and was glad to be there. Two of our preachers were in town ; they have just began to preach in that place, and intend to continue it every Sabbath ; and withal, they contemplate purchasing the old meeting-house, in which I preached, if they can. It has a bell and a steeple, and is fitted out with pews. The next day I crossed

28 *

the river in the Province of Maine, and rode on through York to Kennebeck, and stayed all night at Barnard's tavern.

"Wednesday, August 3d. At Haye's, in the north part of Gloucester, I preached, and I had a great many of my old acquaintances to hear me, and the congregation was so large that we were forced to go into the woods to hold our meeting. I was greatly pleased and comforted among my friends. Many in the neighbourhood have been converted in the course of a few months past. Bless the Lord for his goodness.

"Sunday, 7th. In our meeting-house in Monmouth, at half after 10 o'clock, I preached on Heb. vii. 12. I had a good degree of liberty in speaking to the people, and it was a melting time with many of the hearers, and the word reached their hearts. Joshua Soule exhorted a while, and concluded. At half after 1, I held forth again on James i. 12. We had another good meeting. The congregation was uncommonly large, and many were forced to stay out of doors for the want of room. It was said by many, that they never saw so great a collection of people before, except at a conference. Just before night I attended a prayer-meeting at brother Fogg's, and after several persons had prayed, I prayed, and then spoke a little to the people, and told them I wished that *all* who would engage from that time to try and serve God, and meet me in heaven, would come and give me their hands, in token of it; many came and gave me their hands, and wept, and I could not refrain from weeping. Glory to God for that visit of love.

"Monday, 8th. I preached at a school-house in Winthrop. I had more people to hear me than could get in the house, and many of them wept heartily

under the word. There was great reason to hope
that much good was done. Thank God, I have had
much of the presence and love of God with me every
day for some time. Many of my former friends, who
have grown rather careless, flock out to hear me, and
some of them say they will try again to be more
engaged with God than what they have been heretofore.

"Tuesday, 9th. I preached at ———. My text
was, Deut. xxix. 29. *The secret things belong unto
the Lord our God, &c.* I felt but little faith or satisfaction in the beginning of the discourse. The people
have fixed pews all around the house, and all the rest
have no seats, except a few loose boards on blocks.
Whilst I was preaching, if a well dressed person came
in, the people would jump up in their pews, and slam
open their doors, and thump on their pews, and beckon
with their hands to get the person into their pews. I
was quite displeased with their pews, and with their
conduct. Toward the close of the meeting I felt
pretty well. I rode up to brother Thomas', and stayed
all night.

"Wednesday, 17th. I preached at a school-house
in Linconville, to a good company, who were quite
engaged in religion. The Lord is reviving his work
in this town, and souls are returning home to God. I
lodged at Mr. John Williamson's. What cold weather
for the season! the 17th of August, and frost sufficient
to kill some tender vines. But in many places in the
District of Maine, and in other parts of the country,
it killed whole fields of corn, both the blades and the
ear. Such an early frost has been seldom known.

"Sunday, 21st. I rode up on the east side of
Penobscot river, to Orington meeting-house, and

half after 10 o'clock I preached on Matt. xxv. 10. I
had a large company of people to hear me, and I
spoke with great freedom and faith; and the hearers
felt the power of the word. Then at half after 2
o'clock, I preached to a crowded assembly. When I
called upon them to remember former days, when I
first visited them about fifteen years before, which
was the first time they had ever heard a Methodist
preacher, many of them were bathed in tears; for
many of them, both parents and children, had been
converted under the preaching of the Methodists. It
was indeed a most solemn time, and my soul was much
quickened and blessed. I could truly say, *it was good
to be there.* In the afternoon I preached at Paul Nick-
erson's. My text was Psa. cxlv. 20. I had a crowded
house, and the spirit of the Lord God came upon me
while I was speaking, and I wept, and the people
wept greatly. It was the best meeting that we had
had together in that place. When I dismissed the
people, I told them that I was about to leave them,
and had but little expectation of ever preaching in that
place again. I told them I would be glad for all, who
were determined to try and meet me in heaven,
whether they were converted or not, to come and give
me their hands. Many of them came and gave me
their hands, and with streaming eyes begged my prayers, and wished my welfare. Several came who had
never been converted, and crying aloud, said they
would try to get to heaven if they could. I have no
doubt but a lasting blessing will follow this meeting.

"Monday, 22d. I turned my course back towards
my native country, being then about one thousand
miles from home. I crossed Penobscot river to Hampden; and in the meeting-house at 3 o'clock, I preached

on John vii. 7. We had a good meeting, and were
comforted together. I found some who feared God, in
this place. Among whom are some who say that they
were awakened and brought to God, by means of my
preaching in former years I lodged at brother Joseph
Baker's, a travelling minister.

"Tuesday, 23d. I rode to the Twenty-five mile
Pond, which is now a thickly settled country, most
part of the way through; but when I first travelled
the road, about fifteen years ago, there was not a house
to be seen for twenty miles. The country has been
won 'erfully improved of late years. I came to the
Twenty-five mile Pond, in Unity, and preached at 4
o'clock. I had a tolerably good time; but they were
not notified of my coming until some friends from a
distance, came into the neighbourhood. I lodged at
John Chaise's that night.

"Wednesday, 24th. I rode early, and went through
Clinton, crossed Kennebeck river, and on to Fairfield
meeting-house; in all about twenty-six miles. I
preached at 3 o'clock, and enjoyed a comfortable season; but felt weak and faint from long fasting. I
lodged at Philps' that night.

"Sunday, 28th. At our meeting-house in Farmington, I preached at half past 10 o'clock, on Isaiah
xxxiii. 13. I had a precious meeting, and the congregation was very large, insomuch that there was
not room in the house to contain the people. It was
a melting time indeed, and the people wept in every
part of the house. Then we had the Lord's Supper,
and a great many communicants, together with twelve
preachers. The people were greatly affected at the
table, and many of the spectators who tarried in the
house wept freely. I was pleased and surprised to

see such a crowd of people at the Lord's table. When
I first came among them, about fifteen years ago, they
had never seen a Methodist, and many of them were
afraid that they were a dangerous set of men ; but at
this time, (1808,) we have nine local preachers, and,
I suppose, about one hundred persons to commune
with us. Surely, the Lord hath done great things for
us. At half past 1 o'clock I preached again on Psa.
l. 23. The people were greatly wrought upon by the
word. Allen H. Cobb exhorted, and concluded. I
then had a sorrowful parting with many of my old
friends, whom I never expected to see again. I then
rode to James Couchran's, in Vienna, and stayed all
night."

The next day, he preached in Vienna, to an attentive congregation, from whom he parted with the most
sincere regret. In this place he had preached in
former days. The labours of him and of those who
succeeded him, had been greatly owned of God. "The
society was large and lively."

From Vienna, he visited Strong, near Sandy river,
a place which he had visited about eight years before.
He then went on through Jay and Livermore, Readfield, Durham, Portland and Scarborough ; and then
leaving the District of Maine, he entered the state of
New-Hampshire, and taking Dover in his way, went
to Mr. Church's, in the lower part of Barrington. He
had been in the District of Maine forty-three days,
during which time he had preached forty-seven sermons ; and, to use his own words, "had seen very
few dry or barren meetings." "The visit," continues
he, "was the most profitable and pleasing of any I
had ever made in that part of the world." He also
visited Poplin, Sandown, and Plastow, where he

finished his abours in New-Hampshire state, having
been in it five days, and preached seven sermons.

Wednesday, September 14th. He reached Lynn,
in the state of Massachusetts; here he preached for
the last time in that place, and had a sorrowful parting
with his old friends.

Friday, 16th, found him in Boston, where he
preached and visited, until the 19th, and then proceeded on, through Waltham, Ware, and Wilbraham.

Sunday, 25th. He crossed Connecticut river to
Hartford, and preached in the old play-house, in the
morning, and in the afternoon; "but (says he) there
is a very poor prospect of doing good in that place by
our preachers."

Friday, 30th. He left the state of Connecticut,
having remained six days in that state, and preached
eight sermons, and arrived the same day in Rhinebeck, state of New-York.

Sunday, the 2d October, he preached at Rhinebeck flats in the morning, and in the afternoon, on the
Rev. Freeborn Garrettson's plantation. He then
shaped his course towards the city of New-York,
passing through Poughkeepsie, down the high lands
of Croton river, on by the White Plains, and on the
7th reached the city, at which place he remained until
the 11th. Here he was pleased to find that the Lord
was at work, and graciously visiting the people with
the outpourings of his spirit. "I believe," says Mr.
Lee, "I never knew so great a revival of religion in
the city of New-York before, as what there was at
that time. The work had been great for several
months, and many souls had been converted to God,
and joined our society, and the prospect was still
pleasing."

During the few days which he spent in that place, he had an opportunity of preaching to crowded audiences, and he had great reason to believe that his labour was made a blessing to those that heard.

From New-York, he directed his course to Philadelphia, preaching at several intermediate places, and from the last named place to Baltimore, and then on to Washington city, where he arrived while Congress was in session, and had an opportunity of hearing the debates of that body for a few days. At length, after an absence of about eight months from his relations, he returned to Petersburg on the 9th of December. We will close this chapter with one more extract.

"Saturday, 31st. I was again closely engaged in writing all day. My mind was kept in peace, and my soul was longing after a greater conformity to the will of God. There I finished the day, the week, the month, and the year, all together, and bid farewell to the year 1808 for ever. I look back on the past year, and call to remembrance the trials I have passed through, and bless God, that my face has not been turned back to the world. I think over the blessings which the Lord has conferred upon me, and call upon my soul to bless the Lord, for his great goodness towards my poor soul the past year. If my life is spared, I intend by the grace of God, to push through all difficulties for the time to come, and try to get ready to go to heaven, when I die. Lord prepare me for thyself, and take me home to heaven, to dwell with thee, for ever and ever. Amen!"

CHAPTER XIX.

—◦◦◦—

WE have followed Mr. Lee with much pleasure in his last tour through the New-England states, and have, in some measure, participated in the pure joy he must have experienced in the society of his old friends, and particularly with his spiritual children, many of whom he found *walking in the truth*. From the blessed effects attending his ministry during this long journey, we cannot doubt but that his *steps were directed by the Lord*. And we rejoice, more particularly, to find in him the same devotion to the cause of Christ, the same laborious servant to the Church, while he receives the same returns of gratitude, and of kind attentions from the people among whom he laboured. And though the jealousy of rivalship might have excited some narrow and selfish minds to attempt an eclipse of

29

his well-earned fame during his life, yet, now that he is dead, we cannot, and *they* cannot, withhold their admiration at beholding his undeviating constancy, and persevering diligence in the cause of his Divine Master.

On his return to his native land, probably thinking that he could not much longer continue his itinerating career, he thought it advisable to furnish himself with a place that he might call his own ; and accordingly, in the beginning of the year 1809, he purchased a piece of land in the vicinity of his father's residence. How little could he have accumluated of this *world's goods*, when, after devoting about twenty-six years of his life to the service of the sanctuary, he was only able to pay two hundred dollars towards his small farm, with an engagement for two hundred and fifty dollars more at the end of four years. *Freely he had received, and freely he had given.*

It afforded him a peculiar gratification to meet with many of his old friends and brethren in the ministry, at the Virginia conference, which commenced the first of February, in Tarborough, N. C. At this conference he received his appointment to Brunswick circuit, Virginia, and delayed no time in getting to the place of his destination.

Some notice has been already made of his writing a *History of the Methodists in America.* He had been engaged in collecting materials for this work, which was now nearly ready for the press. It was therefore necessary to go as far north as Baltimore, in order to superintend its publication ; and as Congress was about to meet in the city of Washington, on business of great emergency, Mr. Lee concluded that he would tender his services to that body, to serve them as chaplain. He arrived in Washington the 20th of May, and on the 22d Congress met, and proceeded to the election

of their proper officers.   Mr. Lee was present, and
witnessed their proceedings, and took occasion to
speak to some of the members of his acquaintance,
and let them know that he was in nomination for the
chaplain's place, in the House of Representatives.
On Saturday, 27th, the house proceeded to the election of a chaplain, and after two ballotings, Mr. Lee
was declared to be duly elected, and on the Monday
following, began to officiate in his new office.

In entering upon the important duties of his station,
to which he was called by the representatives of a
free and independent people, it is but reasonable to
suppose, that although he might feel gratified with his
station, yet he was far from being dazzled with those
marks of respect thus shown him.   Respecting this appointment, the following were his views.   " I believe
my intention was pure in offering for this place ; and
I must do the best I can while I am in the office.   I
expect some good will be done directly or remotely.
I wish to leave all to God.   O Lord, thou knowest my
heart, thou knowest I desire to please thee, but unless thou wilt stand by me, I shall labour in vain."

In regard to this appointment, it has been urged by
some to the disadvantage of Jesse Lee's character, as
being incompatible with his prior engagements as an
itinerant Methodist preacher.   But why ?   If his station could be filled by a faithful substitute, does the
being a Methodist itinerant preclude him from obey-
ing the call of his country, to preach to, and pray for,
the representatives of the nation!   Besides, had not
the faithful labours, the long services, the high standing, and the distinguished abilities of Mr. Lee, fairly
purchased hi n privileges which many others had no
right to claim?   But why make this apology for him?
Have not others of our own preachers served in the same

capacity ? But we shall dismiss this subject by observing, that the necessity of any such apology for this
act, instead of lessening the dignity of our beloved
brother, only enhances his worth at the expense of
those whose censures have made this slight vindication
necessary.

In June he made a trip to Baltimore, and issued a
prospectus for his History of the Methodists, and sent
out prospectuses to different parts of the continent.
On returning from Baltimore to Washington, as he
was descending a hill, about two miles south of Elk-
ridge ferry, his horse unluckily fell at full length, and
broke the shaft of his gig, and he was thrown head
foremost from his seat, and in falling, his leg struck
against a screw attached to the gig, making a most
dangerous wound. Some person of his acquaintance
happening to come up just after the accident had hap-
pened, assisted him to a house, where the wound was
dressed as well as circumstances would admit. But.
notwithstanding the pain and inconvenience which he
endured from the wound, he pursued his journey the
same day, and rode to Bladensburg. In a day or two
he began to experience serious inconvenience from
his leg, and was confined several weeks to his room ;
during which time he was attended by a physician.

In the month of July he was able to return to Virginia, and took his circuit once more, though not
entirely recovered from the effects of his fall.

In December he was re-elected chaplain to Congress ; and on the 30th of the same month the first
sheet of his History of the Methodists was printed.

In February, 1810, he attended the Virginia annual
conference, in Petersburg, and received his appointment to the Meherrin district. As soon as conference
adjourned, he hastened on to Washington. Toward

the latter part of April, he finished the last proof sheet of his History of the Methodists. This business had employed his attention a little more than four months, and he was not a little gratified that it was now fast drawing to a close. His book contained three hundred and sixty-six pages.

On Tuesday the first of May, Congress, after an unusually protracted session, adjourned to the first Monday in December. Mr. Lee was enabled, on that day, to distribute several of his books among the members of his acquaintance. From the press of business on his hands at this time, he could not possibly get to his district until the latter part of the month of May. He took his appointments at Roper's meeting-house, on the 27th; but, contrary to his expectations, found that all the preachers of the several circuits in his district had held their quarterly meetings in his absence, with the exception of one. He then concluded that he would attend every place where he had appointed quarterly-meeting, and preach on the Sabbath; thus compensating, in some sort, for the derangement of his plans in the first instance.

He continued on his district, labouring with considerable success, until the latter part of the month of November. He then set out for the Federal City, where he arrived time enough to tender his services to Congress as their chaplain. He proved to be the successful applicant, and was again elected.

In February, 1811, he attended the Virginia conference, held in the city of Raleigh, North Carolina. Here some difficulties occurred relative to the book which he had published; and dissatisfaction expressed by some on account of his being absent from his district for several months during the year. It is unde-

niably true that Mr. Lee published a book, entitled
" A Short History of the Methodists in the United
States of America, beginning in 1766, and continued
till 1809." But, however little this work might have
been estimated by some of his brethren, I am inclined
to think that posterity will thank him for his labour.
It is true, the work may have its imperfections, and
the scientific reader may not relish its style, and the
arrangement of its matter ; and those who read merely
to gratify their petulent disposition to find fault, will
doubtless discover blemishes enough to satisfy their
desire. But it might be asked, who has as yet produced a better? Mr. Lee endeavoured to furnish a
plain people with a plain account of the rise and progress of Methodism in America ; and if he has not
been able to please the fastidious critic, he has unques-
tionably accomplished a very important object, namely,
the furnishing the friends of the cause with an undisguised narration of interesting facts respecting the history of the Methodists. Those who object to the apparent
egotism in this history, should recollect that JESSE LEE
had known the people whose history he writes from
the beginning ; that he had travelled the most extensively of any of the preachers except Mr. Asbury and
Mr. Whatcoat ; that he had kept the most minute account of matters and things of any one else ; that he
took an active and deep interest in most of the events
and transactions which he records ; and finally, that the
greater proportion of his history was composed from
materials of his own composing ; these things considered, it is not to be wondered at that he frequently
speaks in the first person. On this account, so far as
we confide in his integrity, of which we have no
reason to doubt, his history assumes a character of
authenticity which otherwise it could not possess. He

was an eye and ear witness of what he relates. And what stamps it with the most indubitable character of truth, it accords with the public record, (so far as this latter speaks,) of the annual conferences, the printed minutes of conference.

Whoever may hereafter write the history of Methodism in America, will have to acknowledge his obligations to Mr. Lee, for many interesting facts, which, but for his history, would, in all probability, have been buried in oblivion. On this account, we cannot but rejoice that such a record, plain and artless, has been given to the public ; and we shall equally rejoice to see it superceded by a more diffusive, a more elegant, and a less exceptionable history of the Methodist Episcopal Church.

Respecting the censure which he incurred on account of serving as chaplain to Congress, it is scarcely necessary to say any thing more. In this transaction he acted, no doubt, conscientiously, and perhaps was as useful in that station as he might have been elsewhere.

Mr. Lee possessed that buoyancy of mind, and consciousness of integrity which enabled him to bear up under any difficulty with peculiar fortitude. And he uniformly maintained an independence of soul, which procured for him the victory in almost every contest. He was a stranger to that gloominess and dejection, which have been the companions of even some good men ; and he had that perfect command of himself, which never failed to place him in an elevated situation, superior to the assaults of the weak or the malevolent. Sometimes when he saw that his assailants were actuated by improper views, and were destitute of solid ground on which to stand, a humorous anecdote served as a weapon of defence ; and it often proved successful in frustrating his antagonist. His extensive travels, and consequent acquaintance with mankind, furnished him with a fund of instructive anecdotes, which he never failed to use to the best advantage; and, in self-defence, when a consciousness of innocence presided in his breast, he often found it a more successful weapon than the gravity of argument, or the labour of testimony would have been. Though to mortify an enemy as a rival, was never his design, because he possessed too much delicacy of feeling to indulge in this work of humiliation, yet his keen satires were not unfrequently productive of this effect. We do not, however, recommend the frequent use of this dangerous weapon. It must be used as the barber does his razor, to shave off the excrescences of character, when their bushy appearance renders them disgustful.

From the conference in Raleigh, he had to travel through intense cold weather, and bad roads, to Washington, where he continued until Congress adjourned. the 4th of March.

Having some business in Baltimore, he accordingly set out for that place, on the 5th, and arrived there the same day. Here he was much cheered with pleasing tidings from England, respecting the prosperity of the work of God. Having adjusted his temporal business, he left Baltimore on the 11th, and set out for the south, passing through Bladensburg, Georgetown, Alexandria, Dumfries, Fredericksburg, Richmond, and so on to Petersburg, where he attended to some temporal concerns which called his attention, and then visited his father, and employed a day or two in making some improvements on his farm.

During the remaining part of this year, his labours were principally confined to Amelia circuit, and the

Petersburg station. In 1812 he attended the conference in Richmond, and was stationed in that city.
In May he attended the general conference at New
York, and returned to his station about the middle of
June. While in Richmond, he endeavoured to attend
to the interests of the church, by preaching, and by
paying due attention to discipline. Not only did he
enforce the doctrines of repentance, faith, and holiness, but he made it his business to defend those leading doctrines of the gospel, against the cavils of infidels, and fatalists.

In December, he received the intelligence of his
being once more elected as chaplain to Congress.
This news came to him rather unexpectedly, inasmuch
as he made no efforts whatever to obtain the office.
He could not but feel indebted to his friends in Congress, for this mark of attention ; but at that juncture,
he wished to give his services to the church, provided
it had been left to his choice. He finally resolved to
attend to the call, and forthwith repaired to Washington without delay.

In 1813 he was appointed to Brunswick, and was
twice elected chaplain to Congress. In 1814 he was
appointed to Cumberland and Manchester, and in December of the same year, was chosen chaplain to the
Senate. This year he made preparation to publish
a couple of sermons ; the one, a funeral discourse,
which he was called upon to preach in consequence
of the death of Miss Hardy, of Bertie. The other,
a practical discourse, from a favourite text, and well
worthy the perusal of every Christian, who has a real
desire to understand his duty to God, his neighbour,
and himself. The former also has its merits ; but
neither of them has ever had a very extensive circu-
lation.

In February, 1815, he attended the Virginia conference, at Lynchburg, (Va.) and was appointed to travel within the bounds of the Baltimore conference. No particular place was designated. It was intimated to him that this would be made known in due time. Perhaps the bishop concluded, that it would be better for Mr. Lee to have a station near the seat of government, inasmuch as he had been called to that place, to serve as chaplain several years in succession. It is quite reasonable to suppose that the bishop, who, we may presume, had the interests of Mr. Lee at heart, wished to accommodate him in that respect.

A few weeks subsequent to the conference in Lynchburgh, Mr. Lee received a letter from one of the preachers in Baltimore, informing him that he was appointed to Fredricksburg. He refused to fulfil this appointment, being firmly persuaded that it was illegally made. It was the first time in his life in which he refused to fill the station assigned him. Although at first he thought himself justifiable in acting as he did, yet afterward, he regretted that he failed in this instance to conform to the established usage of his church. The writer is disposed to think, and he is not alone in the sentiment, that the superintendent gave him this appointment from a belief that it would suit his convenience.

But, although Mr. Lee did not go to Fredricksburg, yet he was not unemployed. During the year he travelled through that part of Virginia lying between the waters of James and Appomattox rivers, and Roanoak. He made a visit to Norfolk, in the spring; then returned to the vicinity of Petersburg, and spent a few weeks amongst his relations, preaching at frequent appointments, and in the summer and autumn was employed on Brunswick circuit.

Mr. Lee, who previous to this time, had generally enjoyed a portion of health unusually good,
began to find by experience that this state of things
could not always last.   His afflictions were now
more frequent, and more severe than formerly.
In looking into his journal for this year 1815, we
find the following remarks.

"November 9th.   This was a wet day.   I did
not go to meeting, but after dinner I rode to sister
Jane Fisher's, and stayed all night, and was quite
unwell.   These afflictions of the Lord, are designed
for my good, perhaps to give me notice that my
departure is at hand.   Lord, sanctify them to my
spiritual welfare."

In the latter part of November, and first of December, his afflictions seemed to increase so much
that he was confined to his room, and had recourse to medicine, but in the midst of these pre-
sages of approaching dissolution, he was resigned ;
being fully persuaded that "these light afflictions,
which were but for a moment, should work for him
a far more exceeding and eternal weight of glory."

In January, 1816, he attended the Virginia conference, held in Raleigh, then returning to Virginia.
he made arrangements for his journey to the north,
having come to the determination to take his appointment from the Baltimore conference.

Whether he had a real presentiment that he should
never return to Virginia again, I am not prepared
to say ; yet, from the very particular pains he took
to arrange his business before his departure, and
to adjust all his temporal concerns in the best manner he possibly could, leave us grounds to believe
that he had some impression upon his mind to that
effect.

On the 27th of February he took leave of his
friends in Petersburgh, and commenced his journey
to the north, and on the 6th of March arrived in
Georgetown, and on Friday the 8th, the Baltimore
conference met, and did not adjourn until the 15th.
Mr. Lee was appointed to the city of Annapolis,
and entered upon his station the 27th. He commenced his ministerial duties with a determination
to do something for God whilst he remained in that
place.

It is worthy of remark, that about this time the
Methodist church sustained, I might say an irrepa-
ble loss, in the death of the Rev. Francis Asbury.
The whole Methodist church, from the Canadas to
St. Mary's, were ready to pay him that tribute of
respect which was due to his worth.   The estimation in which Mr. Lee held the character of this
good and great man, may be seen by the following
biographical sketch, which he wrote, and published
soon after he received the news of his death.

" Departed this life, near Fredricksburg, in Virginia, on Sunday, the 31st of March, the *Rev. Francis
Asbury*, the oldest bishop of the Methodist Episcopal church, in America ; in the 72d year of his
age, and the 49th of his itinerant ministry. He
was an Englishman by birth, and entered into the
travelling connexion with the Methodists in 1767,
and after travelling four years in England, he came
to America, (then British provinces) in 1771, and
landed at Philadelphia, on the 27th of October. He
was present at the first conference that was ever
held by the Methodist preachers in America, which
began in Philadelphia in July, 1773. He continued
among us during the revolutionary war, and after
travelling upwards of thirteen years in the United

States, he was ordained a deacon, an elder, and a
superintendent, at the conference at Baltimore, which
began on the 25th of December, 1784, and ended
in January, 1785. In February following he visited
Charleston, South-Carolina, for the first time. In
1787, he was the first time called *Bishop*, in the
form of discipline. He acted as superintending bishop
for thirty-one years and a few months. In which
time he attended about two hundred and seventy conferences, and appointed all the preachers to the different circuits. It is supposed that he ordained in
all, three thousand ministers, including travelling and
local preachers. He travelled through seventeen
of the United States, and some of the territories.
He was always of a slender constitution, and yet never
spared himself, but ventured through the greatest
difficulties and dangers, in order to preach to the people, and attend to the preachers. He was an excellent preacher : and his gift in prayer was exceedingly great. He was deeply pious, remarkably fervent and constant in prayer. His peculiar talent
was for governing the preachers, and taking care of
the Church of Christ. He generally rose early in the
morning, travelled many miles in a day, preached
often, and slept but little. He was generally known
throughout the United States ; much esteemed, and
greatly beloved. His presence was generally courted,
his advice requested, and his directions attended to.
It pleased God to spare him for many years ; and at
last to give him an easy, safe, and happy passage out
of this world : and his numerous friends have no room
to doubt but what their loss is his infinite gain. He
has not left behind him many, if any, to equal him in
the church to which he belonged. And notwithstand-

ing his loss is, and will be greatly lamented, we have full confidence in the Lord that he will take care of, and provide for his church."

Such was the tribute which the subject of this memoir paid to bishop Asbury. Little did he think at the time he was penning this sketch, that within a few months some surviving friend would have to perform the same mournful task for him. But such is the feeble tenure by which we hold our lives, that we are treading in the same steps of those who have passed into eternity, and soon will have to realize the same change, and leave others to follow us, as we have followed those who have gone before.

The writer of these pages, had an opportunity, for the last time, of seeing Mr. Lee in the city of Baltimore, during the sitting of the general conference, in the month of May, 1816. One circumstance which occurred at that time, was well calculated to awaken the sympathies, and excite the sorrows of those who attended this conference. Mr. Asbury's remains were brought from the place of their first interment to the city of Baltimore, and were deposited in a vault prepared for the purpose, under the pulpit of the Eutaw church.

The procession was formed in Light-street; perhaps not less than one hundred and fifty ministers, travelling and local, followed as mourners. Mr. Lee, and the compiler of these pages, walked together. The scene was solemn and impressive. Mr. Lee's countenance bespoke the emotions of his mind; a dignified sorrow, such as veterans feel, while following to the grave an old companion in arms, was evinced by his words and countenance. They had suffered together, and had long fought in the same ranks; the one had gained his crown, the other was soon to receive it.

From Baltimore, Mr. Lee returned to his station in Annapolis, in May, and recommenced his labours with zeal and assiduity. While not engaged in his public labours, he took a peculiar pleasure in visiting his friends in the city and its vicinity. The residences of Mr. H. Duvall, Mr. G. Wills, and E. Williams, situated some distance from town, were favourite retreats ; places to which he could at all times go as a friend, and where he was sure to meet with a hearty welcome.

About the middle of July, he made another, and his last visit to Baltimore, and put up at the house of his particular friend, Zachary Myles. Here he adjusted some temporal business, and returned to his station, where he continued, until he went to return no more.

Hearing that a camp-meeting was to be held near Hillsborough, on the eastern shore of Maryland, he resolved to attend it. It commenced on the 21st of August. We do not know the precise day in which he set out to the camp-meeting; his journal is brought down to the 15th of August ; on the evening of which he preached in Annapolis, to a large congregation, on 1 Cor. xv. 33. *Be not deceived; evil communications corrupt good manners.* It was a solemn meeting ; and judging from every circumstance, we are inclined to believe that he spent the Sabbath also in Annapolis. Be this as it may, he attended the camp-meeting ; where, on Thursday 22d, he preached a profitable sermon, on 1 Pet. ii. 5. *Ye also, as lively stones, are built up a spiritual house, &c.*

Saturday, 24th. At 3 o'clock he preached on 2 Pet. iii. 18. *But grow in grace.* This was a favourite text with him, and it was his last ; the discourse which he delivered from it, ending his public labours. A large, attentive, serious, and much affected congregation will not soon forget the sermon, and the feelings on that memorable occasion. The same evening he was taken with a chill that was succeeded by a fever, which continued to the close of his life.

On Saturday the 25th, he was removed to Hillsborough, to the house of brother Sellers, where every attention, by physicians and friends, was given ; but neither medical skill, nor the soothing hand of friendship could arrest the progress of his disease.

Through the first part of his illness, his mind was much weighed down, so that he spoke but little. These were, no doubt, the last struggles with the grand adversary, and the sequel will show the triumphant manner in which he was put to flight ; for, on Tuesday night, September the 10th, he broke out in ecstacies of joy ; also, on Wednesday, 11th, about 9 o'clock A. M. his soul was so overwhelmed with the love of God, that he was constrained to cry out glory ! glory ! glory ! hallelujah ! Jesus reigns. On the evening of the same day he spoke nearly twenty minutes deliberately, and distinctly ; among other things, he directed one* present, who affectionately attended him in his illness, to write to his brother, and inform him that he died happy in the Lord ; and was fully satisfied with brother Sellers' conduct towards him. " Give my respects to bishop M'Kendree, (said he)

* The Rev. Henry Boehm, to whom we are indebted for the particulars of his death.

and tell him that I die in love with all the preachers ;
that I love him, and that he lives in my heart." Then
he took leave of all present, six or seven in number,
and requested them to pray. After this he spoke but
little ; his work was done, and he was in waiting for
the summons of his Master.

Thursday, the 12th. In the early part of the day
he lost his speech, but appeared still to retain his reason. Thus he continued to linger till the same evening about half past 7 o'clock, when, without a sigh or
groan he expired, with his eyes seemingly fixed on his
great recompense of reward. Such was the end of
this faithful servant of Christ. "O ! death, where is
thy sting ? O ! grave, where is thy victory ?"

Thus ended the labours and sufferings of this man
of God aged fifty-eight years and six months ; and
though he left no disconsolate widow, or fatherless
orphan, to shed the tear of sorrow upon his bier, or
strew his grave with flowers, yet he lives in the affections of thousands who knew him, and who were
endeared to him by the strong ties of Christian love
and brotherly affection.

A SKETCH OF HIS CHARACTER.

ACCORDING to the usual custom, we shall endeavour to present the leading features of Mr. Lee's character. But we must premonish the reader not to expect from us an elaborate display of virtues which did not exist, a record of deeds which were never performed, nor of mental and spiritual excellences to which he never attained. It is easy to sketch a character by seizing on some prominent feature, and, aided by an excursive imagination, fill up the outline according to our own ideas of greatness, of goodness, and of perfection; but to represent a man as he in reality was, to exhibit those lights and shades which actually existed, and to draw every line with the pencil of *truth*, so as to leave no artificial colouring, either to gratify an enemy, or to please a partial friend; this requires an intimacy of acquaintance, and a power of nice discrimination, as well as an impartial regard to truth, to which we can hardly dare to lay claim. Reminding ourselves of our own liability to err, and claiming the same indulgence which we wish to extend to others, we will attempt a sketch of the character of our departed brother, JESSE LEE.

1. *His experience of the grace of God.* This was evidently deep and genuine. At the time he first made a profession of experimental religion, the number of experienced Christians was small, and they were often made the subject of obloquy and reproach; but in the midst of these temptations to continue a

life of sinfulness, in the days of his youth, from a conviction of the importance of religion, he turned his
back upon the world, took up his cross, and dared to
be singular for the sake of Christ. And he gave the
fullest evidence of the genuineness of the work of
grace upon his heart by the uniformity of his obedience, in the subsequent years of his active life, to
the commands of God. He rested not his hope of
eternal happiness upon the sandy foundation of a dry
morality; but he built upon Christ; he experienced
justification by faith in the merits of His death; and
persevered in the exercise of this faith and in good
works, *in all holy conversation and godliness*, unto the
end of his life.

2. *His call to, and faithfulness in, the ministry.*—
We have already seen the caution with which he
commenced in this important work. He evidently
acted under the influence of that truth, that a man
must be "inwardly moved by the Holy Ghost to take
upon him this office:" and it was not until, in addition
to his own impressions as to its being his duty, the
frequent and pressing calls of his brethren urged him
forward, that he could persuade himself to embark in,
what appeared to him, so hazardous an undertaking.
And that he commenced without any view to pecu-
niary reward, or from any ambitious views of human
applause, is fully evinced by the circumstances under
which he began. When compelled, contrary to his
inclination, and in opposition to the dictates of his
conscience, to serve as a soldier, he boldly announced
his religious views and principles, and preached
Christ unto his fellow-soldiers; and when money was
offered as a compensation, he disinterestedly and re-
solutely refused it, thinking,—such were the humble
thoughts he entertained of his performance,—that if

they could have "patience to hear him, he could
well afford to preach to them."

Having "put his hand to the plough" he did not,
as many have done, "look back;" but steadfastly persevered, often in the midst of sufferings and reproach,
but as often amidst success, in the awakening and conversion of souls, to the end of his probationary exist-
ence. Nor were his ministerial labours small. He
travelled extensively. Perhaps no man on this continent, except the superintendents of the Church, has
travelled so extensively, and laboured so assiduously,
especially in breaking up new ground, as it has been
called, as the Rev. Jesse Lee. New-England will
long remember his toils, his watchings for the souls
of the people, and his active endeavours to advance
their spiritual and everlasting interests. We find him,
like a *flying angel*, taking his rapid flight, crying to
all who came within the hearing of his voice, *Repent,
and believe in Christ*, from New-York to Boston, to
Rhode-Island, to the Province of Maine, to Vermont,
to Canada; filling up every intermediate place, which
time and circumstances would allow him to reach and
light upon, and in all scattering the good seed of the
kingdom: and when his mission apparently ended
in this part of the country, in which he had laboured
hard and suffered much, he as readily in obedience to
the call of Providence, turned his course southward,
and stopped not until the extreme parts of Georgia,
and even the Floridas witnessed the sound of his
voice. And during the whole course of his ministerial career, though, like all the other of the Methodist itinerants, he was subject to an annual re-
moval by the superintending bishop, only once did he
hesitate or refuse to take his allotted appointment;
and though he might have erred in this, charity, and

the known integrity of the man, both say, that it was
an error of the judgment and not of the heart. We
cannot but venerate the stern virtues of the man,
who, braving all dangers, despising ease, wealth, lux-
ury, and the temporary breeze of popular applause,
should commence, and progress, and continue, even
to the end of life, in the discharge of a ministerial
duty which should drag with it so much toil, in-
volve in it so high responsibilities, and make so little
promise of worldly good. But he judged accurately.
He had counted the cost. He looked higher than
earthly good. He fixed his eye upon the future recompense of reward ; and after this he steadily pursued until it was, through mighty grace, obtained.
Let those who can make sport with such men's characters, blush for their own frivolity, and own that
their trifling shows how little they have learned to
value true worth, and how unworthy *they* are to
compete with *him*, as well as how much they would
suffer by a comparison with *him* whom *they* affect
to despise.

3. *His abilities as a preacher.* Perhaps it will
be somewhat difficult to make a just estimate of these,
because men differ so much as to what constitutes
ministerial abilities. If, however, the being well read
in the sacred scriptures, the having a clear understanding of the grand system of redemption by Christ, and
of salvation through His blood, the being able to deliver oneself in language plain and energetic, the art
of addressing oneself to the conscience so as to awaken
the sinner from his sleep of death ; if so to exhibit
Christ in all his offices, as Priest, King, and Prophet, so
to magnify the merits of His atoning blood, as to induce
the trembling penitent to lay hold on Him for life and
salvation ; if a capacity to explain and enforce all the

great doctrines of the gospel, and particularly the
doctrine of holiness of heart and life ; if an ability to
defend the peculiar doctrines of Christ against liber-
tines and infidels, as well as against " heated Antinomi-
ans," and cavelling controversialists ; if an ability to do
all this may be taken as a sound criterion by which we
may decide on the abilities of a preacher of the gospel,
then we may pronounce Jesse Lee to have been a
GREAT preacher, and, what is incomparably better,
and has a much pleasanter sound, a GOOD preacher ;
for this he did, and that for a length of time of which
few can boast, very successfully.

But if it be necessary to constitute a man of great
abilities, to be *profoundly learned*, he has no claim to
that distinction. He, it is true, cultivated an acquaintance with his vernacular language, had a taste for
reading, and, according to the opportunity afforded
him amidst his extensive travels and numerous labours,
he improved himself by the study of theological, and
other books ; but he never made any pretensions to
human learning, neither do his friends think it necessary to put in this claim for him, in order to rescue his
name from oblivion, or his character from reproach.
He, however, was deeply read in the school of Christ,
being inwardly taught by the Holy Ghost, was soundly
experienced in divine things, and had acquired, from
his various travels and continual intercourse with all
sorts of people, an extensive acquaintance with human
nature, in all its varied hues ; this gave him that perfect command over himself and over others, especially
an audience and an antagonist, which generally secured
to him respect and attention. Those who fre-
quented the house of God with a view to *profit* by the
word, were seldom disappointed when Jesse Lee occupied that " holy place," the pulpit ; and those who

went from other motives, sometimes repented of their temerity, and came again to atone for their fault, by confessing their sins, and supplicating for mercy in the name of Jesus. These are the evidences of his abilities as a preacher of righteousness.

Neither do we claim for him those rare talents of elocution which are supposed requisite to constitute the orator. His eloquence was the simple eloquence of truth, warmly addressed to the heart, unadorned with any other flowers, than such as he had gathered from the garden of the Lord, the holy scriptures ; for he seldom quoted from any book except the book of God. And it may be said to his praise, that he never disgusted the good taste of his hearers by assuming the airs of some popular speakers, in order to gain applause ; nor of copying the defects of others under an erroneous idea that they were excellencies which might enhance his own worth. To this worse than worthless traffic, his lofty soul never stooped. He doubtless acted under the impression that truth shines by its own light, and that it presses upon the conscience by its own weight ; and therefore, it only needed to be presented plainly to the understanding in order to be either cordially received, or wilfully and criminally rejected.

4. *His love to the souls of men.* This evinced itself on all occasions. The personal sacrifices which he made to save them, and the vehemence with which he urged upon them the tremendous truths of God, sufficiently prove his thirst for their salvation, without adding one word more on this head.

5. *His plainness of dress and manners,* give him a rank among the primitive Christians, and evangelists. He abhorred all worldly pomp and parade, much more, *religious* pomp, esteeming it as the relic of an apostate church. In this, some have thought he carried

his aversion to an inexcusable extreme. But, doubtless, if we must err, this is the safest side of the "golden
mean." His extreme aversion to the "priestly robe"
made him so zealously oppose its introduction among
the Methodist clergy, at the time of the organization
of the church. How far this may have been justifiable, we leave others to judge, who have searched
the records of ancient times, and have considered the
garments by which the ministry was distinguished. It
is certain, however, that the *pride of dress* is one of
the reprehensible things which the holy scriptures
condemn..

6. *His ambition.* It may seem strange to some that
this should be enumerated. Though we think it perfectly commendable to be ambitious to obtain and to do
good, or, in other words, "earnestly to covet the best
gifts," yet we have introduced the notice of this here,
principally for the purpose of repelling, what we consider, an unfounded accusation which some have preferred against Mr. Lee. In the course of the preceding memoir, we have noticed his having been a
candidate for the office of a bishop, and the nearness
of his election. We are willing to grant that he was
disappointed,—that he did expect the office. And had
he not a right to expect it? Had not Mr. Asbury more
than once signified his intention to bring him forward?
Had he not formally recognized him as either his suc-
cessor or coadjutor, by using him as his substitute in
attending the annual conferences, and stationing the
preachers? And would Mr. Asbury thus have presented him to the notice of preachers and people,
had he not believed Mr. Lee a suitable person to fill
that highly responsible office?

31

But, say some, he was *desirous* of being a bishop, and therefore indulged in a criminal ambition. Allowing that he was *desirous*, does this *criminate* him ? By no means. Does not the apostle Paul say, " He that desires the office of a bishop, desires a good thing ?" And is it *criminal* to desire a good thing ? Allowing, therefore, that elder Lee was desirous of being a bishop in the Methodist Episcopal Church, it by no means follows as a necessary consequence, that he indulged in any reprehensible ambition.

Besides, the objection takes for granted, the very thing to be proved, namely, that elder Lee ever did *desire* the office of a bishop, *abstractedly* considered. That he might have desired it in subserviency to the wishes of many of his brethren, who had expressed their wishes to him, and to the calls of the church, which now demanded an additional officer under that title, and also with a view to more extensive usefulness, may be granted without any impeachment of the integrity, the honesty, or even the meekness and humility of our deceased brother. Every *good* man, and especially every *good* minister, desires every gift, and every qualification, and every station, in which he may *do* the *most good* to the souls of men ; and such is the wide field of labour expanding before a Methodist bishop, that it presents a vast opening for extensive and permanent usefulness to the church, and to the world ; and a man duly qualified for this station, may, we believe, desire it on the same principle, and from the same motives, that he may desire to preach the gospel at all.

Look for a moment, at the labours, the privations, the sufferings, and the poverty, as well as the many perplexing difficulties, fully known only to those who have an experience of them, which are connected with this high station, and then judge, if a man must not be the merest novice among men, to desire the office from any other motive than to comply with the imperious calls of divine Providence. *Jesse Lee was ambitious to do good.* And if any used an improper influence to prevent him from doing all he might otherwise have done, let the stone fall at his feet, and not be lodged in the forehead of him whom the people, and whom God delighted to honour.

7. *That he enjoyed much of the consolations of the Spirit,* is evident from the numerous instances in which he records the happiness he possessed in communion with God, and the times of refreshing which accompanied his ministry. And the influence of the divine Spirit he considered not only as essential to c institute the real Christian, but also to enable the minister of Jesus Christ to understand and " rightly to divide the word of truth." Through this influence he was inwardly supported, and comforted, during his toils and sufferings, in the cause of Christ. This also enkindled that ardent *zeal* which burned so steadily and uniformly, and which sometimes burst forth in flames of divine love, in shouts of praise to God, and on all occasions, evinced itself in his efforts to do good to the souls of men.

8. *He was a great lover of the doctrines and the discipline of the church of which he was a member.* In days of dissention and division, when the church has been torn by factious spirits, he stood " as an iron pillar strong," turning the whole weight of his influence to preserve the " unity of the Spirit in the bonds of peace." In forming his plans, he used cau-

tion and deliberation, but was prompt to execute them.
Neither could small matters turn him aside from his
purpose, when his judgment was finally made up . If,
in the opinion of some, he manifested too much tenacity in adhering to his peculiar sentiments, we r ay
safely attribute it to a conscientious regard to what he
considered right and important, and not to that contracted spirit which defends a purpose, a plan, or a
proposition, merely because he was its author.   He
knew how to estimate the judgment of others too well,
not to yield in peace, when the majority decided against
him.   The early attachment which he had formed for
the peculiarities of Methodism, and his firm conviction,
that they were subservient to the advancement of the
eternal interests of men, made him adhere to them
with that firmness and resolution, which sometimes
exposed him to the suspicions of bigotry ; and, perhaps in some instances, when he found himself obliged to differ from others in matters of opinion and
judgment, he did not evince that modesty which a just
regard to our fallibility inspires, nor that yieldingness
of spirit which is needful to prevent unnecessary alter-
cation.   But these may be ranked among those infirmities of our natures, which originate from ignorance,
(for who so wise as to comprehend every subject
clearly ?) and from those biases which grow out of
our peculiar circumstances of life, and habits of thinking.   That Jesse Lee was subject to such like infirmities, and that he would have evinced fewer of them,
had his mind been more exclusively devoted to science,
we are willing to admit ; and it is admitted without
any impeachment of his motives, the purity and integrity of his conduct, or of his inflexible regard to justice and mercy.

In his last will and testament, he bequeathed a legacy to the three oldest travelling preachers of the Virginia conference, and likewise left a donation to the Charter Fund, whose annual revenue is appropriated to the support of the travelling preachers, their widows and orphans. Thus evincing in his last moments, his unalterable attachment to the cause, for the support of which he had devoted his whole life. But he left neither widow nor child to weep over his tomb, having never been married; and it seems he never thought of changing his state of celibacy until within a few years of his death, and even this thought was relinquished soon after it was formed, as he could not succeed according to his wishes in the person of his choice. In this, as in all the other events of his life, he bowed with that submission to an inscrutable Providence which became the christian and the christian minister.

Mr. Lee's countenance generally indicated a calm and peaceful mind, and was expressive of much shrewdness of observation. And that he sometimes indulged himself in sallies of innocent witticisms, and could point the weapon of irony so as to render the absurd ridiculous, is granted. How far these dangerous weapons may be indulged without injury to ourselves and to others, is one of those nice points which the casuist may find it somewhat difficult to determine. If time is devoted to this which ought to be employed upon graver subjects; if its indulgence at any time unfits the mind for the solemn exercise of devotion; if it is suffered to obtrude itself into the awful solemnities of announcing the counsels of infinite wisdom and goodness, to "court a smile," instead of "wooing a soul;" it is undoubtedly reprehensible, and ought to be chastised with a just severity. Perhaps had he, whose character we are contemplating, laid a more strict embargo upon a disposition naturally facetious, he might have saved himself from some just censure, and his friends, who sometimes felt the strokes of his wit, from the flush of mortification. But after subtracting somewhat of our reverence for his character, on account of those infirmities which marked the features of a fallible being, we shall be pleased and edified by beholding in our departed brother, an assemblage of those virtues and christian graces, which are the offspring of a heart renewed in the image of God, and which adorn the soul of that minister of Christ, who unreservedly devotes himself to the services of the sanctuary.

In the latter part of his life, he was quite corpulent, commonly weighing about two hundred and fifty pounds. This, as has been well observed, was not the effect of intemperance, nor of inactivity ; for he was both temperate in his mode of living, and very active and diligent in his business, as the preceding memoir abundantly shows. In his peregrinations through the country, he always rode on horse-back, until the latter period of his life, when by age, and its attendent infirmities, it became convenient and needful for him to accommodate himself with a carriage.

It is unnecessary to say more. He rests—after spending thirty-six years in the faithful performance of the duties of an itinerating minister in the Methodist church—he rests from his labours, while thousands, converted through his ministry, remember him with gratitude.

APPENDIX.

IN the course of Mr. Lee's ministry, he preached between eight and nine thousand sermons, and delivered nearly six hundred public exhortations.

With the greatest accuracy he noted down all the texts on which he ever preached, with the time when, and the place where, he delivered each discourse. In the early part of his ministry, he frequently set down the outlines of the discourse, or manner in which he divided his text, but this he discontinued after the year 1786, a circumstance much to be regretted, as it would certainly have given greater interest to his journals, than barely the transcribing the text alone.

His manner of preaching, as has already been observed, was plain and artless, but generally full of energy, and always perspicuous and pointed. Like the most, and perhaps all, of the Methodist preachers, he never either read or memorized his sermons, seldom commiting any thing more of them to paper, than merely the leading ideas, or general propositions. He thought, and very justly thought, that the method of reading sermons, or of delivering them from memory, had a tendency to dampen the ardour of devotion, and to prevent the speaker from availing himself of those thoughts, which suddenly arise in his mind, and which often produce the greatest and most beneficial effect in the hearer's mind. He, therefore, after previously digesting the outlines of a sermon, entered the pulpit in the name of the Lord, confiding in the aids of the Holy Spirit to assist his powers of invention as well as delivery, and he was seldom disappointed in either.

We take the liberty of presenting the reader with a small collection of the texts of sacred scripture, and of his manner of treating them, as we find them recorded in his journal. Those who have often heard him preach in the name of Jesus, will doubtless recognise his manner in this specimen, and others may be edified by thus seeing the weapons (and the manner of using them) with which Mr. Lee defended the sacred cause of Christianity. These, however, are not presented as the most perfect models of sermonizing, but merely to show *his* method of dividing the word of God, in order to instruct mankind in the all-important truths of the Gospel of Christ.

JOHN V. 40.

" And ye will not come to me, that ye might have life."

I. Show how man has gone from God.

II. The necessity of coming to Christ.

III. The reasons why he will not come.

IV. The manner in which he is to come.

V. Invite all to come to Christ.

HEBREWS VI. 1.

" Therefore, leaving the principles of the doctrine of Christ, let us go on to perfection."

I. Speak of the principles of the doctrines of Christ, and show what they are.

II. How we are to leave them.

III. The perfection attainable in this life, and how we are to go on unto it.

AMOS V. 6.

" Seek ye the Lord, and ye shall live."
I. Show the necessity of seeking the Lord.
II. How we are to seek him.
III. The effect.—Ye shall live.

EZEKIEL XXXIII. 11.

" Say unto them, as I live saith the Lord God, I have
no pleasure in the death of the wicked." &c.
I. God has no pleasure in the death of the wicked.
II. His pleasure is that they should turn and live.
III. The exhortation, turn ye.
IV. The argument, or expostulation ; why will ye
die, O house of Israel.

LUKE XV. 2.

" This man receiveth sinners."
I. Show what right this *man* has to receive sinners.
II. Upon what conditions this *man* receiveth sinners.
III. Invite sinners to come to Christ.

AMOS IV. 12.

" Prepare to meet thy God, O Israel."
I. Show what is implied by being prepared to meet
God. 1. Repentance toward God. 2. Faith in our
Lord Jesus Christ. 3. Holiness, without which no
man shall see the Lord in peace.
II. Exhort the people to prepare to meet God.
III. The consequence of being prepared.

EPHESIANS V. 8.

" For ye were sometimes darkness, but now are ye
light in the Lord ; walk as children of light."
I. Show how we are by nature in darkness. 1.
The darkness of sin. 2. The darkness of ignorance.
3. The darkness of unbelief.

II. How we must become light in the Lord.

III. How we are to walk as children of the light.

MARK XIII. 33.

" Watch and pray."

I. Show how we are to watch, and what we are to watch against.   1. The world, the honours, the profits, and the people of the world, and the love of the world.   2. The flesh, the lust of the flesh ; namely, in eating, drinking, sleeping, uncleanness ; of dress, behaviour, of action.   3. The lust of the eye.   4. The pride of life.   5. The devil.

II. What we are to watch over, thoughts, words, and actions.

III. For what we are to watch, for all opportunities of doing good to ourselves or others, temporally, or spiritually ; we must watch for death and judgment.

IV. How we are to pray.   1. The manner how we are to pray.   2. Where we are to pray.   3. When we should pray.   4. For what we are to pray, &c.

COLOSSIANS III. 1.

" If ye then be risen with Christ, seek those things which are above."

I. Show what is implied in being risen with Christ.

II. What things we are to seek.   1. Grace.   2. Glory ; the glory of God below, and the glory of heaven above.

2 PETER III. 18.

" But grow in grace."

I. Speak of the different degrees of grace.

II. Show the hindrances to a growth in grace.

III. The helps to a growth in grace.

IV. Lay down some marks by which we may know whether we grow in grace or not.

PSALM LXXXIX. 15.

" Blessed is the people that know the joyful sound : they shall walk, O Lord, in the light of thy countenance."

I. Show what is implied by the joyful sound.

II. Who are they that know the joyful sound.

III. The blessed consequences which will result, they shall walk, O Lord, in the light of thy countenance.

1 THESSALONIANS V, 19.

" Quench not the Spirit."

I. Show the different ways in which the Spirit of God operates.

II. How it may be quenched.

III. Enforce the exhortation, Quench not the Spirit.

MATTHEW XI. 28.

" Come unto me all ye that labour and are heavy laden, and I will give you rest."

I. Describe those that labour and are heavy laden.

II. Show how they are to come to the Lord.

III. The rest which is promised. 1. In this world. 2. In the world to come.

MATTHEW VI. 33.

" But first seek the kingdom of God, and his righteousness ; and all these things shall be added unto you."

I. Show what we are to understand by the kingdom of God, and his righteousness.

II. How we are to seek it.

III. Why we should seek it first.

IV. Explain the promise by showing what things shall be added unto you.

TITUS II. 14.

"Who gave himself for us that he might redeem us from all iniquity, and purify unto himself a peculiar people, zealous of good works."

I. Show who it was that gave himself for us; Christ the Son of God.

II. What he gave himself for, for us.

III. The manner in which the gift was bestowed; in the manner best calculated to propitiate the Father's wrath; to excite our humility and gratitude—he died for us.

IV. The end which he had in view in thus giving himself for us, that he might redeem us from all iniquity, and purify unto himself a peculiar people, zealous of good works.

GALATIANS V. 1.

"Stand fast therefore in the liberty wherewith Christ hath made us free, and be not entangled again with the yoke of bondage."

I. Show the bondage which man is under by nature.

II. How he may be made free.

III. What this liberty is.

IV. How we are to stand fast in this liberty, and not be entangled again in the yoke of bondage.

It would be an easy matter to give many others, but these may suffice.

FINIS.

DUE

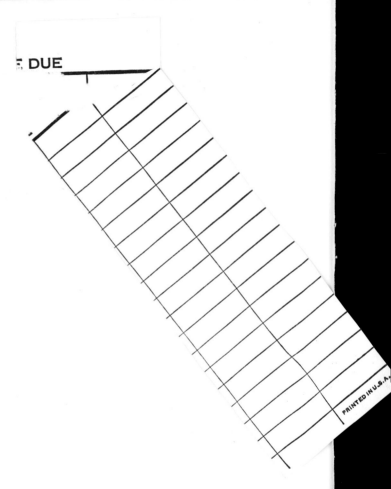